Beneath the Banner

Archaeology of the M18 Ennis Bypass
and N85 Western Relief Road, Co. Clare

Beneath the Banner

Archaeology of the M18 Ennis Bypass and N85 Western Relief Road, Co. Clare

Nóra Bermingham, Graham Hull and Kate Taylor

with contributions by
Sian Anthony, Edward Bourke, Miriam Carroll, Michelle Comber, Maria FitzGerald,
Steve Ford, Simon Gannon, Matilda Holmes, Carleton Jones, Lynne Keys, Tessa Machling,
Clare McCutcheon, Declan Moore, Ciarán Ó Murchadha and Annette Quinn

NRA SCHEME MONOGRAPHS 10

First published in 2012 by
The National Roads Authority
St Martin's House, Waterloo Road, Dublin 4
Copyright © National Roads Authority and the authors

Library of Congress Cataloging-in Publication Data are available for this book.
A CIP catalogue record for this book is available from the British Library.

Material from Ordnance Survey Ireland is reproduced with the permission of the Government of Ireland and Ordnance Survey Ireland under permit number EN0045206.

ISBN 978-0-9564180-7-4
ISSN 2009-0471
NRA Scheme Monographs 10

Copy-editing: Editorial Solutions (Ireland) Ltd
Cover design, typesetting and layout: LSD Ltd
Index: Julitta Clancy
Printed by: Nicholson & Bass Ltd

Front and back cover—An engraving of Clare Abbey from Francis Grose's *Antiquities of Ireland,* London, 1791.

Frontispiece—Detail from an engraving of Clare Abbey from Francis Grose's *Antiquities of Ireland,* London, 1791.

CONTENTS

CONTENTS OF CD-ROM

The final excavation reports for all the archaeological sites excavated on the route of the M18 Ennis Bypass and N85 Western Relief Road, Co. Clare are presented in PDF format on the CD-ROM that accompanies this book. These are copies of the fully illustrated stratigraphic and interpretive reports, with specialists' analyses of samples and finds that form part of the national archive of excavation reports curated by the National Monuments Service.

Licence number	Site code and townland	Site type	Excavation director
03E1291	Testing (TVAS Ireland): southern sector	Scheme footprint	Graham Hull
03E1293/ 03R130	Testing (Moore Group): northern sector	Scheme footprint	Tom Roger
03E1426	M27 Carrowdotia	Pits (iron-working); road, ditches, furrows and pits	Kate Taylor
03E1442	AR25 Carrowdotia	Cashel; burnt spreads; quarry pits, field boundaries and furrows	Kate Taylor
03E1443	AR27 Carrowdotia	Clearance cairns	Kate Taylor
04E0019	AR123 Clareabbey	Pit and hearth cluster	Graham Hull
04E0022	AR124 Clareabbey	Burnt mound	Graham Hull
04E0023	AR125 Clareabbey	Burnt mound	Graham Hull
04E0024	AR126 Cahircalla Beg	Burnt mound	Graham Hull
04E0025	AR129 Keelty	Limekiln	Graham Hull
04E0026	AR131 Claureen	Ring-ditch / barrow	Graham Hull
04E0027	AR120 Clareabbey	Brick kiln clamps	Kate Taylor
04E0028	AR127 Cahircalla More	Burnt spreads; field boundary and furrows	Kate Taylor
04E0029	AR128 Cahircalla More	Cremation pit; enclosure, smithy and field system; road, bank and ditch complex	Kate Taylor
04E0030	AR130 Keelty	Late 19th-century dump	Kate Taylor
04E0031	AR121 Clareabbey	Burnt mounds	Kate Taylor
04E0032	AR122 Clareabbey	Burnt spread and pits	Kate Taylor
04E0050	AR105 Manusmore	'Prayer stones' modern	Markus Casey
04E0052	AR106 Barefield	Charcoal production pit	Markus Casey
04E0053	AR107 Ballymacahill	No archaeological significance	Markus Casey
04E0054	AR108 Ballymacahill	Pits (purpose unknown)	Markus Casey
04E0055	AR109 Ballaghboy	No archaeological significance	Markus Casey

Licence number	Site code and townland	Site type	Excavation director
04E0056	AR110 Kilbreckan	Hearth	Markus Casey
04E0187	AR100 Manusmore	Cremation cemetery	Graham Hull
04E0188	AR101 Manusmore	Brick kiln clamp	Graham Hull
04E0189	AR102 Manusmore	Cremation cemetery; hearth/food preparation pit	Graham Hull
04E0190	AR103 Killow	Burnt mound	Kate Taylor
04E0191	AR104 Killow	Burnt mound; cremations (probable); double ditches	Kate Taylor
04E0192	AR54 Knockanean	Field system	Kate Taylor
E2021: C020	Clareabbey	Augustinian Abbey	Graham Hull
E2022: A025	Clareabbey	Augustinian Abbey	Graham Hull

FOREWORD

This book represents the completion of a complex programme of investigations that commenced with exploratory fieldwork and concludes with the publication of the results. The mill of activity between these 'bookends' included test excavations and surveys, documentary researches and laboratory analyses and, of course, intensive manual excavations. No less than the road scheme itself, all of this represents the work of a large team of people with diverse skills and specialisms. This is particularly evident in *Beneath the Banner* and readers will be fascinated to discover what insights into past human communities can be teased from a handful of cremated prehistoric human bone or the waste products of an early medieval smithy.

These past human communities were the people of the Fergus river valley and its catchment area. This landscape was a constant backdrop to their affairs, in every period, and is the scene of the archaeological stories told in this book. What we learn in *Beneath the Banner*, however, is that the relationship between a human community and the landscape it inhabits is dynamic and reflexive. That is to say, the natural environment provides the basic pre-conditions for human life—climate, soil, water, wood, iron and other raw materials—but humans also change the places they inhabit in visible and sometimes permanent ways. Primeval forests give way to grass pastures and tillage lands. Routeways become established. Field banks and stone walls parcel up the countryside. Rivers are canalised and bogs are drained. Buildings are raised and sometimes survive as monumental ruins. Some of the most visible evidence of these changes is relatively recent and a welcome feature of *Beneath the Banner* is that it records post-medieval routeways and early modern limekilns with the same attention to detail as prehistoric cemeteries and early medieval farmsteads. Change is the only constant in the landscape and, as the centuries pass, all of these relics of former communities become 'archaeological remains' in time.

The biggest change in this landscape in recent years has been the construction of the M18 Ennis Bypass and N85 Western Relief Road. The road was opened in January 2007 and is hailed as a success by the public, delivering shorter and safer journeys to road users in this important transport corridor in the mid-west region. The NRA is happy to publish this account of archaeological discoveries along the routes. We are grateful to TVAS (Ireland) Ltd for assisting us in this and to Clare County Council—as the Roads Authority for the M18 Ennis Bypass—for commissioning and managing their work. We especially congratulate Dr Nóra Bermingham, Graham Hull and Kate Taylor for taking the archaeological project across the finishing line with *Beneath the Banner*, the latest title in the NRA scheme monograph series.

Fred Barry
Chief Executive
National Roads Authority

APPRECIATION OF MARKUS CASEY
(1957–2008)

Markus Casey MA, MIAI, was an archaeologist and aviator whose contributions to our understanding of promontory forts, in particular, will be lasting, as will the discoveries he made while excavating medieval Galway in the late 1980s. He was cast in a similar mould to that other great flying digger, the late Leo Swan: both men were equally at home in the sky and in the field. But perhaps the most lasting memory for all who knew him was Markus's often roguish personality and his mischievous smile.

He was a graduate of the National University of Ireland, Galway, where he was awarded both his Bachelor's Degree (1981) and Master's Degree (1999). The latter, entitled *The coastal promontory forts of Ireland: a survey of counties Sligo, Mayo, Galway and Clare*, was a major contribution on a hitherto neglected site type, and the aerial reconnaissance that was an important feature of this research allowed Markus to combine his twin passions, fieldwork and flying.

His major excavations were on promontory forts and urban sites. These include 'Doonamo' promontory fort on the coast of County Mayo (published in the *Journal of the Galway Archaeological and Historical Society*, Vol. 51, 1999) and 'Doonagappul' promontory fort on Clare Island (published in the *New Survey of Clare Island*, Vol. 5, 2007). Of his Galway City excavations, those at the Spanish Parade-Fishmarket in 1998–99 were the most fruitful (published in *Archaeological Investigations in Galway City*, 2004).

Markus died in an airplane crash near Ireland West Airport, Knock, Co. Mayo, on Sunday 11 May, 2008. His loss was, and still is, immense, both to his family, colleagues and many friends, but also to Irish archaeology as a whole.

Paul Gosling

ACKNOWLEDGEMENTS

All of the archaeological investigations on this road scheme were commissioned by Clare County Council with funding from the NRA. The excavations were authorised by the Minister for the Environment, Heritage and Local Government, through the National Monuments Service, in consultation with the National Museum of Ireland. Contour vector, settlement boundary and soil data were supplied by Clare County Council.

Test excavations in the southern sector of the scheme were by TVAS (Ireland) Ltd, managed by Graham Hull and Kate Taylor, and in the northern sector by Moore Group, directed by Tom Rogers and managed by Ken Fitzsimmons.

Full excavations were by TVAS (Ireland) Ltd, managed by Graham Hull and directed by Graham Hull, Kate Taylor and Markus Casey (†). The excavation supervisors were Lee Roy Krakowicz, Matthew Logue, Astrid Lesley Nathan, Richard Oram, Edel Ruttle and Sean Wallis. The site assistants were Connor Conroy, Tim Dean, Elisabeth Dos Santos, Lewis Goodman, Allan Grassie, Toby Graystone, Vincent Hanley, Callum Hillary, Áine Kelly, Paddy Lawrence, Patricia Long, Fiona McAuliffe, Margaret McNamara, Siobhán McNamara, Frank Mulcahy, Fergal O'Shea, Michael Parks, Jamie Parra Rizo, Alan Smart, Tom Varley and Sarah Webb.

Post-excavation analyses and reporting were managed by Kate Taylor. Specialist reporting and conservation were by ArchCon Labs, Sian Anthony, Beta Analytic Ltd., Edward Bourke, Miriam Carroll, Michelle Comber, Lucy Cramp, Martin Feely, Maria FitzGerald, Steve Ford, Val Fryer, Simon Gannon, Matilda Holmes, Lynne Keys, Tessa Machling, Stephen Mandal, Clare McCutcheon, Declan Moore, Lorna O'Donnell, The Chrono Centre Queen's University, Belfast, Annette Quinn, Edel Ruttle and Alan Vince (†). Illustrations for all Final Reports and for the publication were prepared by Aisling Mulcahy, Astrid Lesley Nathan and Eimhear O'Brien. Paul Gosling prepared the appreciation for Markus Casey.

The NRA project archaeologists were Sébastien Joubert and Jerry O'Sullivan.

This book was prepared for publication at TVAS (Ireland) Ltd by Nóra Bermingham and was copy-edited at Editorial Solutions (Ireland) Ltd in Belfast, by Sheelagh Hughes. Typesetting and design were by LSD Ltd also in Belfast.

1
INTRODUCTION

Nóra Bermingham and Graham Hull
with contributions by C Jones, M Comber and C Ó Murchadha

Cruit i Bhriain fá sirim beoir
(fá hiad mo thrí ceoil do ghnáth)
faoidh chluig Innse don taobh thiar
nuall na lice ag triall sa sál.

The harp of O'Brien while sipping back beer
(one of my three usual melodies here)
The bell of Ennis from the western side
The murmur of flagstones against the tide.

Inis ar Fhorgas na bhfian
noch timchilleas grian is muir
do ba mhaith linn dul dá bruach
Is ní dfuath an tighe a bhfuil.

Ennis on Fergus of the warrior band
The water and the sun encircle your land
Along by your shore I would like to roam
Though not for dislike of my present home.

Duanaire Ghearóid Iarla (VII:3:249–51 and VII:6:261–4, Mac Niocaill 1963, 22; translation Ó Dálaigh 1987, 26–7).

County Clare is a cultural and heritage hotspot within the island of Ireland. Tourists meander through the stark Burren landscape to ponder over the region's signature stone-built forts, dolmens, wedge tombs and walls. The great cliffs at Moher are often a starting point for journeys up and down the coast that take in the rounded limestone peaks that give way to Galway Bay in the north and the long beaches that soften the coastline to Loop Head in the south. The majesty of this landscape can, at least initially, make one forget that there is another Clare: an inland, low-lying gentler landscape carved and shaped by retreating ice sheets. It is this territory that the 14th-century poet, Gearóid Iarla, evokes in verse purportedly composed while in captivity after a slew of battles between warring factions of the O'Briens of Thomond (Mac Niocaill 1963, 22). It is this landscape and its antecedents that this volume attempts to illuminate. The archaeological sites described here were discovered in advance of construction of the M18 Ennis Bypass and the Western Relief Road that skirts Ennis. The volume builds on the wealth of historical and archaeological resources for the county; many of which can be accessed via the County Library website (http://www.clarelibrary.ie). The discoveries provide new insight into periods under-represented in the archaeological and historical records of the county. New information that elucidates past ritual, secular, economic, agricultural, craft and industrial practices has resulted from the excavations and associated investigations.

The road scheme represents the central portion of the M18 through County Clare and a new relief road that skirts the south-western fringes of Ennis. The scheme totals 21 km in length. The M18 runs almost north–south, traversing the lowland between the Slieve Aughty and Slieve Bernagh

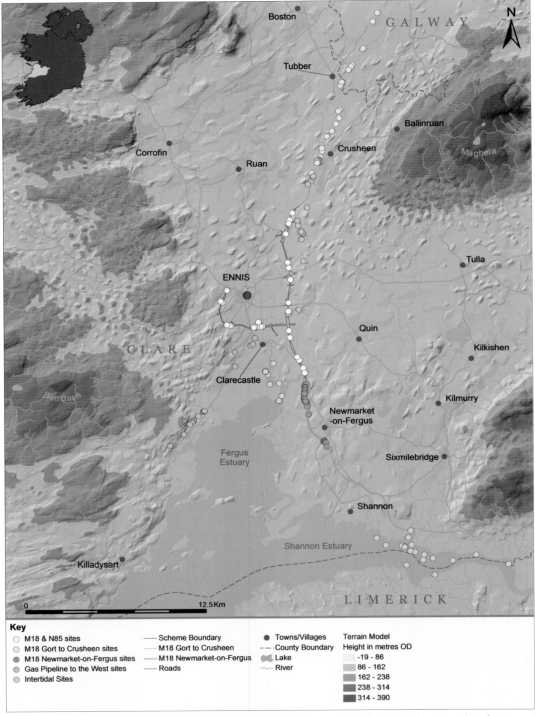

Illus. 1.1—Location map of the M18 and N85 Western Relief Road showing distribution of archaeological sites on the road scheme and on other linear projects in the region.

Mountains in the east and Ben Dash, Slieve Callen, Clifden Hill and the Burren in the west (Illus. 1.1). The route is bookended by the townlands of Barefield in the north and Latoon in the south, north of Newmarket-on-Fergus. It bypasses Ennis to provide a direct connection between Limerick and Galway and is linked with the N85 Western Relief Road to Ennistymon from a junction in Killow to the N85 in Claureen, north west of Ennis.

Excavations were conducted under licence at 27 sites with Ministerial Consents and Directions provided for excavations at Clare Abbey (Illus. 1.2). The excavations recorded both multi-period and single-event sites with habitation, agricultural and industrial sites as well as funerary sites, burnt stone mounds (hereafter referred to as burnt mounds) and a range of agriculturally related features. The earliest sites date from the Chalcolithic with later activity dating to the early and later Bronze Age, the Iron Age, the early medieval and late medieval periods. The latest sites excavated are post-medieval or early modern in origin.

The M18 Ennis Bypass joins with the M18 Gort-Crusheen scheme in the north and with the Newmarket-on-Fergus Bypass in the south (Illus. 1.1). Archaeological investigations on these routes involved excavation of an array of previously unknown archaeological sites. Between Gort and Crusheen almost 30 prehistoric sites were excavated. The majority were Bronze Age in date, mainly burnt mounds with sites from the Neolithic, Iron Age and medieval periods also occurring (Delaney 2011). Funerary sites included a Bronze Age cremation pit and two Iron Age ring-ditches from Ballyboy, Co. Galway. Other site types included Iron Age metal-working sites in Derrygarriff, Co. Clare and Rathwilladoon, Co. Galway; also a multi-phase prehistoric settlement at Rathwilladoon; and a complex of medieval corn-drying kilns from Curtaun, Co. Galway. In contrast, burnt mounds did not feature greatly in excavations on the Newmarket-on-Fergus Bypass. The majority of archaeological sites discovered were small features, seemingly isolated pits and/or post-holes, excavated during monitoring of the scheme (Hull 2001; Hull & Tarbett-Buckley 2001). An early medieval ringfort containing at least one contemporary kiln was excavated in Ballyconneely, Co. Clare. Nearby in the same townland excavations revealed a complex of possible prehistoric and early medieval pits and post-holes as well as post-medieval human burials. A probable ring-ditch, represented by a sub-circular gully containing significant quantities of cremated human bone, was excavated in the adjacent townland of Ballygirreen, Co. Clare.

Along with the road schemes already mentioned, the construction of the Gas Pipeline to the West resulted in the excavation of about 20 new archaeological sites occupying the same lowland zone traversed by much of the M18 in Clare. The investigations included burnt mounds (characterised as either *fulachtaí fia* or burnt mounds), a small number of cremation burial sites, including a single ring-ditch, as well as an array of pits, burnt spreads and post-medieval features (Grogan et al. 2007, 167–216). Some of the excavated sites on the Gas Pipeline to the West were within townlands that also revealed new sites during investigations on the M18. Finally, archaeological surveys conducted in the 1990s populated the mudflats and floodplains of the Fergus and Shannon estuaries with fishtraps, post-rows and structures dating from early prehistory to the modern era (O'Sullivan 2001).

Between them, the five projects described above have augmented the archaeological record, providing new evidence for settlement, burial, industry and craft in periods and areas where such activities had previously been under-represented or unknown and it is within this context that the archaeological sites excavated on the Ennis Bypass and Western Relief Road are considered.

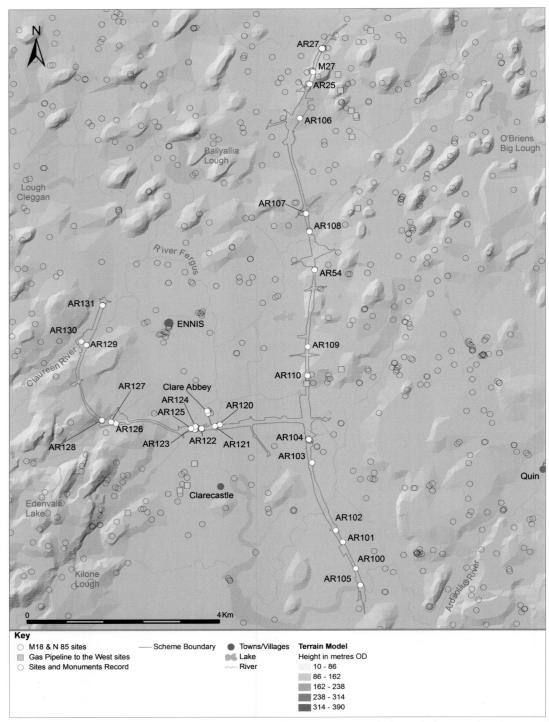

Illus. 1.2—Detailed location map of the M18 and N85 Western Relief Road showing distribution of archaeological sites on the scheme and on the Gas Pipeline to the West (2007).

Archaeological investigations on the new road

In advance of the construction of the new roads, an Environmental Impact Statement (EIS) was prepared in 2000 (Babtie Pettit). The Archaeology chapter of the EIS included a desk-based assessment of cartographic and aerial photographic sources, and information from the Sites and Monuments Record of Ireland (SMR), the Record of Monuments and Places (RMP) and the finds database and files of the National Museum of Ireland. These investigations were supplemented by a field inspection or 'walkover survey' of the whole scheme, and by architectural (Aegis Archaeology Ltd), underwater (Doland Boland; Babtie Pettit 2000) and geophysical surveys (Earthsound Archaeological Geophysics 2003). A programme of archaeological testing involving the mechanical excavation of test trenches throughout the footprint of the new road was undertaken 2003. In total, 29 sites were subsequently targeted for full manual excavation between September 2003 and November 2005. Of these, 25 are reported on here as four were either of very recent origin or not archaeologically signficant.

The excavations were carried out under licence and involved the stripping of identified sites by mechanical excavator under archaeological supervision. At Clare Abbey much of the topsoil stripping was completed by hand. All topsoil removal was followed by hand-excavation and the excavated features and deposits were recorded following the *TVAS Ireland Field Recording Manual* (TVAS 2003).

Presentation of archaeological findings

In this volume, the archaeological sites are primarily categorised as prehistoric, early medieval, medieval and post-medieval/early modern in origin. Within each of these categories, the sites are described in chronological order with sites grouped on the basis of type within the prehistoric period. Here there are two groups, namely burnt mounds, also known as *fulachtaí fia* and funerary sites.

Chapter 1 places the discoveries within their landscape, geological and topographical context. Next, the chronological framework adopted in this volume is defined before recounting the archaeological and historical background of each period represented on the scheme. These are followed by consideration of the parishes and townlands traversed by the route and a brief outline of the origins of Ennis and Clarecastle. Finally the historic development of the region's infrastructure is chronicled. The results of each excavation are described in summary form in Chapters 2, 3 and 4. Each chapter concludes with a discussion of the excavated sites and their wider interpretation and significance. Chapters 5, 6 and 7 describe the cremated human bone, animal bone and wood charcoal from sites on the scheme. These chapters illustrate the interplay between past human populations and their contemporary environment. Fourteen sites on the scheme yielded artefacts. These are described in Chapter 8, with sections on prehistoric pottery and lithics, metal-working slag, historic stone and metal objects, and diverse individual finds including wooden, glass, textile, metal and ceramic items. The volume concludes in Chapter 9 with a brief overall discussion of the findings.

Landscape, geology and drainage

The Ennis Bypass and the Western Relief Road lie within central Clare. This is a large lowland zone coated with glacial drift and its surface is peppered with rock outcrops, drumlins, lakes, rivers, turloughs and peat bogs (Illus. 1.3). Ennis occupies a central position in the south-west part of this lowland with marshy ground to the east towards the River Fergus. A slightly elevated and rugged area with frequent rock outcrops surrounds this central area and this in turn is surrounded by a series of low drumlin hills (Brady Shipman Martin 2000, 5).

The mixed, low-lying terrain characterising the road corridor represents a very different landscape to the flanking uplands of the Burren and the Slieve Aughty and Slieve Bernagh Mountains. The majority of archaeological sites identified on the route occupy elevations between 2 m and 35 m above Ordnance Datum (OD), with most lying between 2 m and 10 m OD. In dramatic contrast, the Burren can exceed 300 m OD with the Aughty and Bernagh Mountains rising to between 300 m and 500 m. Drumlins and other glacial ridges represent the most prominent topographical features along the route with a range of archaeological sites situated on and around these localised high points.

The gross landforms were shaped by repeated episodes of glaciation, the latest of which ended around 13,000 years ago (Aalen 1997, 7–10). Nestled between the limestone peaks and pavements of the Burren, and the sandstone, slate and grit formations of the mountains in the east, the soils of the lowland zone are characterised by weathered glacial till derived from carboniferous limestone bedrock. Peaty soils and bog occupy former open water bodies, river floodplains and areas of poor drainage.

Illus. 1.3—Aerial view of the landscape traversed by the northern part of the scheme, with archaeological test trenches (left).

Illus. 1.4—Map showing the distribution of the soil types on the route and in the wider area (after Clare Co. Council).

The modern soil types along the route are varied, with brown earths, podsols, rendzinas, gleys, peat and alluvial silts all occurring (Finch 1971) (Illus. 1.4). In agricultural terms, the soils can be described as being largely of good quality, though agriculture intensity is limited as much of the land is not free-draining and is liable to flooding in spring and winter. Today, these soils typically support permanent grassland with pastoral farming, including dairying and dry-stock rearing, representing the primary agricultural activities along the route. In addition to cattle, sheep are grazed in the more southerly part of the area. Field sizes are typically small to medium with tree-lined hedgerows on the drumlin landscape. East of Ennis, where more marshy ground exists, hedgerows are lower and there are fewer trees (Brady Shipman Martin 2000, 5–6).

At various times throughout the past, land use was more varied, with woodland, tillage and pasture implied in the archaeological record (see Chapters 6 and 7). Less than 50 years ago farming was much more diverse in Ireland, with smaller fields, and lots of root crops and cereal crops as well livestock. In addition to grassland there are several areas of wetland and scrub-to-woodland along the route, echoed by the charcoal remains from many of the excavations. Hazel, gorse and other scrub are common on unenclosed rock outcrop areas and large areas of hazel scrub woodland are present at Knockanean for example (ibid., 6). Nineteenth-century plantations of woodland survive around former Ascendancy period houses in townlands such as Manusmore, Ballymacahill and Knockanean.

The River Fergus, an important river for salmon, trout and eel, is the main drainage artery within the study area (Illus. 1.5). Alluvium blankets the floodplains on both sides with areas of peat lying behind the river silts on the east. The river drains into the Fergus estuary, in the south and, along the way is crossed by the Western Relief Road between the Augustinian foundation at Clare Abbey and the small town of Clarecastle. This crossing recalls an earlier ford at Clarecastle, which linked east and west Clare, and was a crucial element on a major prehistoric routeway leading into the county from the east (Grogan 2005a, 27). The relief road also crosses the Claureen or Kilmaley River near the junction with the N85 Ennistymon Road. This river is a significant salmon and trout-spawning nursery ground for the River Fergus.

Other tributaries of the Fergus are crossed by the Ennis Bypass. The largest of these, the Latoon Creek, is also known as the Ardsollus River and the River Rine. The Fergus, and probably the Ardsollus, were factors in the siting of archaeological sites excavated within the scheme (see Jones, Chapter 2). Access to water was clearly important, as the siting of burnt mounds and later industrial sites attests. Proximity to water could also be problematic. In more recent times, the difficulties of controlling drainage is to some extent reflected in the enthuasistic but failed attempt to drain the basin of the River Fergus in the 19th century (see Ó Murchadha, this chapter).

Chronology

Perhaps the one thing that is consistent about chronology is that it is never truly absolute or fixed. The periods into which the past is separated have flexible and permeable boundaries that can change following, for example, new archaeological discoveries, refinements in dating techniques and/or changes in interpretation and approach. Hence the chronological framework adopted here can appear significantly different from those applied 50, 40 or even 20 years ago, or even in other

Illus. 1.5—Archaeological test trenches show the line taken by the road scheme at the River Fergus crossing, by Clare Abbey (top left).

publications today. This framework remains quite broad (Table 1.1); for example, some individual periods are not subdivided into early and late phases because the character of the discoveries described by this book does not warrant it.

Table 1.1—Chronological framework adopted in this volume.
★ This column reflects the multi-period nature of some sites, which are represented in more than one period.

Period	Date range	Dated sites (n.) per period ★
Mesolithic	7000 – 4000 BC	n/a
Neolithic	4000 – 2500 BC	n/a
Chalcolithic or Final Neolithic (Copper Age)	2500 – 2100 BC	5
Early Bronze Age	2100 – 1500 BC	
Later Bronze Age	1500 – 600 BC	8
Iron Age	600 BC – AD 400	4
Early medieval	AD 400 – 1169	9
Medieval	AD 1170 – 1550	2
Post-medieval/early modern	AD 1550 – 1850	5

The majority of archaeological sites on this scheme returned samples suitable for radiocarbon dating. Forty-one individual radiocarbon dates were returned using charcoal, wood, plant macrofossils and animal bone samples. Artefact typology and, in some cases, documentary and cartographic sources provided additional dating evidence. Thus, for the most part, the archaeological sites have been securely dated (Illus. 1.6 and 1.7).

All radiocarbon dates are based on the Accelerator Mass Spectrometry (AMS) method and have been calibrated (i.e. translated into calendrical date ranges) using OxCal v4.1.7 (Bronk Ramsay 2009). Within the text the calibrated results are cited as either BC or AD inclusive of laboratory code and in all cases the second level of probability (2-sigma) is cited. A full list of dates is provided in Appendix 1.

Radiocarbon dating results

Of the prehistoric sites, 12 returned 33 radiocarbon determinations (Illus. 1.6). The earliest sites date from the Chalcolithic with archaeological activity occurring throughout the prehistoric period into the Late Iron Age. The record suggests a reasonably constant human presence in this part of County Clare and this is discussed further by Jones (see Chapter 2).

It is apparent that multiple episodes of activity occurred at both burial and burnt mound sites, e.g. Manusmore AR100 and Cahircalla Beg AR126. In fact all funerary sites, with the exception of a ring-ditch at Claureen AR131, involved repeated use for burials. In contrast most burnt mounds appear to represent single events, e.g. Clareabbey AR121 and AR122; Cahircalla More AR127i–vi and Killow AR103 though the intact mound at Cahircalla Beg AR126 demonstrates that certain burnt mounds were reused repeatedly over centuries.

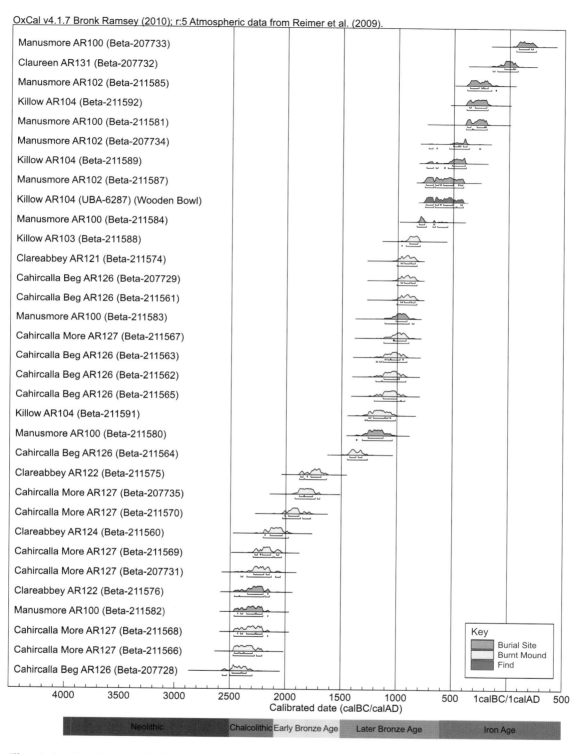

Illus. 1.6—Distribution of radiocarbon dates from prehistoric sites on the scheme.

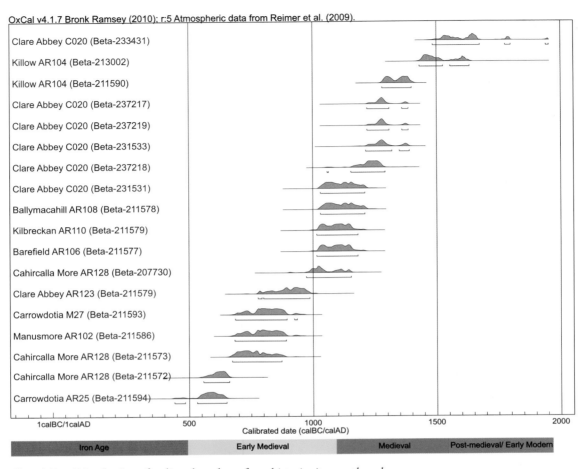

OxCal v4.1.7 Bronk Ramsey (2010); r:5 Atmospheric data from Reimer et al. (2009).

Illus. 1.7—Distribution of radiocarbon dates from historic sites on the scheme.

The archaeological record on the scheme in the historic period opens in the second half of the first millennium AD, at the beginning of the early medieval period in Ireland (Illus. 1.7). Ten sites returned 18 radiocarbon dates, with six of these derived from excavations at the Augustinian house at Clare Abbey. Most of the early medieval dates derive from pits that served a range of purposes, including charcoal production, iron-working and food preparation. Some of these features are associated with settlement enclosures but others are from sites of unenclosed activities, away from settlement sites.

Archaeological and historical background

Occupation in prehistory
Carleton Jones

The Mesolithic (c. 7000–4000 BC) and Neolithic (c. 4000–2500 BC)
No evidence from these two periods was recovered during the present study. Both periods are, however, in evidence at other locations in the county. A small number of finds and sites indicate

Mesolithic activity focused on the River Shannon (Collins & Coyne 2003; Condit & O'Sullivan 1999; Lynch 2002). The Neolithic is known primarily through its megalithic tombs (excluding wedge tombs), three of which have been excavated on the Burren, showing that some parts of Clare were being farmed from c. 3800 BC (Jones 2004, 27–54).

Close to the present study area, three pits in a cremation cemetery just north of Newmarket-on-Fergus at Ballyconneely yielded sherds of Neolithic pottery (Read 2000a & b), demonstrating some level of Neolithic occupation in the vicinity of the present study.

The Chalcolithic and Early Bronze Age (c. 2500–1500 BC)

The 1000-year span between c. 2500 BC and 1500 BC encompasses many significant phenomena, which overlapped in time but which did not all begin and end at the same time. Technologically, the Chalcolithic is divided from the Early Bronze Age by the introduction of tin-bronze alloying c. 2100–2000 BC (O'Brien 2004a & in press). In terms of pottery, Beaker pottery (c. 2450/2400–1900 BC) is followed by food vessels and urns (c. 2200–1500 BC) (Brindley 2007). The construction of wedge tombs (c. 2500–1800 BC) (O'Brien 1999 & in press; Schulting et al. 2008) is a feature of the earlier part of the period, but ritual and funerary practices become diverse after this. Cist and pit inhumations and cremations in flat cemeteries, cairns, and mounds, and a variety of other funerary monuments including barrows and ring-ditches all occur. (Some of these monuments have earlier beginnings and some are actually more common in the later Bronze Age and into the Iron Age: Grogan & Condit 2000; Waddell 1998, 140–62.)

In many parts of western Ireland it is not until this period that we see evidence for significant population levels (O'Brien 2009; Jones 2004) and this may be the case in the present study area as well. A pollen core from Mooghaun, near to the present study area in central Clare, shows evidence of farmers opening only small clearances in the woodland in the Neolithic, but in the period between c. 2250 BC and 1800 BC, there is evidence for the first substantial woodland clearance in the area accompanied by low-level but sustained farming (Molloy 1997 & 2005). Perhaps significantly, this period correlates

fairly closely with the earliest radiocarbon dates in the present study (Illus. 1.6). On the thinner soils of the Burren in north-west Clare, tree clearance seems to have occurred earlier, sometime in the Late Neolithic or Chalcolithic (Crabtree 1982; Watts 1984).

In Clare, the most visible sites dating to the earlier part of this period are the numerous megalithic monuments known as wedge tombs. Research on the Burren has revealed that they are closely linked to contemporary farms (Jones 1998; Jones et al. 2011). Although some wedge

Illus. 1.8—Prehistoric houses and tombs on the Burren indicate a settled population in the region in the Late Neolithic/Early Bronze Age period. Wedge tomb on Roughan Hill, Co. Clare (Con Brogan, Department Arts, Heritage and Gaeltacht).

tombs cluster around the earlier Neolithic monuments, a more dispersed spread of wedge tombs stretching from the Burren in the north-west down into south-east Clare (de Valera & Ó Nualláin 1961) suggests that this was a time of population growth and possibly population expansion (Grogan 1996, 26–44; Grogan & Condit 2000; Jones et al. 2011). In the later part of the period, the small number of dated sites makes it difficult to discuss population patterns but the evidence that is available suggests continuity of occupation in most areas and possibly continuing expansion as well (Illus. 1.8).

Finds of Beaker pottery in both domestic and burial contexts in Clare (Jones 1998; Hencken 1935) demonstrate that the area was linked into the widespread exchange networks that are characteristic of this period, while finds of early metal artefacts are further evidence of exchange networks and possibly an emerging social hierarchy in the area (O'Brien 2004a; Jones et al. 2011).

The later Bronze Age (c. 1500–600 BC)

The Burren, in north-west Clare, seems to have undergone large-scale tree clearance in the Late Neolithic or Chalcolithic, and the Mooghaun pollen core shows the first substantial woodland clearance and sustained farming in central Clare in the Early Bronze Age. However, the Mooghaun core also shows that it was probably not until the later Bronze Age that central Clare was subjected to a period of major woodland clearance accompanied by an increase in both pastoral and arable farming (Molloy 1997 & 2005). A similar pattern has recently been revealed in north Clare where a pollen core from Caheraphuca shows woodland clearance and farming impact in the early Chalcolithic, another farming phase with greater farming impact in the Early Bronze Age, and an even more significant phase of woodland clearance and farming impact in the later Bronze Age (Molloy & O'Connell 2012).

Some of the most common sites of this period in Clare, as in many parts of the country, are burnt mounds. Studies across Ireland have shown that most of these sites date to the Bronze Age (from the earlier stages right through to the later stages of the Bronze Age but with a concentration in the later Bronze Age), but also that a minority are earlier and later than the Bronze Age (Brindley et al. 1990; Grogan et al. 2007, 96). In Clare, they occur in large numbers in the central part of the county and in the eastern Burren and are probably a good indication of settlement concentrations at this time. In central Clare, it has been shown that burnt mounds tend to occur in groups and that they are associated with other possibly Bronze Age sites such as standing stones, habitation enclosures and hilltop enclosures. Grogan (2005b, 73–5) has suggested that these site clusters are the remains of small Bronze Age farming communities occupied by closely-related kin groups.

A substantial cremation cemetery that was excavated on a hilltop just south of the current study area at Ballyconneely also dates mainly to the Bronze Age (Read 2000a & b). In the present study, the discovery of more cremation cemeteries and other sites of a more domestic nature add to the growing evidence indicating that the Ennis/Newmarket-on-Fergus area was densely populated in the later stages of the Bronze Age.

By around 900 BC, distinct political territories that were probably occupied by ranked chiefdoms seem to have emerged in many parts of Ireland. The hillfort of Mooghaun, just north-east of Newmarket-on-Fergus, was built at this time (c. 950 BC). This hillfort seems to have served as the central site for a powerful chiefdom that probably controlled most of central and south-east Clare for the remainder of the Bronze Age (Grogan 2005b, 95–101). It has been suggested that the Mooghaun territory was subdivided into smaller sub-territories, each with its own less substantial hilltop enclosure, and further down the hierarchy, multiple individual farmsteads (Grogan 2005b, 97–101; O'Sullivan 2001, 254–56; O'Sullivan & Condit 1995), but most of the sites postulated to have filled these roles remain undated and their role in the Late Bronze Age landscape remains speculative. Further east, at Formoyle Beg, is another large, triple-ramparted hillfort on the south side of the Broadford Gap (Condit & O'Sullivan 1996), which may have been the central site of a chiefdom independent of Mooghaun, or it may have been somehow linked to the Mooghaun chiefdom.

The wealth and power of the Mooghaun chiefdom is demonstrated not only by the vast amount of labour that had to be co-ordinated to build the hillfort, but also by the various deposits of high-status metal-work found in the surrounding territory, including the large hoard of gold ornaments known as the 'Mooghaun hoard' (Armstrong 1917).

The Iron Age (c. 600 BC–AD 400)

Pollen cores in both central Clare (Molloy 1997 & 2005) and on the Burren (Watts 1984) show a regeneration of the tree cover in the Iron Age. This suggests that fields cleared and farmed in the Bronze Age were no longer used. A similar pattern is shown on a recent pollen core from Caheraphuca in north Clare (Molloy & O'Connell 2012). This correlates with a general paucity of evidence for settlements, burials and metal-work in Clare at this time. It is unclear what factors were behind this decline in activity but they were probably not solely local as a similar pattern of declining activity is found in many parts of Ireland.

There is not, however, a complete lack of evidence for activity in Clare in the Iron Age. Iron Age artefacts have been found in different parts of the county from Killaloe in the south-east (Condit & O'Sullivan 1996) to the Burren in the north-west (Jones 2004, 79–83). A recent radiocarbon date from a west Clare promontory fort, in the mouth of the Shannon at Horse Island, suggests that the site was first fortified in the Iron Age (Lynch & Jones forthcoming). This opens up the possibility that some of the other promontory forts in west Clare may have Iron Age origins as well.

A Gaelic kingdom
Michelle Comber

The early medieval period is well represented in the archaeological record of County Clare, especially by the ringforts and cashels, associated field systems and early ecclesiastical sites on the Burren uplands. Today, the surrounding lowlands are much more thinly populated by archaeological monuments. This probably reflects the gradual destruction/damaging of monuments in the course of more wide-scale tillage and farm improvements in the easily accessible lowlands. That a greater density of remains once existed in these areas is supported by the evidence from large linear developments like road schemes. These can reveal buried landscapes of levelled ringforts or ringfort-like enclosures (such as Carrowdotia AR25 and Cahircalla More AR128), related enclosures and field systems (such as at Cahircalla More AR128), ecclesiastical remains and dispersed unenclosed features (such as the pits at Carrowdotia, Manusmore, Kilbreckan and Clareabbey). Evidently the lowland zone was equally well populated in the early medieval period, though the surviving remains are not as visible as their counterparts on the Burren (Illus. 1.9). Furthermore, these excavated lowland features are yielding important evidence of function and chronology that complements what is known of some better-preserved, but as yet unexcavated, remains in the Burren, thus enhancing our knowledge of the early medieval period in County Clare as a whole.

Until at least the fifth century, this part of Clare (part of the petty kingdom or *tuath* of Thomond/ *Tuath Mumhain*) fell under the sway of Connaught and the ruling Connachta. Tradition dates the conquest of Thomond by the Déis Becc (the 'little Déis', a branch of the Déisi of south-east Munster) to the fifth century (Byrne 2001, 180). In reality, however, Connaught influence continued into the seventh century under the rule of Guaire of the Uí Fiachrach Aidne, and may only have ended

Illus. 1.9—Ploughed down remains of early medieval enclosures and field systems in the lowlands can have counterparts in the well-preserved cashels or stone forts of the Burren uplands. Cahercommaun, Co. Clare (Con Brogan, Department Arts, Heritage and Gaeltacht).

with the Battle of Carn Feradaig in AD 627 (ibid., 239). The Connaught rulers were replaced by the northern branch of Déis Becc, the Déis Tuaiscirt, who controlled Thomond during the eighth and ninth centuries. At the start of the 10th century the Déis Tuaiscirt came under pressure from the newly established Viking settlement at Limerick, and were pushed back into east Clare. By the mid 10th century, however, a series of military victories over the Vikings and native neighbouring groups, in conjunction with the gradual weakening of Éoganacht power throughout Munster, saw the ruling dynasty of Déis Tuaiscirt, Dál Cais, emerge as rulers of Munster. Under the leadership of Brian Boru and his brother Mathgamain, the Dál Cais (now the O'Briens) established control over Munster and much of Ireland, and held it throughout much of the following centuries. With the death of Muirchertach O'Brien in AD 1114, however, Munster influence outside the province began to decline (ibid., 181).

These events provide the historical background for the early medieval archaeological evidence uncovered on the road scheme. Perhaps the construction of the cashel at Carrowdotia AR25 and the enclosure at Cahircalla More AR128 are representative of Déis Tuaiscirt efforts to establish themselves and claim territory from the ruling Connaught dynasties in the sixth/seventh centuries AD. The more stable atmosphere of Déis Tuaiscirt/Dál Cais/O'Brien rule from the eighth to the start of the 12th centuries saw the continued use of settlements like Cahircalla More AR128 and its associated field system. It may also have facilitated the safe movement of people across the local landscape and the use of unenclosed spaces for domestic and semi-industrial purposes, as represented by the apparently isolated pits of varying function found in several townlands traversed by the scheme.

Thomond and the O'Briens
Nóra Bermingham

In the mid 12th century the kingdom of Thomond included all of Clare, Limerick, North Tipperary and part of Offaly and was held by the O'Briens. Under the kingship of Domnall Mór (1168–94), the O'Briens strongly opposed Norman advances on Thomond following their arrival in Leinster in AD 1169. The 13th and 14th centuries in Thomond are marked by power struggles within the O'Brien clan fuelled by the reduction of the kingdom to an area the size of Clare by AD 1200. O'Brien alliances with Norman lords such as Robert de Muscergos and Thomas de Clare advanced the Norman Conquest and resulted in castle-building projects with strongholds established at Clare Castle, Bunratty and Quin in the second half of the 13th century. These castles were subject to repeated destruction and re-building as different branches of the O'Briens attempted to assert control over Thomond and limit Norman power within the kingdom (Nally 2008). The Battle of Dysert O'Dea (AD 1318) was decisive in ending Norman inroads into Thomond. Here, Richard de Clare, son of Thomas, challenged Conor O'Dea, an ally of Muirceartach O'Brien, who had gained control of Thomond in AD 1317. At Dysert, de Clare was killed and his army routed, leaving Muirceartach unopposed in Thomond for more than two decades. The supremacy of the O'Briens prevailed in Thomond without serious contest until the 16th century when the Tudor Crown returned its attention to Ireland. In 1534 the then king of Thomond, Murragh O'Brien, submitted to Henry VIII and opened the way for the imposition of the Crown administration and control of Thomond.

While political control of Thomond was hotly contested throughout much of the medieval period, the other major player in the kingdom was the Church and, more specifically, the Augustinians. In the early medieval period a monastic system had prevailed across Ireland. Though there are few upstanding churches from this period known in Clare, Harbison (2008, 9) suggests that there may be up to 170 surviving ecclesiastical sites. The candidates include many round enclosures 70–120 m in diameter. The numbers reflect the Church's position in society often predicated on close and often familial connections with the ruling élite. By the 12th century the monastic system was subject to scrutiny and reform by modernisers who sought centralised control and conformity with a universal Church system (MacMahon 1993).

Twelfth-century episcopal reform paved the way for the establishment of a diocesan system with the Canons Regular of St Augustine playing a fundamental part in this process. Within Clare, the Augustinians established six houses on charter lands, i.e. lands listed within the charter for the foundation at Clare Abbey in AD 1189. In addition to Clare Abbey, houses were later established at Canons' Island, Inchicronan, Kilshanny, Killone and St Peter's Cell in Limerick. These foundations ensured the religious and economic hegemony of the Augustinians in Clare. By the end of the 12th century the Augustinians had become the most influential religious order in Ireland. Their ascent in Clare is closely linked to the rise of Domnall Mór O'Brien, the 'famous [church] builder' (Harbison 2008, 12), whose patronage facilitated church building across Thomond.

Smaller churches were also a feature of medieval rural Clare and within 2 km of the road scheme a handful are listed in the Sites and Monuments Record of Ireland (SMR). These include churches, some with graveyards and typically in ruins, at Killow (Recorded Monument CL034-102), Kilbreckan (CL034-104), Newhall (CL041-062) and Drumcliff (CL033-033), with a possible church site in Ballymacahill (CL034-003) (Illus. 1.10 and 1.11).

To some degree, medieval churches are better represented in the archaeological record than contemporary Gaelic settlement. In Gaelic dominated areas, settlement occurred in moated sites, *crannóga*, *longphorts* (earthwork enclosures sometimes associated with landing places on rivers), cashels, and possibly ringforts (O'Conor 1998, 94). Of these, cashels and ringforts are common

Illus. 1.10—Church and graveyard at Killow (CL034-102).

Illus. 1.11—Church and roundtower at Drumcliff (CL033-033).

within the study area. Typically regarded as early medieval in date, later examples of each are known from elsewhere in Clare (Comber & Hull 2010, 133–72) and Ireland (O'Conor 1998, 89–94). The O'Briens appear to have built at least one ringfort in the 13th century: an historical reference to 'a circular hold and princely residence of earth' may refer to a ringfort built by Donnach O'Brien at Clonroad some time before AD 1242 (ibid., 92). Of the cashels and ringforts within the study area, medieval examples may yet be identified. Several cashels and ringforts in neighbouring County Galway, recently excavated on national road schemes, have also produced evidence of continuing occupation in the later medieval period. These would have been within Gaelic territories that were annexed to the de Burgo Lordship of Connacht in the mid 13th century (J O'Sullivan, pers. comm.).

Of the other settlement forms listed above, there are no *crannóga, longphorts* or moated sites known in the study area. Moated sites are typically, although not exclusively, regarded as an Anglo-Norman settlement form and as such their absence is unsurprising in an area under the control of Gaelic lords (Barry 2000, 6). In the 13th and 14th centuries the Irish did not build castles and their tower houses were typically built after AD 1400 (Nugent 2008, 91–6). This includes remnants of two tower houses in Ennis, recorded by the SMR. The SMR also includes a handful of 'unclassified castle' entries, broadly dated to the medieval period (Illus. 1.12). While some high-status buildings survive, such as tower houses, other unequivocally secular rural and medieval settlement forms are not known in the current record for County Clare. The apparent under-representation of Gaelic rural settlement is repeated across the country although this is changing as more research into contemporary

Illus. 1.12—Castlefergus House, a tower house close to the River Ardsollus and west of Quin (CL042-059).

settlement attests (Corlett 2009; O'Conor 2001, 2004). There are about 170 undated earthworks and enclosures listed within the SMR for the study area and it remains to be determined if any of them is the remains of later medieval settlement.

Tower houses account at least for élite dwellings in the later medieval period, but there is little excavated evidence for the sorts of dwellings built and occupied by ordinary people in rural locations between AD 1200 and 1600. Two sites in Munster—at Ballysimon, Co. Limerick and Mooghaun, Co. Clare—suggest that circular *creat*-like structures were built in the 13th and 14th centuries (O'Conor 2001, 204). A *creat* was a small one-roomed house, typically circular and windowless, and constructed from post-and-wattle panelling with a roof of thatch or sods. Their slight construction, in perishable materials, means they are poorly represented in the archaeological record. As yet, examples of such dwellings remain to be identified from elsewhere in Clare.

Conquest, re-conquest and plantation
Nóra Bermingham

The post-medieval/early modern period in Ireland (AD 1550–1850) commenced at a time when Henry VIII had determined that Ireland would be 'reduced and restored to good order and obedience' (Lennon 1994, 87). Plantations and military campaigns featured greatly during the early part of this period of conquest as the Crown attempted to consolidate its power over the 'Old Irish' (Gaelic) lords. Ultimately, the plantations would come to have a profound long-term impact on the social, political, religious and economic organisation of the island. By the end of the 17th century, the legacy of successive conquests and re-conquests was the dispossession of the Irish and Old English Catholics of their lands and political authority, which passed to a landed class of English Protestants, who would retain their 'Ascendancy' status until the early 20th century (Gillespie 2006, 185–94). The consequent formation of great rural estates in the ownership of the Ascendancy and the corresponding development of market towns was concomitant with improvements in rural roads, agricultural practices and rural industries driven largely by these estate owners (sometimes via the Grand Jury system—precursor to the modern local authority system). The collapse of cheap labour and a populous countryside after the Famine (1845–9) led ultimately, to the wane of the great estates and—hastened by popular and political reform movements—their ultimate dispersal into smaller freeholds, for the benefit of former tenantry, by the Land Commission.

Land, ownership and commerce
In the late 16th century the Fourth Earl of Thomond, Donnchadh O'Brien, was the principal landowner in Thomond with control of the baronies of Islands and Bunratty (Upper and Lower). The O'Brien earls had become loyal Protestants by now and adopted a policy of anglicising landholdings within Thomond and, along with other local élites, created personal estates based on an English pattern. For example, the O'Brien stronghold at Bunratty, for which the Earl received title from James I in 1621, extended over 2,000 acres. The Earl's success at securing English, and, indeed, Dutch, tenants for his estates is reflected by the mix of Irish (49%), English (47%) and Dutch (4%) surnames listed in a breakdown of rates and revenues from the Earl's estates across Clare from 1626 (Cunningham 2008, 72–5). Not content with settling estates the Earl also sought out settlers for towns, specifically Sixmilebridge, where records show an English merchant, tanner and yeoman leased lands and houses (ibid.). Similarly, English settlers including tradesmen, carpenters and weavers were attracted by the growing commercial success of Ennis in the 17th century (Spellissy 1998, 13; and see Ó Murchadha, this chapter).

The emerging colony suffered a terrible setback during the 1641 rising, when English planters were targeted and very frequently murdered by the rebels, but a new influx of planters would soon arrive in the county. Following the Cromwellian war in Ireland, former royalists from other parts of the island were resettled in confiscated lands west of the Shannon, under the *Act of Settlement* (1652). Thus, in the latter part of the 17th century, Clare was principally in the hands of the Earl of Thomond, Catholic families loyal to the Crown and transplanters (Gillespie 2006, 186–9). Within the study area, contemporary surveys record that, in addition to lands posessed by the Earl, lands were held by the MacNamaras, Neylans, the Bishop of Killaloe and Lord Inchquin, among others

(Simington 1967; Frost 1893a). Following the Cromwellian campaigns, transplanters accounted for up to 20% of the county's population in the late 1650s and had settled exclusively within four baronies, including two relevant to the present scheme, Islands and Bunratty (Nugent 2008, 80). The transplanters in effect redressed a population collapse following a decade of warfare in the 1640s and all the associated ravages of famine and disease.

The Williamite-Jacobite Wars (1689–91) brought the 17th century to a turbulent close. Following defeat at Aughrim, Jacobite resistance was finally quashed in Limerick after the city was besieged for a second time in 1691. Little substantial military action appears to have taken place in County Clare but those loyal to James II were 'despoiled of every thing, with no prospect before them but exile and poverty' (Frost 1893a, 570). Estates were confiscated, transferred and sold to Protestant families from County Clare who retained possession and largely controlled the wealth of the county until the mid 19th century (Ó Dálaigh 2008, 114–15). In contrast, in the decades preceding the Famine, and at the other end of the social spectrum, much of the population of Clare lived in landless or near landless households with landholding labourers and cottiers only marginally better off (Ó Murchadha 2008, 245).

Despite the upheavals of the 17th century and the neglect of their estates, successive Earls of Thomond managed to retain possession of their lands; in the late 1660s the seventh Earl owned approximately 18% of the county. Throughout the 18th century, sales necessitated by debt reduced the size and extent of the Thomond estates and in the pre-Famine decades the estate was fragmented and scattered across the county. Some of the larger land blocks included tracts between Crusheen and Ennis (Lynch 2008, fig. 13.1). By the 19th century the O'Brien legacy had passed to Colonel George Wyndham, an important figure in Clare in the pre- and post-Famine eras. His grandson, George Wyndham, played a crucial role in paving the way for the dismantling of landed estates and the transfer of ownership from landlords to tenants in the early 20th century, with the Wyndham *Land Purchase Act* of 1903 (ibid., 330).

Monuments and dwellings

The archaeological record includes visible traces of the changes in everyday life that were played out against the backdrop of changing élites. The SMR for Clare lists a diversity of post-medieval monument types encompassing gun batteries, castles and mansion houses, brickworks and limekilns, roads and bridges, children's burial grounds and Mass rocks. Many are small-scale monuments, representing local responses to evolving agricultural, industrial, domestic and commercial needs of the day, while others met more institutional military and religious needs. On the present road scheme, the range of post-medieval site types excavated was limited to features of an agricultural and industrial nature (Chapter 4). Most were newly identified features, found by testing, with only one excavated example of a visible, upstanding monument—the limekiln at Keelty AR 129.

By the late 17th century across Ireland, the preference was for Jacobean style manor houses, most of which either extended or incorporated pre-existing tower houses. These mansions lay within planted demesnes, with houses of estate workers (kennel keepers and stablemen, herds, gatelodge keepers) typically occurring only on the margins. The ordinary rural tenantry lived elsewhere on the lands forming the total estate holdings. Townhouses of the period stand in Ennis and a handful of contemporary structures are listed in the SMR in townlands within the vicinity of the scheme:

e.g. Tooreen (CL034-054), now restored (Illus. 1.13); and Newpark (CL034-043), a mid 17th-century house later added to and altered. The 18th century saw the rise of the estate house, or 'Big House', with tenants housed peripherally to the house giving rise to more dispersed settlement (Nugent 2008, 94–6). The landlord estate structure prevailed into the post-Famine era; within the study area this includes Hermitage House (CL033-081), an 18th-century

Illus. 1.13—The restored gentry house at Tooreen (CL034-054).

'Gentleman's House' in which the Keanes, relatives of the notorious land agent Marcus Keane (1815–83), resided throughout the 18th and 19th centuries (Lewis 1837; Guy 1893; Burke 1912). Most of the gentry's residences in proximity to the route, however, date from the 19th century, including examples from Clareabbey, Claureen and Kilbreckan.

As we have seen, from the late 17th century in Clare, landed estates with lands leased to tenant farmers became the norm. In the east and south of the country this new landholding structure resulted in the imposition of a different pattern of enclosure with larger, more regular field systems imposed either on older systems or within unenclosed landscapes (Aalen & Whelan 1997, 136). In the 18th century most farmers in the West of Ireland typically operated at subsistence level and those on marginal lands farmed communally, in a rundale system, with the *clachan* at the centre of activities. A *clachan* was a cluster of dwellings, outbuildings and small gardens inhabited by the rural poor. As a settlement form it survived into the 20th century, though many were wiped out in the mid 19th century by the Famine (Feehan 2003, 81–5; Bell & Watson 2008, 24–8). There are few surviving visible remnants of clachans today but many are recorded on the first edition Ordnance Survey map of 1840, which captured a snapshot of rural settlement in the county before the devastation of the Famine. One such clachan has been excavated at Moyveela, in County Galway. Here 18 buildings and a trackway, bank, pavement and multiple platforms were investigated. Tenant farmers from the Moyveela estate are thought to have built it and resided there until it was abandoned in the early 19th century (Tierney 2011, 64–6).

Placenames and settlements
Ciarán Ó Murchadha

The route of the Ennis Bypass and the Western Relief Road takes in six civil parishes, spread over the three baronies of Islands, Bunratty Upper and Bunratty Lower. The parishes are: Clareabbey and Drumcliffe (Islands), Doora, Kilraghtis and Templemaley (Bunratty Upper) and Kilnasoolagh (Bunratty Lower). Six townlands of Clareabbey parish are crossed by the new roads (Ballybeg, Carrowgar, Clareabbey, Killow, Manusmore, Skehanagh); four in Doora (Ballaghboy, Kilbreckan, Knockanean, Knockaskibole); six in Drumcliffe (Ballymacaula, Cahircalla Beg, Cahircalla More,

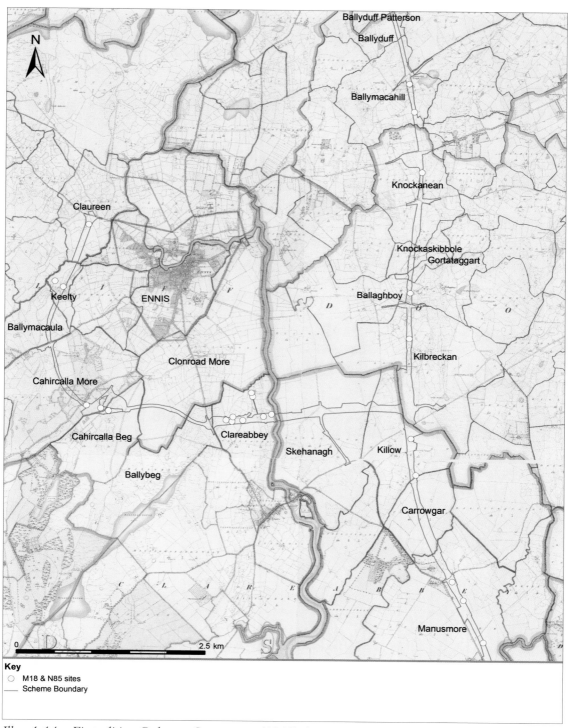

Illus. 1.14—First edition Ordnance Survey map (1840) showing townlands traversed by the new M18 and N85 Western Relief Road.

Claureen, Clonroad More, Keelty); two in Kilnasoolagh (Latoon North, Latoon South); five in Kilraghtis (Ballyduff, Ballymacahill, Carrowdotia, Cragard, Drumquin); and three in Templemaley (Barefield or Gortlumman, Ballyduff Patterson and Ballyduff Blake) (Illus. 1.14). While not all these townlands produced new archaeological sites requiring excavation on the course of the new roads, each has the potential to inform the archaeological and historical record.

Some of these townland names are obscure in derivation, but most of them offer linguistic clues to the historical experience of the stretches of landscape they designate (D'Auria & O'Flaherty 2005; Ó hÓgáin 1938; Frost 1893b). Some of these placenames identify the kinship groups that once occupied them, such as Ballymacahill, from *Baile Mhic Cathail*, the townland of the Mac Cathail, or Ballymacaula, the townland of the Mac Amhlaoibh. Other townland names derive from ancient land measurements or furnish indications of ancient land-use (Carrowgar, from *Ceathrú Gearr*, the short quarter; Carrowdotia, *Ceathrú Dóite*, the burnt quarter), while others again describe topographical features (Cragard, from *Creag Ard*, the high crag; Skehanagh, from *Sceachánach*, bush-covered terrain), man-made structures (Claureen, from *cláirín*, little bridge; Knockaskibbole, from *Cnoc an Sciobóil*, hill of the barn) or ecclesiastical sites (Kilbreckan, from *Cill Breacáin*, Church of Breacán of Doora; Killow, *Cill Lua*, the Church of Lua).

Most of these townland names are readily identifiable in the *Book of Survey and Distribution* and other cadastral sources drawn up in the 17th century, when the Irish landscape received its modern administrative overlay (Simington 1967). Many others may be much older, some dating as far back perhaps as the 12th century when ecclesiastical/administrative divisions first emerged in Ireland.

Typical of sparsely inhabited rural hinterlands in Ireland, the individual townlands have left little in the way of documented source material, and with little to go on—apart from the clues furnished by placenames, the findings of archaeologists published in the present volume and elsewhere, in addition to the fine detail of some local histories—the past experience of these little territories is largely beyond retrieval. We are left only with impressions of a long-sustained continuity of human occupation, and a cultural tenacity that has lasted until close to our own day.

We have seen how the road scheme bisects lowland rural Clare and skirts towns and villages in the county. The history and development of these habitation centres in proximity to the new roads provides information essential to understanding the pattern of human interaction with the Clare landscape. The two most significant centres of population in the vicinity of the new roads are Clarecastle and Ennis.

Clarecastle and its hinterland

The village of Clarecastle, or Clare as it was known until the 19th century, is often said to have originated in a settlement built around the Norman keep constructed by Robert de Muscegros in AD 1250, at a strategic crossing point on the River Fergus (Power 2004, 22). However, it is probable that two *loci* of settlement already existed in the immediate area prior to this, one of them adjacent to the Augustinian foundation established by Domnall Mór O'Brien in AD 1189, and the other at the crossing point itself. Throughout the medieval period the river was spanned by a massive bridge of oak timbers, between two weirs. From this is derived the earliest known name, the *Clár-atha-dá Choradh* (literally, 'the bridge between two weirs') and the *Clár Mór* ('the great wooden bridge') (Ó hÓgáin 1938, 11, 70). In the Tudor period, after the Gaelic lordship of Thomond was reconstituted as an English earldom under the O'Briens, the new shire that replaced it was given the designation

Clare, with the intention that its county capital could be developed at this advantageous location at the highest navigable point of the Fergus estuary, as it appeared to be ideal for the construction of port facilities (Power 2004, 44).

All the major upheavals of the 17th century had their local reverberations in the Clarecastle area and, in such conflicts as the 1641 rising and Confederate Wars, the Cromwellian conquest and the Williamite wars, the castle assumed a certain strategic military importance (Frost 1893a, 379; O'Brien 1986, 179). During the long peaceful interlude of the 18th century, however, both castle and settlement lapsed into insignificance. By 1800 the castle had become the location of a transit depot for the standing British army in Ireland and, throughout the 19th century, there was a constant movement of infantry and cavalry regiments through the depot en route to different destinations. In addition to the depot/barracks, in the early 19th century Clarecastle also boasted an elegant new bridge and there was also a series of improvements to the quays. These combined architectural innovations seemed to portend a prosperous future for the village. However, for a number of reasons, this bright new era was never to dawn, and Clarecastle would remain the very under-developed port for Ennis, the county capital, its chief function being the export of corn and other agricultural commodities from the immediate hinterland.

Throughout the 19th century Clare village remained a desperately impoverished place. In 1841 the population stood at 879 persons and it was not until modern times brought industrial employment and the gradual absorption of Clarecastle into the suburbs surrounding Ennis that the population increased significantly again.

Origins and history of Ennis

Settlement in the Ennis area began early in the 13th century when Donnchadh Cairbreach Ua Briain, the ruling Uí Bhriain dynast, moved his capital to a new location at *Cluain Ramhfhada* on the banks of the Fergus (Ó Dálaigh 1987, 20). Over the centuries a small independent settlement would flourish at *Cluain Ramhfhada*/Clonroad, but the town of Ennis proper developed to the west of it, around the Franciscan abbey established in 1247 by Donnchadh Cairbreach (Gwynn & Gleeson 1962, 268 et seq.; Ó Dálaigh 1987, 19, 22). From the late 16th century, substantial numbers of English Protestants settled in the town under the protection of the O'Briens, formerly Gaelic chieftains and now anglicised, Protestant earls of Thomond. In 1576, Ennis became the county seat of the new county of Clare, favoured over Clarecastle probably for the sole reason that its abbey buildings provided a large enough meeting place for the assizes, an advantage that Clarecastle could not match (Frost 1893a, 245–6).

As owners of Ennis, successive earls of Thomond sought to develop the town by requiring their settled English and native Irish tenants to improve their leased tenements and plots, which would be handed back in this improved condition on the expiry of their short leases. Mercantile activity was encouraged, as Clarecastle became the port for the new town, and seagoing ships docked at its quays, their cargoes freighted upriver to Ennis in small barges or 'lighters' (Ó Murchadha 1998, 3). Street nomenclature along the riverfront in Ennis preserves fossilised memories of the places where these goods were then unloaded: e.g. Harvey's Quay, Parson's Quay and Wood Quay. In the town, a wealthy, enterprising merchant class developed, composed of English Protestant settlers and Irish and Old English Catholics. After the 1650s, when their ranks were swelled by Limerick merchants transplanted into County Clare by the Cromwellians, the Old English would become the dominant

1.15—Ennis in the early 1800s. Turner de Lond's painting (c. 1820) shows a bustling town square and courthouse in Exchange Place (reproduced in Ó Murchadha 1998, np).

influence in town affairs through their control of the Ennis borough corporation (Ó Murchadha 1984, 66–7).

By pre-Famine times, Ennis was a bustling provincial town with a rundown, quasi-medieval appearance, its small central area of three narrow streets surrounded by extensive shantytown suburbs, with lines of hovels extending into the countryside on all its approach roads. The major market and distribution centre for the county of Clare, Ennis was also the seat of administration, commerce and courts in the county (Illus. 1.15). The only substantial business enterprise in Ennis at this time was its extensive corn-milling complex, and with no other employment available, the bulk of the town labourers and tradesmen remained idle and impoverished for much of the year.

Devastated during the Famine, the population of the Ennis borough area dropped sharply from 9,318 in 1841 to 8,623 in 1851 (Census 1852). The drop would have been considerably greater but for the fact that these years also saw a large-scale increase in administrative, police and judicial personnel living in the town, which also became a magnet for thousands of evicted tenants and their families.

In the latter half of the 19th century Ennis went into an inexorable state of decline, and by 1911 there were just 5,472 persons living in its central urban area (Census 1912). For 50 years the population of this tiny area (which was far from including the entire town) remained stagnant, and as late as 1966, had increased only to 5,834 (Census 1967). By the 1980s when the economic situation of country and town had altered greatly, it was still only 5,917 (Census 1986). At that point, however, the bulk of the town's population was living in the newer streets outside the old borough boundary and in the burgeoning housing estates that formed its suburbs. In 2006 the population of Ennis and environs was 24,253 (www.clarelibrary.ie).

Infrastructure and reclamation
Ciarán Ó Murchadha

The N18 Ennis Bypass, together with the ancillary works on the Western Relief Road, represents the latest in a series of civil engineering projects impacting on the greater Ennis area since the 1700s, including drainage works, bridges and quays, a railway and, of course, roads.

Grand Jury county roads

Before the 19th century the main road from Limerick to Galway took a route through Cratloe and Sixmilebridge, Quin, Moyriesk, and Spancillhill, entering Crusheen just beyond Inchicronan Lake. This is clear from late 18th-century maps produced by George Taylor and Andrew Skinner from 1777 onwards (1783, 200) (Illus. 1.16) and Henry Pelham (1787). The general route followed by the modern N18, from Newmarket-on-Fergus through Clarecastle and Ennis, also features on these maps, although, at that time it was of lesser significance. These roads were part of a county system built and maintained by the Grand Jury forerunners of Clare County Council. Around Ennis, the generally favoured route proceeded east of the town. After 1800, the rapid expansion of Ennis and its increasing commercial and administrative importance led to the concentration of traffic on the county roads that converged on it. By 1820 inter-city traffic between Limerick and Galway, as well as that generated locally, was now moving through the town itself.

As to local traffic, information is limited to anecdotal reportage from local newspapers and the published experiences of travel writers. Many of the travel writers availed of the county roads radiating from Ennis in order to access the interior and coastal regions in search of material that would interest the armchair tourists at whom their works were directed. Both these sources confirm that Ennis was now the nexus of an extensive local and inter-county road network (Ó Dálaigh 1998, 172–213). There is strong anecdotal evidence that traffic passing through Ennis now included private and public carriages and coaches, agricultural, commercial and other horse-drawn vehicles, and a wide diversity of slow-moving pedestrian traffic, including cattle drovers with their herds, military forces, and escorted prisoners, as well as a great mass of individual travellers, bound on short and long journeys.

Famine relief roads

During the Great Famine, roadworks formed a major part of the relief schemes operated by government and private agencies. In the Ennis area, however, as in Ireland as a whole, this amounted to a huge investment of manpower in minor repairs along existing roads, involving cutting hills, filling in hollows and rounding corners. The value of this as long-term infrastructural investment was negligible. However, the Famine-era road schemes did produce at least two entirely new county-grade roads that, unusually, were of lasting infrastructural value. These were the roads between Ennis and Quin, now the R469, and the road to Tulla, the modern R352. Both routes were restored to the management of the Grand Jury after 1847, and in the well-documented case of Quin road, it would be years before it was completed (Ó Murchadha 1998, 85–6).

For the post-Famine period the volume of pedestrian and wheeled traffic no longer posed the same difficulties within the town and environs that it had previously. This was because of the sharp drop in population resulting directly from the Famine and the continuing demographic drain in the

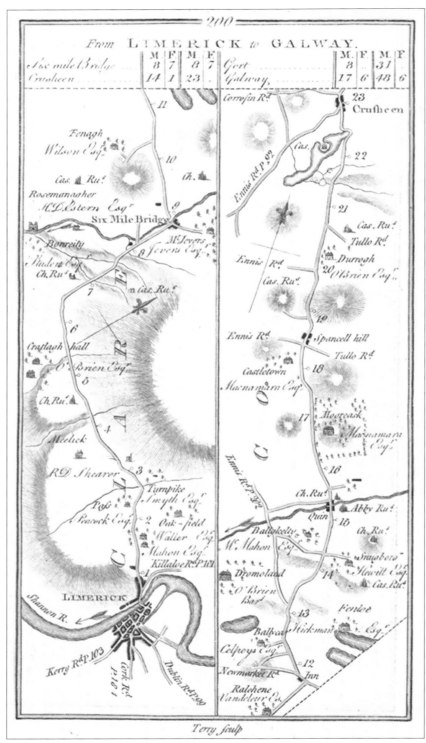

1.16—Taylor and Skinner's map of the main Limerick to Galway route 1783.

decades afterwards. It also coincided with the advent of the railway, in the 1860s, which diverted much of the longer-distance private and commercial traffic to the passenger and freight carriages of the trains operating the new line east of the town.

The coming of the railway

Two separate companies opened lines through Clare during the post-Famine era of railway expansion in Ireland: the Limerick and Ennis Railway (1859), and the Athenry and Ennis Junction Railway (1869) (Mulligan 1983, 57; Lenihan 1990). Eventually, the entire line was taken over by the Waterford and Limerick Railway, which maintained the route until a State takeover in the 20th century. The railway line was built in parallel with the main roadway and in one sense the new railway line constitutes an early transport bypass for Ennis, in that it served to relieve the traffic within the town centre.

Land reclamation: the Fergus drainage

An enormous acreage of land in the basin of the River Fergus was rendered useless through frequent and sometimes catastrophic flooding. A great project to drain, and thereby reclaim this land was begun as an immediate response to Famine conditions in 1846 (Ó Murchadha 1998, 259–66). The project was pushed forward intermittently until well into the 1850s, although it was never to be fully completed. Among the lands affected were all those through which the 19th-century railway and 21st-century bypass would be constructed.

Illus. 1.17—Clare Abbey stands high and dry above the floodwaters of the Fergus River in 2009 (Department Arts, Heritage and Gaeltacht).

The entire scheme was designed by a Board of Works engineer named John W Kelly, and its immediate objectives were the removal of artifical and natural obstacles in the Fergus and the deepening of the river channel. At Clarecastle, one great obstacle was a submerged shelf of rock at the bridge whose removal was integral to the entire plan, the theory being that the downriver flow from the cleared and deepened channel above Ennis would be strong enough to prevent a tidal backwash that might otherwise lead to inundations in the town. In the event, an insufficient number of the riparian landowners were willing to participate in the second, crucial phase of the reclamation, and the project lapsed. Since the ledge at Clarecastle had not been fully removed, the lands south and east of Ennis were once again subject to flooding, despite the continued maintenance and improvement of a double system of embankments along the river.

Late in the 19th century a barrage with sluices was installed on the channel at Clarecastle. This was a woefully inadequate solution to the problem, however, and even after a major upgrading in the late 1940s, flooding in these lands remained frequent and chronic (Dáil Éireann 1943). Owners and occupiers of lands above Ennis, on the other hand, benefited greatly from the overall drainage scheme, which liberated large tracts of land that were previously useless for agriculture. At the same time the failure to complete the project meant that much of the lands that were successfully drained were also subject to occasional flooding (Power 2004, 119–21) (Illus. 1.17).

Between 1864 and 1894 another major engineering project took place on the Fergus. This was the attempt to drain some 2,000 acres of mudflats below Clarecastle (Ó Murchadha 1998, 266; Power 2004, 117–19; Becker 1881, 167–83). However, because this was on the estuary, the effects on the local region under discussion were far less significant than the main Fergus drainage works.

2
PREHISTORIC SITE EXCAVATIONS

Nóra Bermingham, Graham Hull and Kate Taylor
with a contribution by C Jones

Evidence for prehistoric occupation of the landscape was revealed on 14 sites (Illus. 2.1). The excavated sites included burnt mounds and funerary deposits ranging in date from the Chalcolithic to the Late Iron Age. Evidence of prehistoric funerary activity occurred on five sites and in all cases was in the form of cremation deposits, mainly in pits. A single ring-ditch represents the only burial monument excavated. Nine sites yielded burnt mound remnants, typically truncated, and shallow deposits, some of which had associated pit and/or trough features. Less substantial examples were recorded as burnt spreads. Unusually, the scheme provided the opportunity for excavating one intact burnt mound with a stone-lined trough. The recovery of a palstave axehead during testing further attests to the significant prehistoric occupation of the area.

Burnt mounds and spreads

Cahircalla Beg AR126: burnt mound with trough[1]

Cahircalla Beg AR126 is distinguished from other burnt mounds excavated on the scheme as it was intact and retained a stone-built trough. The site's location, on a limestone outcrop within an area of bog formed in a shallow valley, protected it from agricultural damage. (Many other burnt mounds on the scheme were truncated by agricultural works resulting in comparatively shallow or remnant mounds.) Cahircalla Beg was covered in hazel scrub prior to excavation and, although subject to root damage, represents an excellent example of an intact, multi-period burnt mound (Illus. 2.2).

Multiple phases of activity were identified spanning several centuries. This repeated use resulted in the accumulation of a crescent- or kidney-shaped mound around a centrally placed trough (Illus. 2.3 and 2.4). The mound measured 13.5 m by 17.5 m with a maximum height of 1.6 m and comprised an estimated 400 tonnes of stone. Three phases of activity have been defined using radiocarbon dating of charcoal derived from distinct deposits.

Phase 1
In the years 2550–2300 BC (Beta-207728), a burnt stone layer (22) was deposited onto limestone bedrock. The deposit comprised heat-shattered sandstone with charcoal, and measured 4 m wide

---

1 Cahircalla Beg, Co. Clare; barony Islands; NGR 132803 175465; height 10 m OD; Excavation Licence No. 04E0024. Excavation Director: Graham Hull.

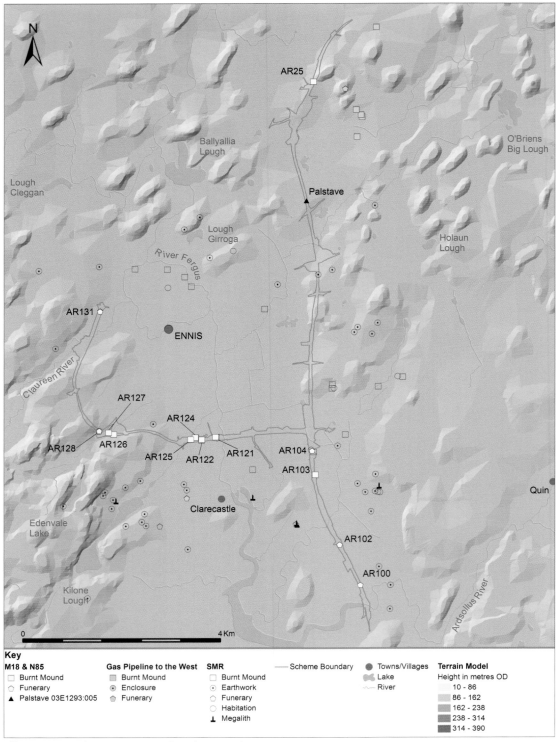

Illus. 2.1—Prehistoric sites on the scheme and in its environs.

and 0.15 m deep. Charcoal of hazel, ash, cherry/blackthorn, oak and yew was present. There was no evidence for a trough during this phase, which probably represents a single event. Broadly contemporary burnt spreads are situated 220 m to the north and west with dates between 2470 BC and 2150 BC (see Cahircalla More AR 127).

Illus. 2.2—Cahircalla Beg AR 126. Intact burnt mound prior to excavation.

Phase 2

In the same location, around 1440–1280 BC (Beta-211564), a second horizon (21) of heat-shattered stone and charcoal was deposited, which measured 4 m wide and 0.3 m deep. In contrast to the earlier deposit, limestone accounted for approximately 80% of the stone. A similar range of woodland taxa provided firewood with hazel, ash, oak and pomaceous fruitwood occurring. Again, there was no evidence for a trough during this phase.

Phase 3

This phase is represented by a series of deposits that radiocarbon dating has revealed as multiple episodes of deposition over a relatively short period. During this phase, in which the stone-built

Illus. 2.3—Cahircalla Beg AR 126. Stone-lined trough.

trough was erected and reinforced, five main deposits were made which overlap in time: deposit 18 dates to 1190–930 BC (Beta-211565), deposit 19 to 1140–920 BC (Beta-211562), deposit 20 to 1130–920 BC (Beta-211563) with deposits 16 and 17 each dating to 1000–820 BC (Beta-207729 and Beta-211561). These deposits mainly represent material taken from and dumped around the trough, except where access was required in the north–west. Virtually all the stone was limestone with less than 1% sandstone occurring. Deposit 20 was a discrete deposit of burnt limestone within the larger mound deposit and represents a fire on the surface of the mound.

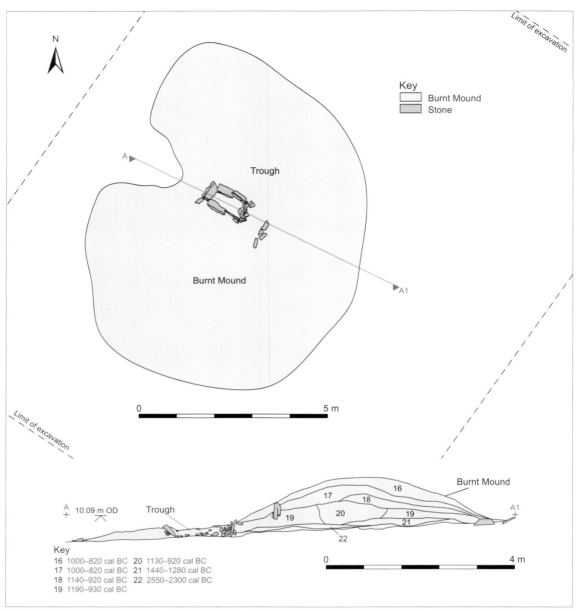

N

Key
Burnt Mound
Stone

Trough

A ▶

◀ A1

Burnt Mound

Limit of excavation

Limit of excavation

0   5 m

Burnt Mound

A 10.09 m OD   Trough   16
                                    17   18
+   19   20   19
                                              21
                        19   22

A1
+

Key
16 1000–820 cal BC   20 1130–920 cal BC
17 1000–820 cal BC   21 1440–1280 cal BC
18 1140–920 cal BC   22 2550–2300 cal BC
19 1190–930 cal BC

0   4 m

Illus. 2.4—Cahircalla Beg AR126. Burnt mound in plan and section.

The trough was constructed from six limestone slabs set on edge to form a rectangle and measured 1.8 m by 0.9 m, 0.45 m deep, with an approximate volume of 0.75 m^3 (Illus. 2.3). The trough did not yield evidence for a lining though its construction suggests one would have been required to retain water. In places the slabs sat directly on the underlying bedrock but were also stratigraphically later than the earliest deposit in Phase 3 (deposit 19). At some stage after its formation, four limestone slabs were inserted into the mound behind the trough and served to protect it from mound slippage (Illus. 2.4).

Plant macrofossils and animal bone

The broadest range of woodland taxa occurs in Phase 3. Charocals of hazel, alder, ash, pomaceous fruitwood, cherry/blackthorn, willow/poplar, oak, yew and elm occur in varying proportions. Other than charcoal, charred plant remains were not represented but a small quantity of unidentifiable burnt mammal bone was retrieved from within the mound. A single cattle rib fragment recovered from the trough cannot be assigned with certainty to a specific deposit within Phase 3. A number of well-preserved bone fragments bearing saw marks, retrieved from the uppermost mound deposit, are of recent origin.

Cahircalla More AR127: burnt spreads[2]

Excavations at Cahircalla More comprised eight individual trenches distributed across rough pasture reclaimed from bog (Illus. 2.5 and 2.6). Archaeological features included seven amorphous burnt spreads. All were shallow, up to 0.1 m thick, were between 3 m and 13 m wide and mainly comprised sandstone, although limestone and igneous rock did occur. There was no evidence of hearths or of cut features such as troughs. The relatively small volume of material and simple stratigraphy at each site suggests short periods of use, probably single episodes.

Table 2.1—Cahircalla More AR127. Radiocarbon-dated burnt spreads.

Site	Date (2σ)	Lab. Code
AR127i	2470–2210 cal. BC	Beta-211566
AR127ii	1100–900 cal. BC	Beta-211567
AR127iii	1910–1700 cal. BC	Beta-207735
AR127iv	2450–2150 cal. BC	Beta-211568
AR127v	2330–2060 cal. BC	Beta-207731
AR127vii	2290–2040 cal. BC	Beta-211569
AR127viii	2020–1770 cal. BC	Beta-211570

Dating evidence The seven seemingly discrete burnt spreads were deposited within the margins of a peat basin at various times in the Chalcolithic, the Early Bronze Age and later in the Bronze Age (Table 2.1; Illus. 1.6).

Plant and animal remains Each spread contained charcoal with ash, alder, elm, hazel, oak, pomaceous fruitwood and yew occurring. Pieces of hazelnut shells were the only other plant macrofossils recovered, namely from AR127i, ii, iii and viii.

Artefacts Nil.

---

2   Cahircalla More, Co. Clare; barony Islands; NGR 132700 175500; height c. 9 m OD; Excavation Licence No. 04E0028. Excavation Director: Kate Taylor.

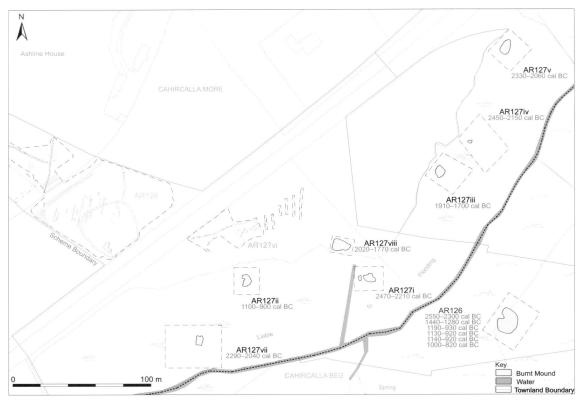

Illus. 2.5—Cahircalla More AR127 i–v, vii–viii and also (bottom right) the burnt mound at Cahircalla Beg AR126.

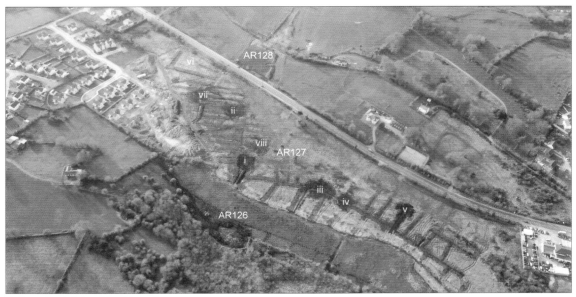

Illus. 2.6—Cahircalla More AR127 and AR128; Cahircalla Beg AR126. Aerial view of the excavations showing the wetland area or bog in which the sites were located.

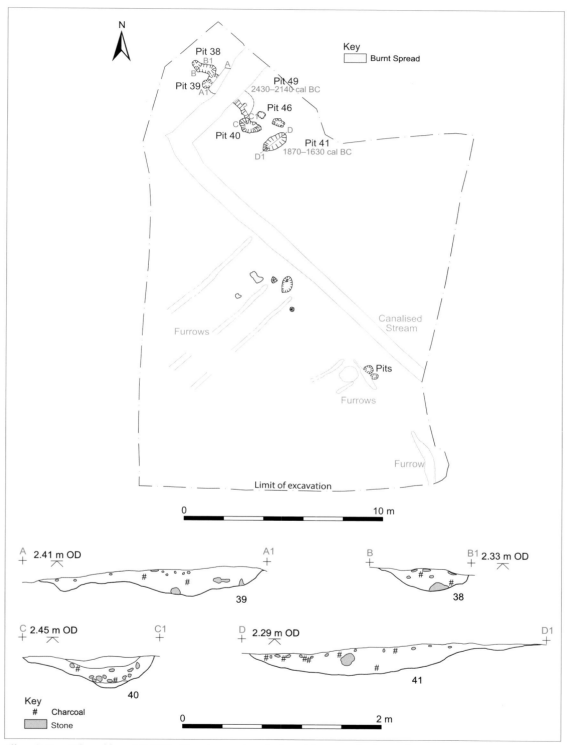

Illus. 2.7—Clareabbey AR122. Burnt spread and pits with examples in section.

Clareabbey AR122: burnt spread and pits[3]

Situated at the edge of a bog were a single burnt spread and a series of 10 pits containing charcoal and heat-shattered stone (Illus. 2.7). Two phases of prehistoric activity were identified across the north, centre and south of the excavation area and not all features can be assigned to one phase or the other. Located towards the centre, within a shallow depression, was the burnt spread. The pits were typically oval or circular in plan and concave in profile and were infilled with charcoal and heat-shattered stone. The pits in the north contained similar fills while those in the centre generally contained little or no stone.

Dating evidence Hazel/alder charcoal from Pit 49 was dated to 2430–2140 BC (Beta-211576). Activity several centuries later is implied by a date of 1870–1630 BC (Beta-211575) from hazel charcoal from Pit 41.

Plant and animal remains Charcoal included alder, ash, hazel, pomaceous fruitwood, cherry/blackthorn, oak, willow, yew, elm and rose/briar—the latter representing a unique instance within the scheme. Two pits yielded small quantities of burnt and unidentifiable mammal bone though Pit 40 contained a single, probable red deer metapodial.

Artefacts Nil.

Clareabbey AR124: burnt mound and troughs[4]

Excavations revealed a burnt mound overlying a pit or trough with a second nearby pit/trough. Beneath the mound was a circular, flat-bottomed pit filled with the same material as in the overlying mound. Similarly filled was a second pit or trough exposed in the baulk of the excavation trench.

Dating evidence Hazel/alder charcoal dated to 2200–1960 BC (Beta-211560) places the site in the opening centuries of the Bronze Age.

Plant and animal remains Charcoal represented included hazel, alder, ash and yew with ash the most abundant.

Artefacts Nil.

---

3   Clareabbey, Co. Clare; barony Islands; NGR 134587 175350; height 2.2–3.6 m OD; Excavation Licence No. 04E0032. Excavation Director: Kate Taylor.
4   Clareabbey, Co. Clare; barony Islands; NGR 134456 175394; height 2.3 m OD; Excavation Licence No. 04E0022. Excavation Director: Graham Hull.
5   Killow, Co. Clare; barony Bunratty Upper; NGR 136822 175115; height c. 2.5 m OD; Excavation Licence No. 04E0191. Excavation Director: Kate Taylor.

Killow AR104: burnt mound[5]

The excavation straddled an area of reclaimed peatland punctured by a substantial gravel island or drumlin, and the edge of nearby higher ground. Excavations revealed multiple phases of prehistoric and medieval activity with the earliest phase represented by a burnt mound (Illus. 2.8). The mound

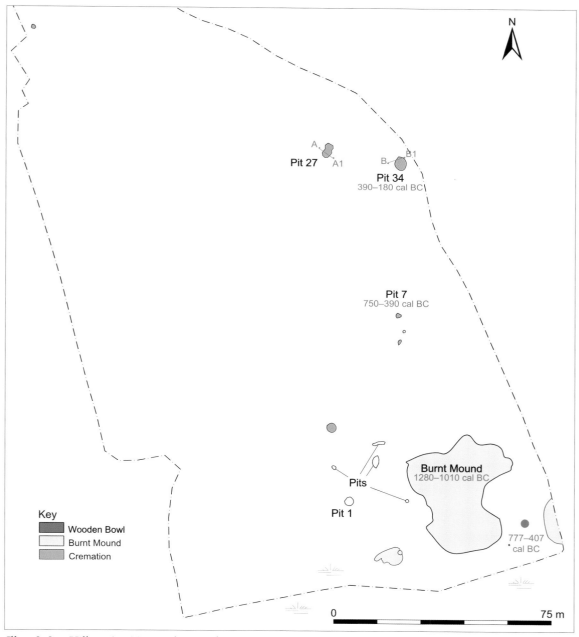

Illus. 2.8—Killow AR104. Prehistoric features.

occupied the south-east corner of the excavation where it survived in two parts and overlay a peat-filled hollow. Overall, the mound was concave or bowl-shaped in profile, mirroring the morphology of the underlying hollow.

Immediately south-west of the mound was a second smaller burnt spread that overlay a small circular pit with charcoal. Six other pits were identified north-west and south of these features (Illus. 2.8). Charcoal and heat-shattered stones occurred in varying amounts though not every pit contained both. All the above features were eventually sealed by peat as the mire expanded over the slopes of the gravel island.

Dating evidence Charred hazelnut from the mound returned a date of 1280–1010 BC (Beta-211591).

Plant and animal remains The mound, the nearby spread and pits yielded small quantities of unidentifiable mammal bone, most of which was burnt. The bone appeared to be from cattle-sized animals, but one pit contained a single unburnt horse tibia. Charcoal was retrieved from all but one of the pits with hazel, ash, pomaceous fruitwood, cherry/blackthorn, oak and willow/poplar with hazel and ash the only taxa represented in the mound.

Artefacts Nil.

Clareabbey AR121: burnt spreads[6]

Two burnt mounds were excavated. The larger mound comprised an amorphous spread. The smaller example, a shallow oval deposit, was approximately 25 m to the south-east and within peat. Although this mound is undated, its proximity to the larger mound and their shared characteristics suggest they are contemporary.

Dating evidence Hazel charcoal from the larger mound returned a date of 1000–820 BC (Beta-211574).

Plant and animal remains Charcoal was abundant and included alder, ash, cherry/blackthorn, pomaceous fruitwood, hazel, oak, willow/poplar and yew.

Artefacts Nil.

Killow AR103: burnt mound[7]

A burnt mound, 11 m by 8 m by 0.25 m, was situated at the base of the slope of a peat-filled river valley. Two deposits formed an amorphous mound. The lower deposit (51) was a loose silty layer

---

6 Clareabbey, Co. Clare; barony Islands; NGR 134863 175403; height c. 2 m OD; Excavation Licence No. 04E0031. Excavation Director: Kate Taylor.

7 Killow, Co. Clare; barony Bunratty Upper; NGR 136888 174611; height 1–3.5 m OD; Excavation Licence No. 04E0190. Excavation Director: Kate Taylor.

while the upper horizon (52) formed the bulk of the mound. A large pit south of the mound and a drain east of it were interpreted as modern features of no archaeological interest.

Dating evidence A fragment of hazelnut shell from the mound returned a date of 920–800 BC (Beta-211588).

Plant and animal remains Charcoal was abundant in the upper mound deposit and included pomaceous fruitwood, alder, dogwood, hazel, ash, cherry/blackthorn, oak and willow/poplar. This deposit also yielded 5 g of burnt animal bone fragments, none of which could be identified to species.

Artefacts Nil.

Carrowdotia AR25: burnt spreads[8]

Excavations in the vicinity of a medieval cashel (see Chapter 3) recorded a series of burnt stone spreads at the edge of a bog at the foot of a steep hill. (The cashel was located about 50 m uphill and to the north.) The presence of a substantial sink-hole in the adjacent bog hampered their investigation (Illus. 2.9). The spreads were generally thin, with little or no charcoal inclusions, comprising largely degraded or burnt sandstone. The deposits were sealed by 0.3 m of peat, from which a single chert flake was retrieved (03E1442:40). These features are probably prehistoric in date.

Dating evidence Nil.

Plant and animal remains Nil.

Artefacts Chert flake (03E1442: 40).

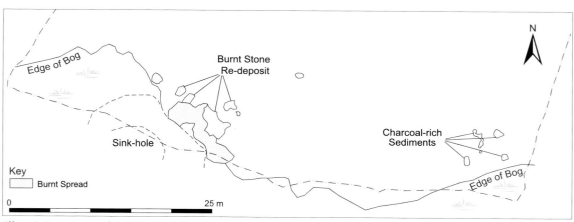

Illus. 2.9—Carrowdotia AR25. Burnt spread and associated deposits with sink-hole in adjacent bog indicated.

8   Carrowdotia, Co. Clare; barony Bunratty Upper; NGR 136850 182830; height 19 m OD; Excavation Licence No. 03E1442. Excavation Director: Kate Taylor.

Illus. 2.10—Clareabbey AR120, AR121, AR122, AR123 and AR125. Aerial view of the excavation sites from west with the Augustinian foundation at Clare Abbey (centre left) and the River Fergus (top).

Clareabbey AR125: burnt mound[9]

Archaeological testing in advance of road construction had revealed a burnt mound on the edge of a bog (Illus. 2.10). The site was destroyed in error before it could be fully investigated. Nearby was a smaller spread of similar composition. Due to its premature destruction the site remains undated and could not be sampled but is likely to have been prehistoric in date.

Dating evidence Nil.

Plant and animal remains Nil.

Artefacts Nil.

9   Clareabbey, Co. Clare; barony Islands; NGR 134366 175353; height 2.35 m OD; Excavation Licence No. 04E0023. Excavation Director: Graham Hull.

Fire, water, wood and stone

Nóra Bermingham

The intact burnt mound at Cahircalla Beg contrasts markedly with the other burnt mounds and spreads excavated on the scheme. About 15 of these smaller burnt mounds/spreads were identified at eight locations, which represents a significant increase on the number of previously known sites within the study area. (Eighteen burnt spreads and 10 *fulachtaí fia* are listed within the SMR for the area.) The scheme sites shared many similarities in terms of their morphology, composition and location. Typically, they comprised a simple deposit of heat-shattered stone and charcoal revealed either as an amorphous or an irregular deposit. The smallest, Clareabbey AR122, measured 1.07 m by 0.7 m and the largest, Clareabbey AR121, was up to 15 m wide. The deeper deposits retained a slightly domed profile but most were relatively level. In depth, the deposits ranged between 0.1 m and 0.4 m with most (nine of them) being less than 0.2 m. At only one site, Killow AR103, were two distinct and overlying deposits identified. The estimated maximum volume of the deposits at seven sites at Cahircalla More AR127 ranges from 0.5 m³ to 8 m³ with an average volume of 4.4 m³. The relatively small volume of material and simple stratigraphy is repeated at sites excavated in Galway (Delaney & Tierney 2011, 41) but contrasts with significantly larger examples in, for example, Killoran, Co. Tipperary (Cross May et al. 2005a, 272–4).

These smaller burnt mounds and spreads were formed by heat-shattered stone and charcoal. Various combinations of limestone, sandstone, igneous rock and even quartz were utilised, with all available locally in the glacial till. Sandstone was the dominant stone type at three locations (Cahircalla More AR127, Clareabbey AR124 and Carrowdotia AR25) with limestone more frequent elsewhere. The selection of sandstone in preference to other stone types might suggest these sites can be associated with cooking, with other activities occurring at sites where limestone was heated. The immersion of roasted limestone in water results in the production of noxious calcium hydroxide which could render the resulting hot water unfit for cooking. It has been suggested, however, that contamination was unlikely to have reached harmful levels and that wrapping meat in straw when cooking protected it from contamination (Grogan et al. 2007, 96–101).

Three sites had associated pits with one at Clareabbey AR124, six at Killow AR104 and 10 at Clareabbey AR122. In only one case, Clareabbey AR124, was a pit found under a burnt mound but all pits contained heat-shattered stone and charcoal and were unlined. At each site, the pits had been cut into the underlying glacial till which at these locations is capable of retaining water, at least in the short-term. The general absence of linings contrasts with pits/troughs excavated on the M18 in County Galway. Here, pits from Ballyglass West and Moyveela retained evidence for stone, daub and wattle linings. Delaney & Tierney (2011, 41) suggest pits with a measurable volume of less than 1 m³ and that are unlined represent non-boiling pits that served a function other than heating water. The lack of a lining may, however, require qualification depending on the permeability of the sediment into which a pit or trough was cut. The noticeable clay content of the glacial till on the route would have negated the need for a pit lining. Where pits or troughs are absent, it may be that water was both transported and heated in a portable container. The water needed to fill the stone-lined trough occupying the rocky outcrop at Cahircalla Beg was presumably carried up from the bog below in some sort of a container. The capacity of Bronze Age ceramic vessels to hold hot stones and water has been dismissed as the pots were insufficiently robust to withstand the process (Grogan et al. 2007, 100). It is possible another form of vessel, such as a leather or wood one, was used in this way but as yet there is no evidence. Where pits or troughs are lacking, the hot stone may have been used for something other than heating water.

Burnt mounds are typically positioned within wetland margins where there is easy access to groundwater and ease of access from drier ground. In Derryville bog, large multi-phased examples occupied the fen margins (Cross May et al. 2005b, 217–20). Of the sites excavated on the Gas Pipeline to the West, all were located at the wetland/dryland interface with two sites positioned in relation to on-site springs and one having evidence for water management (Grogan et al. 2007, 87). Similarly, the sites on the route occupy wet, marshy ground fringing an area of bog or a river floodplain, in this case the floodplain of the Fergus River. The occurrence of seven sites within the bog margins at Cahircalla More AR127 illustrates that the location requirements changed little through time. These, and the other sites excavated were accessed from nearby higher ground, presumably the source of the stone and firewood utilised on site. Wood was gathered from smaller trees and shrubs (see Chapter 7). Two sites at Cahircalla More AR127 involved lighting fires on the surface of the bog: burnt peat was identified amongst plant macrofossil remains from the sites. Hearths are lacking on all the sites on the scheme suggesting fires were probably lit on the surfaces of developing mounds (Cross May et al. 2005b, 219).

The dated burnt mounds and spreads (including Cahircalla Beg AR126) provide some of the earliest occupation evidence on the scheme. Four sites returned Chalcolithic dates; two straddle the Chalcolithic and Early Bronze Age period; three are Early Bronze Age with five dating to the later Bronze Age (Illus. 1.6). As more burnt mounds are excavated and dated, the chronological distribution of this site type is being redefined. In addition to the Chalcolithic and Early Bronze Age sites on the route, excavations on the Gas Pipeline to the West yielded six sites falling within these periods—almost one third of the dated burnt mounds on the pipeline (Grogan et al. 2007, 87). Twelve others dated between 1500 BC and 800 BC, centuries in which burnt mound numbers across the island are highest (Brindley et al. 1990; Ó Néill 2004). Similarly, most of the burnt mounds excavated on the M18 in County Galway returned later Bronze Age dates but six date from the Early Bronze Age (Delaney & Tierney 2011, 33).

Burial sites

Manusmore AR100: multi-period cremation cemetery[10]

Excavations at Manusmore revealed a multi-period prehistoric cremation cemetery located in pasture near the top of a gentle south-facing incline. The site overlooks the floodplain of the Ardsollus River, the modern course of which is located 120 m to the south-east (Illus. 2.11). The location is exposed and has views across the Fergus estuary to the west and the south-west. Within an excavation area of 8,693 m², 61 prehistoric cut features were recorded, mainly cremation pits and possible post-holes. All of these features were cut into glacial till and overlain by 0.4 m of ploughsoil. Dates from six pits indicate cremations were deposited in the Chalcolithic, at the emergence of the Bronze Age, on at least three occasions in the later Bronze Age, and at least twice in the Iron Age (Illus. 2.12).

10   Manusmore, Co. Clare; barony Islands; NGR 137800 172333; height 8 m OD; Excavation Licence No. 04E0187. Excavation Director: Graham Hull.

Illus. 2.11—Manusmore AR100 and AR102. Aerial view of the excavations with the River Ardsollus to the south.

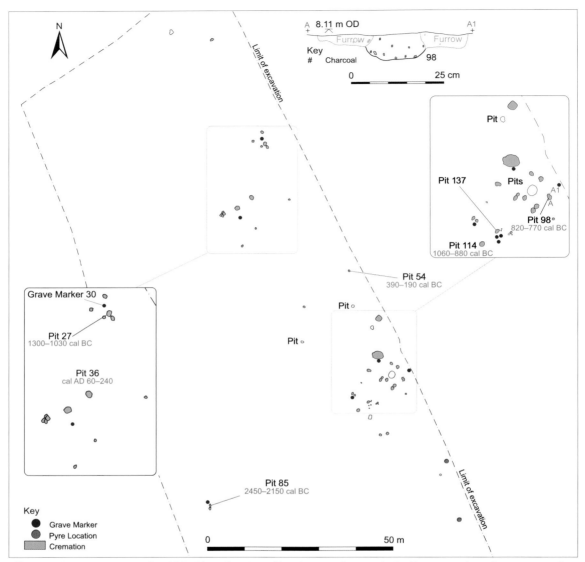

Illus. 2.12—Manusmore AR100. Plan showing all prehistoric features including cremation pits, grave markers and pyre locations with (top) section of Pit 98.

Cremation pits

Twenty seven pits had cremated bone inclusions and a further five contained flecks of burnt bone that suggest these pits also had a funerary connection. These 32 pits were typically circular or sub-circular in shape, with diameters of 0.45–0.9 m and were 0.07–0.4 m deep. Most had vertical or near vertical sides with either concave or flat bases (Illus. 2.13).

Dating evidence shows that the ridge was used on several occasions as a focus for funerary activity. The earliest episode, represented by Pit 85, occurred at 2450–2150 BC (Beta-211582). Later Bronze Age episodes are represented by hazel charcoal from Pit 27 dated to 1300–1030 BC (Beta-211580)

Illus. 2.13—Manusmore AR100. Possible marker post-pits (left) and cremation Pit 24 (right).

and Pit 98, 820–770 BC (Beta-211584). Charred barley from Pit 114 was dated to 1060–880 BC (Beta-211583). Iron Age activity is represented by Pits 54 and 36 with dates at 390–190 BC (Beta-211581) and AD 60–240 (Beta-207733). In addition to cremation pits, two small areas of burnt glacial till were also recorded. These heat reddened and oxidised patches of ground may represent pyre locations. The cremated human remains retrieved at Manusmore are discussed in more detail in Chapter 5 but, in summary, are represented by less than 700 g of cremated bone inclusive of skull and limb bone fragments. The minimum number of individuals represented is unknown as is the gender or age of any of the individuals represented.

Post-holes

Thirteen small cut features were found in close proximity to many of the cremation pits. These were circular to sub-circular in plan, with diameters of 0.15–0.48 m and were 0.11–0.32 m deep. They typically contained silty fills and charcoal but not bone. In some cases they may represent post-holes that held timber uprights, possibly grave markers (e.g. Pits 30, 45 and 68). Six post-holes, albeit in a somewhat irregular arrangement, are situated immediately east of cremation Pit 137. They may represent the remains of a fence or screen erected next to the pit (Illus. 2.12).

Plant macrofossils

Charcoal from the pits included a wide range of woodland taxa including alder, birch, hazel, ash, pomaceous fruitwood, cherry/blackthorn, oak, willow/poplar, yew and elm. Species representation differed slightly between pits and phases but overall varied local woodland is implied, regardless of period.

Other charred plant remains identified were tuber and root/stem fragments, cereals and hazelnut shells. These occurred occasionally and in low numbers; uprooted dried plant material represented by tuber and root/stem fragments was possibly used as kindling. The cereal contents of two pits suggested the deliberate deposition of charred cereal rather than accidental inclusion in pyre residue. Pit 27 and Pit 7 contained moderate to high densities of wheat grains, some wheat chaff and barley.

Artefacts

Pottery was found in seven pits; five also contained small amounts of metal-working slag and nine included flint and/or chert lithics. The pottery was confined to the pits in the southern half of the excavation area and slag was restricted to pits in the northern half. Lithics were distributed across the centre and the south but were absent in the north (see Chapter 8).

Pottery

The pottery comprised poorly preserved and undecorated body sherds and scraps most likely derived from multiple vessels (see Chapter 8). The fragments were unburnt, heavily abraded and eroded and probably represent disparate sherds from old and/or reused broken vessels (Illus. 8.1). One sherd from Pit 174 derived from an urn but otherwise vessel form was indeterminate. The coarsely gritted/voided fabric of the pottery indicates a date in the later Bronze Age and this is supported by the radiocarbon dates from the site which range from the 14th century BC to the 9th century BC. It is probable the pottery was manufactured from clay sources available locally.

Slag

Five pits yielded fragments of slag with a total weight of 16 g including two dated pits, 36 and 54; both are Late Iron Age with dates of AD 60–240 (Beta-207733) and 390–190 BC (Beta-211581). All but four fragments of hammerscale (i.e. flake and sphere microslags produced during the working and welding of iron pieces) from Pit 38, could not be assigned specifically to iron-working. While the amount of slag is insufficient to suggest metal-working occurred on site it is possible that charcoal deposited in Pit 38 was brought from the vicinity of smithing activity, inadvertently introducing hammerscale into the pit (see Chapter 8).

Lithics

An assemblage of 89 pieces of chipped stone was retrieved and included items made from flint (67 pieces) and from fine-grained chert (22 pieces). It mainly comprised spalls, the majority of which were minute; also some flakes and lumps with flaking traces. None of the items was chronologically distinctive. The lithics were retrieved from a range of pits, including the earliest dated example, Pit 85, and one of the latest examples, Pit 54, which also included slag. Most pits contained fewer than 10 pieces but one contained 24 items, albeit minute spalls (see Chapter 8).

Manusmore AR102: multi-period cremation cemetery[11]

Situated near the top of a south-facing slope with views overlooking the Ardsollus River to the south and the Fergus estuary to the south-west, a series of 36 pits and possible post-holes was recorded at Manusmore AR102 (Illus. 2.14). All had been cut into the underlying glacial till and were sealed by up to 0.5 m of ploughsoil and topsoil. Ploughing had resulted in truncation of the archaeological features; plough scars and a plough headland were evident and the landowner reported tillage in the 1950s. Five pits, and possibly an additional three others, yielded cremated human remains, illustrating

---

11 Manusmore, Co. Clare; barony Islands; NGR 137380 173160; height c. 12.5 m OD; Excavation Licence No. 04E0189. Excavation Director: Graham Hull.

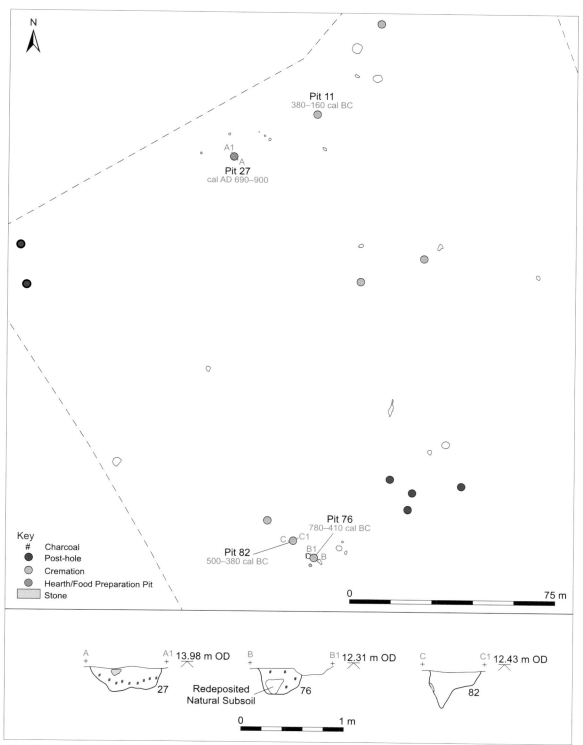

Illus. 2.14—Manusmore AR102. Iron Age cremation cemetery with early medieval pit (Pit 27).

the funerary nature of activity on the ridge. Radiocarbon dates place the activity at the Bronze Age/ Iron Age transition and in the Late Iron Age with dates of 780–410 BC (Beta-211587), 500–380 BC (Beta-207734) and 380–160 BC (Beta-211585). The site is contemporary with episodes of similar funerary practices at Manusmore AR100, 900 m to the south-west.

Cremation pits and possible post-holes

The pits were roughly circular or oval in plan and were typically 0.5–1 m in diameter and 0.3–0.5 m deep. In profile, the pits ranged from steep-sided with flat bases to shallower, concave examples (Illus. 2.14). Nine possible post-holes were identified. These were typically smaller than the pits with diameters of 0.22–0.4 m and depths of 0.1–0.32 m. Pit and post-hole fills were sandy silts with varying quantities of charcoal. Other pit-fill inclusions were cremated bone fragments, slag, pieces of limestone and sandstone and burnt clay. Also, soil sample analysis identified archaeobotanical remains including charred cereal grains and tree/shrub macrofossils. This cemetery did not yield pottery or lithics. Cremated human remains were interred here from at least 780–410 BC (Beta-211587) when Pit 76 was cut and filled. Hazel charcoal from Pit 82 returned a date of 500–380 BC (Beta-207734); this pit also contained cremated human bone. In contrast, the latest prehistoric date, 380–160 BC (Beta-211585), derives from Pit 11, which did not contain human remains. Although not a cremation burial, the pit probably represents activity related to the use of the site as a burial place. The cremated human remains are discussed in detail in Chapter 5. In summary, c. 165 g of cremated human bone was recovered from five pits in which a range of body parts, including skulls and limb bones, was represented. The age and gender of the individuals represented could not be established.

Plant macrofossils

The charcoal recovered from cremation pits is likely to derive from wood burnt in funeral pyres. During the Bronze Age/Iron Age transition, oak, hazel, ash and pomaceous fruitwood were selected for use (Pit 76) with oak and hazel abundant. This continued to be the case throughout the Iron Age. Pit 82 yielded the same woodland taxa with one addition, cherry/blackthorn. The latest dated pit, Pit 11, contained only oak and hazel charcoal. Undated pits contained more or less the same taxa listed above with alder, willow/poplar and elm occurring occasionally and in small amounts. In general, the tree species identified suggest mixed woodland and although similar to contemporary charcoal assemblages from the other excavated site with cremation pits, at Manusmore AR100, the abundance of oak at the more northerly Manusmore AR102 may be significant, as this wood would no doubt have been highly valued in all periods (see Chapter 7).

Low densities of other charred plant macrofossils were identified from assessments of soil samples from 14 pits including those with human remains. Cereal grains of oats and barley, hazelnut shell and sloe fruit-stone fragments occurred in dated and undated pits. All of this material is food waste, but whether it represents ritual offerings in the context of funeral ceremonies, or funerary feasting or, more mundanely, food processing unrelated to funerary activity, cannot be said with total confidence. On balance, however, it is more likely to be associated with the cremations and funerary ritual than not.

Slag

Slag was present in four pits including the earliest and latest dated examples, Pit 76 and Pit 11, respectively. A combination of microslag, fuel ash slag and undiagnostic pieces, with a total weight of 52 g, was retrieved by means of sieving soil samples. None of the slag could be identified with either iron-smelting or smithing.

Killow AR104: probable cremation cemetery[12]

As described above (Killow AR104: burnt mounds and pits), this excavation site straddled an area of reclaimed peatland, a substantial gravel island or drumlin, and the edge of nearby higher, dry ground. Excavations revealed multiple phases of prehistoric and medieval activity (see Chapter 3) with the earliest phase represented by a late second millennium BC burnt mound and associated pits. The site also revealed evidence for funerary deposits made on at least two occasions in the first millennium BC. These events are represented by eight cremation pits and possibly by the deposition of a wooden bowl into the adjacent bog. Pottery or lithics were not found directly associated with the cremation burials though stray lithics were retrieved from the topsoil during testing and excavation. As the lithics could conceivably belong to any phase of activity on site they are described elsewhere (see Chapter 8).

Cremation pits

The pits were distributed on the higher ground in the north and centre of the excavation area (Pits 7, 12, 14, 15, 25, 27, 32 and 34; Illus. 2.8). They are some of the largest examples excavated on the scheme, with diameters of 0.5–1.8 m and depths of 0.8 m–0.4 m (Illus. 2.15). (Pit 34 was truncated by a medieval ditch, Ditch 11.) Three pits (25, 27 and 34) retained evidence for *in situ* burning. Burnt soil concretions and/or fragments of heavily

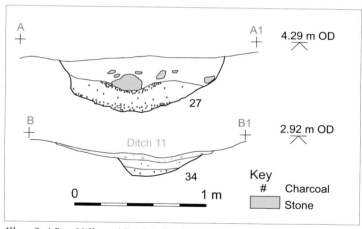

Illus. 2.15—Killow AR104. Sections of cremation pits.

burnt peat were abundant in Pit 7 and may reflect the use of peat in a funeral pyre. Hazelnut shell from Pit 7 returned radiocarbon date ranges of 750–390 BC (Beta-211589). A later, and considerably narrower, date range was returned for hazel charcoal from Pit 34, at 390–180 BC (Beta-211592). These dates encompass a very long period of time, but as they are contiguous at 390 BC it is possible that they represent a single event. It is more likely, however, that they represent at least two episodes of activity on the site. All pits contained burnt mammal bone with human bone clearly identified in Pits 12, 15 and 27 and possible human bone in 7 and 14. Animal bone, horse and sheep-sized animals were represented in Pits 12 and 14 respectively and are discussed in Chapter 5.

---

12 Killow, Co. Clare; barony Bunratty Upper; NGR 136822 175115; height 3–5 m OD; Excavation Licence No. 04E0191. Excavation Director: Kate Taylor.

Illus. 2.16—Killow AR104. Wooden bowl (04E0191:1).

Plant macrofossils

Charcoal from the pits included hazel, oak, ash, pomaceous fruitwood, cherry/blackthorn, willow/ poplar, alder and yew. Two pits each contained charcoal from a single species: oak was exclusively represented in Pit 15, and Pit 34 contained only hazel charcoal. These two taxa were typically the most abundant in all pits.

In addition to charcoal, two cremation pits contained charred plant remains including hazelnut shell fragments and cereal grains. Barley and wheat were present in low densities in Pit 12. This contrasts with Pit 27 where oats, barley, six-row barley, wheat, bread wheat, indeterminate cereal grains and weed seeds were present in relative abundance. The quantity of grain in Pit 27 suggests a deliberate deposit, perhaps similar to that in Pits 7 and 27 at Manusmore AR100. The grain here at Killow was typically poorly preserved, however, and may have undergone several firings.

Artefacts

Two wooden items were recovered from the peat in the south-east corner of the excavation area: an incomplete bowl of carved ash, retrieved in multiple pieces (04E0191:1), and a hazel stake (04E0191:47) (Illus. 2.16). A sample from the the bowl was dated to 777–407 BC (UBA-6287), suggesting its deposition in the bog was contemporaneous with the earliest episode of burial on site. Broken wooden objects were commonly deposited in bogs in the Iron Age and the bowl's proximity to a cremation cemetery may reflect perceived links between the dead and wetlands. The stake had a minimum length of 0.26 m and was c. 8 mm in diameter, with a chisel-point made with a metal tool, perhaps a convex-edged axe. The purpose of the stake and its relationship with the bowl and nearby archaeological features are unknown.

Cahircalla More AR128: cremation pit[13]

Cahircalla More AR128 was located on a south-east facing slope overlooking a wide bog (Illus. 2.6). The main phase of activity at this site is in the early medieval period, when a ditched enclosure and field system were established (see Chapter 3). Their construction resulted in the destruction of at least one prehistoric cremation burial and the incorporation of lithics and Bronze Age pottery in the ploughsoil and ditches of the later enclosure and field system.

Evidence for prehistoric activity came from the southern end of the excavation area, in the vicinity of the later enclosure ditches (Illus. 3.4). A single oval pit (Pit 137), which contained cremated human bone, represents the only *in situ* feature that can be ascribed to the prehistoric period with any degree of certainty. The pit measured 0.40 m by 0.17 m and was 0.23 m deep, with steeply sloping sides and a concave base. Miscellaneous human bone and fragments of vertebrae with a total weight of 3 g were retrieved from the pit fill. Fragments of cremated human bone were retrieved from an early medieval enclosure ditch about 15 m east of this location and is likely to represent material disturbed from an early burial truncated by the ditch.

Other prehistoric activity is suggested by the presence of struck chert in the ploughsoil and as residual material in another early medieval ditch. Several pieces of quartz, possibly worked, may also be of this period. A small amount of prehistoric pottery, probably later Bronze Age in date, was also recovered from the ploughsoil (see Chapter 8).

Claureen AR131: ring-ditch/barrow[14]

Excavations at Claureen AR131 revealed a single ring-ditch or truncated ring-barrow containing cremated human remains and with glass beads in the fills of the ditch (Illus. 2.17). The site was located in a pasture field and covered by c. 0.20 m of ploughsoil. Cut into glacial till, the ditch had been truncated by post-medieval ploughing with plough scars evident across the excavation area. There was no evidence for a mound or enclosing bank associated with the ditch and there was no central pit. Ploughing may have resulted in the loss of original deposits and the ditch had also been cut by a large post-medieval or modern pit. Ash charcoal from the ditch was dated to 100 BC–AD 70 (Beta-207732), placing it in the Late Iron Age.

The ditch was continuous, unlike many penannular ring-ditches. It had a diameter of 6 m and was 0.5 m wide by 0.15 m deep (Illus. 2.18), with two stratigraphically distinct fills. The primary deposit was dark, sandy silt with moderate inclusions of charcoal and cremated bone. It was found exclusively on the inner edge of the gully and was up to 0.15 m deep. The secondary ditch fill was brown, sandy silt with pebbles and appeared to have accumulated naturally—perhaps hastened by tillage. Small pieces of clay pipe, brick and tile within this deposit represent intrusive modern material.

---

13 Cahircalla More, Co. Clare; barony Islands; NGR 132511 175537; height 13 m OD; Excavation Licence No. 04E0029. Excavation Director: Kate Taylor.
14 Claureen, Co. Clare; barony Islands; NGR 132527 178047; height 5.9 m OD; Excavation Licence No. 04E0026. Excavation Director: Graham Hull.

Illus. 2.17—Claureen AR131. Ring-ditch prior to full excavation.

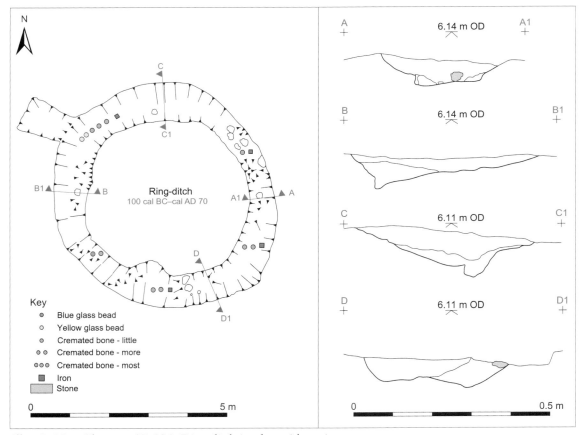

Illus. 2.18—Claureen AR131. Ring-ditch in plan with sections.

Cremated human remains

The ditch included multiple small, human bone cremation deposits with a total weight of 117 g. The distribution of cremated bone, as well as charcoal and glass beads, suggests a bias in deposition in the western arc of the ditch. Identified bones include skull, scapula and pelvis fragments, though many pieces were recognised only as limb bone pieces. The overall assemblage weight indicates that the deposits of bone retrieved are not *in situ* pyre deposits of whole cremated individuals, but rather represent token burials (see Chapter 5).

Plant macrofossils

Firewood used to fuel the cremation pyres came from ash with some hazel. Other tree species represented in low densities include pomaceous fruitwood, cherry/blackthorn, oak and willow/poplar. Other plant remains included hazelnut shell and a single fruit of a dock.

Artefacts

Three glass beads were found within primary ditch fills. These were not heat affected, suggesting they had not been placed in a pyre but had been buried with the bone, as part of the funerary ritual, after it had been burnt. The beads, two blue and one yellow, are opaque annular objects with flattened surfaces and rounded edges (Illus. 8.4). The recovery of such glass beads from Iron Age burial contexts is not unusual (see Chapter 8).

Other artefacts retrieved from the ring-ditch included fragments of quartz, iron and a small amount of slag. With the exception of the quartz fragments, all are regarded as intrusive inclusions. Quartz is represented by 19 minute pieces that may be either natural occurrence or 'retouch' chips from stone tool manufacture. This stone type is found locally in glacial drift but it is unclear if in this case the tiny assemblage was a deliberate inclusion.

Prehistory in the Fergus Valley

Carleton Jones

Cremation cemeteries

Two cremation cemeteries in Manusmore and another probable cremation cemetery in Killow were excavated. Cremation cemeteries seem to be a particular feature of the Bronze Age and Early Iron Age (Grogan et al. 2007, 115–24; Raftery 1994, 188–99; Waddell 1998, 156–62) and this held true in the present case where dates from the sites ranged from the Chalcolithic through to the Iron Age. These sites consisted of multiple pits containing token amounts of cremated bone and, in some cases (Manusmore AR100), heat-reddened and oxidised patches of ground that may represent pyre locations.

These sites point to fairly substantial population levels in the area in the Bronze Age and into the Iron Age. The occurrence of multiple cemeteries within a few kilometres of each other suggests that they were used by groups who lived in the immediate vicinity. The setting of the two cemeteries in Manusmore, along with another nearby cremation cemetery at Ballyconneely (Read 2000a & b), suggests that wider considerations were also at play in the siting of these cemeteries, to do with the relationship between the physical landscape and beliefs about the afterlife (see below).

Ring-ditches

Claureen AR131was either a small ring-ditch or a truncated ring-barrow, and produced an Iron Age date. Ring-ditches (a circular ditch with no internal mound and no bank) and ring-barrows (a circular ditch with a central mound and/or an external bank) are part of a related group of ritual monuments that emerged in the Bronze Age and continued through at least the first half of the Iron Age (O'Brien 2004b; Raftery 1941; Raftery 1994, 189; Waddell 1998, 156–62). At Claureen, the small amounts of cremated bone along with the small number of glass beads that were found throughout the ditch fills suggest that token amounts of cremated remains from several individuals were deposited in the ditch. This is typical of monuments of this type. These monuments often occur in groups and it is possible that further related monuments await discovery in the Claureen area.

Death and the River Fergus

The two cremation cemeteries at Manusmore share similarities in their siting that may provide insights into why these particular locations were chosen. Both sites occupy gentle south-facing inclines about 2 km east of the River Fergus and both sites have views to the south-west across its estuary. (It should be borne in mind, however, that the similar distances from the Fergus may be a result of the path of the bypass). The Manusmore sites are not the only cremation cemeteries that share this particular landscape setting. Just over 2.5 km to the south, there is another cremation cemetery with over 80 cremation pits (most seem to be Bronze Age) at Ballyconneely (Read 2000a & b). Like the Manusmore sites, the Ballyconneely site is also located about 2 km east of the Fergus estuary on a south-facing slope (in this case, on a natural platform on the slope). Also in common with the Manusmore sites, the Ballyconneely site has views to the south-west across the Fergus estuary, and in this case also south to the Shannon estuary, that were described by the excavator as 'panoramic' (Read 2000b). It is located roughly midway between the estuary to the west and the Late Bronze Age hillfort of Mooghaun to the east, and many other prehistoric sites of a ritual nature have also been found in this zone such as standing stones, barrows, a ring-ditch, and other cremation pit burials (ASI 2008; Breen & Hull 2002; Read 2000a & b; Tarbett-Buckley & Hull 2002). It may be that this was an important ritual zone in prehistory but many prehistoric sites of a secular nature (such as burnt mounds and possible areas of occupation) have also been located in this zone, so we should not envisage an area set aside solely for ritual but instead, perhaps a zone where ritual and day-to-day activities intersected. Again, however, at least some of the patterning of the known sites is due to the path of the motorway.

Wet areas were frequently used as sites for ritual deposits in prehistory and the upper Fergus estuary has produced a later Bronze Age gold dress-fastener and a gold bracelet (O'Sullivan 2001, 127–28). It may be that the cremation cemeteries overlooking the Fergus estuary and the metal finds from its margins are two components of the same funerary ritual focused on the estuary. The cremated remains in the pits were only small fractions of the material that would have been left over after the funeral pyre and this begs the question of what happened to the rest of the cremated remains. Given the views from the cemeteries out over the estuary and the fact that contemporary ritual involved the deposition of metal-work on its edges, one possibility is that the bulk of the cremated remains were deposited in the water of the estuary. At the Manusmore sites, the proximity of the Ardsollus River, which flows west into the Fergus estuary, suggests the possibility that cremated remains may have been deposited in the Ardsollus.

As the cemeteries are located on the east side of the Fergus, the views from the cemeteries over the estuary are directed to the west and south-west, the direction of the setting sun. The south-west was associated in medieval texts with the pagan god of death and it has been suggested that the south-western orientation of wedge tombs may indicate that this association between death and the south-west might go all the way back to the Chalcolithic (O'Brien 2002). This would certainly add another symbolic dimension to the sites. If the bulk of the cremated remains were deposited in the Ardsollus and the Fergus, the flow of the Ardsollus west into the Fergus which then flows south to the Shannon, which in turn flows west to the sea, may have been viewed as instrumental in transporting the souls of the dead into the land of the setting sun (while still leaving token remnants of the dead on the hill, close to the land of the living).

Time and continuity in the Ennis region

One of the most striking features of several of the prehistoric sites excavated on this project is the long stretch of time over which they were used and the apparent continuity of their function over that time. The cremation cemetery at Manusmore AR100, in particular, stands out. Here it seems that the same south-facing slope was used as a cremation cemetery over at least two and a half millennia from the Chalcolithic through to the Iron Age. The post-holes that may have held grave markers might have enabled some continuity, but the proximity of an even more important and 'timeless' feature—the River Fergus with its tributary, the Ardsollus—may have been a significant factor determining the longevity of this site. The river, and its possible associations with death, may have provided the common thread through the centuries that kept the site at Manusmore an appropriate place for burial for successive generations.

The longevity of the Manusmore cremation cemetery is not unique. The nearby cremation cemetery at Ballyconneely also seems to have been used over a long span from the Neolithic through the Bronze Age (Read 2000a & b) and, even more remarkably, a site on the south bank of the River Shannon at Castleconnell has produced cremation pit burials where the earliest radiocarbon-dated burial is separated from the latest radiocarbon-dated burial by nearly five and a half millennia (Collins & Coyne 2003). All these sites show an amazing continuity of sacred use over very long spans of time and it does seem likely that some consistent belief (such as a belief in the sacredness of rivers and their association with death) lies behind the continuity.

The living

The numerous burnt mounds excavated on the present project are good evidence for some of the day-to-day activities of those who lived in the area in prehistory. Burnt mounds encountered in the present study ranged from a substantial crescent-shaped mound with a central trough (Cahircalla Beg AR126) to more amorphous spreads of burnt stones. Many of the latter appear to have been truncated and/or eroded by post-depositional processes and are, therefore, probably best interpreted as having functioned similarly to the more substantial burnt mounds. Like burnt mounds elsewhere, the burnt mounds encountered in the present project were located in wet areas or at the edges of wet areas and the burnt stones seem to have been used to heat water. A number of functions have been proposed for burnt mounds including cooking places (O'Kelly 1954), sweathouses or bathing places (Barfield & Hodder 1987; Ó Drisceóil 1990; Ó Néill 2004), or perhaps sites for some more industrial purpose such as cloth dyeing (Jeffrey 1990). None of these proposed functions can be accepted without caveat and some sites probably had multiple uses. Their use as cooking places, however, does seem to be a viable interpretation in many cases. Radiocarbon dates throughout the country have shown that burnt mounds are typically a feature of the Bronze Age (Brindley et al. 1990; Grogan et al. 2007, 96–101), and the radiocarbon dates from the present study conform to this pattern.

Burnt mounds appear to be just one element in a settlement landscape that would have included nearby habitation sites on higher and drier ground. In addition to the information from the excavations of the burnt mounds themselves, therefore, their locations probably also give us some indication of the location and density of contemporary habitation sites.

Like the cemeteries, some of the secular sites excavated on the current project also show a remarkable continuity of function over long stretches of time. At Clareabbey, the various burnt mounds and other features indicate that this area was probably used intermittently throughout the Bronze Age as a place where water was heated (probably for cooking) by people who lived on the nearby higher ground to the west. The radiocarbon dates suggest that this activity took place over at least 11 centuries. Radiocarbon dates from burnt mound sites at Cahircalla Beg and Cahircalla More indicate that similar activities took place there over at least 13 centuries.

Summary

The two themes to emerge from this analysis are the possible association of the River Fergus with death rituals and the remarkable continuity of use of both ritual and more mundane sites over long spans of time in the Ennis area. Previous work has described many of the landscape aspects of a Late Bronze Age chiefdom centred on the Mooghaun hillfort (Grogan 2005a & b). We can now add the possible identification of a 'funerary ritual' zone located just west of Mooghaun and focused on hilltops and slopes that overlook the Fergus estuary. Of significance to the study of Irish prehistory in general is the highlighting of the extraordinarily long spans of time over which some burial grounds were used and the possible continuity of beliefs linking death and rivers that may be behind this longevity.

3
EARLY MEDIEVAL AND LATER MEDIEVAL EXCAVATIONS

Nóra Bermingham, Markus Casey, Graham Hull and Kate Taylor
with a contribution by M Comber

Eight sites produced radiocarbon dates in the early medieval period with another site undated and two sites dating to the medieval period (Illus. 1.7). With the exception of the Augustinian house at Clare Abbey all sites represent new discoveries that lacked surface expression and were only identified upon testing (Illus. 3.1). Most early medieval sites comprised seemingly isolated pits, some of which could be assigned a particular function such as charcoal production or iron-working. The most significant early medieval site was an enclosure with a smithy and an associated field system. This complex at Cahircalla More AR128 suggests a well-established, rural economy supported by local crafts and long-term settlement and management of the landscape. In the later medieval period, the role of the Church in these and other aspects of rural life is illustrated by the results of the excavations at Clare Abbey.

Site summaries

Cahircalla More AR128: enclosure, smithy and field system[15]

A previously unknown early medieval enclosure was excavated on high ground overlooking a bog at Cahircalla More AR128. The site is a sub-circular ditched enclosure with an associated field system dating from the second half of the first millennium AD (Illus. 3.2). Remains of a smithy and a series of small pits were identified in the interior. This enclosure and field system were located on the site of what may have been a Bronze Age cemetery (see Chapter 2), though there is no evidence for continuing occupation of the site in the intervening periods.

Excavations at Cahircalla More AR128 extended over a total area of 8,570 m², with the main focus of excavation in the south, adjacent to the N68 Ennis to Kilrush road. Prior to excavation the land was under pasture with soil cover of topsoil and colluvium, or hillwash, 0.4 m to 0.95 m deep over glacial till. Plough furrows were evident across the entire site and ploughing, mainly dating from the 19th and 20th centuries, had done considerable damage to the archaeological deposits.

The enclosure
The enclosure (100) was elliptical or sub-circular in plan and the southernmost extent had been truncated by the construction of the N68 road (Illus. 3.3 and 3.4). The enclosure had a maximum

---

15 Cahircalla More, Co. Clare; barony Islands; NGR 132511 175537; height 11–33 m OD; Excavation Licence No. 04E0029. Excavation Director: Kate Taylor.

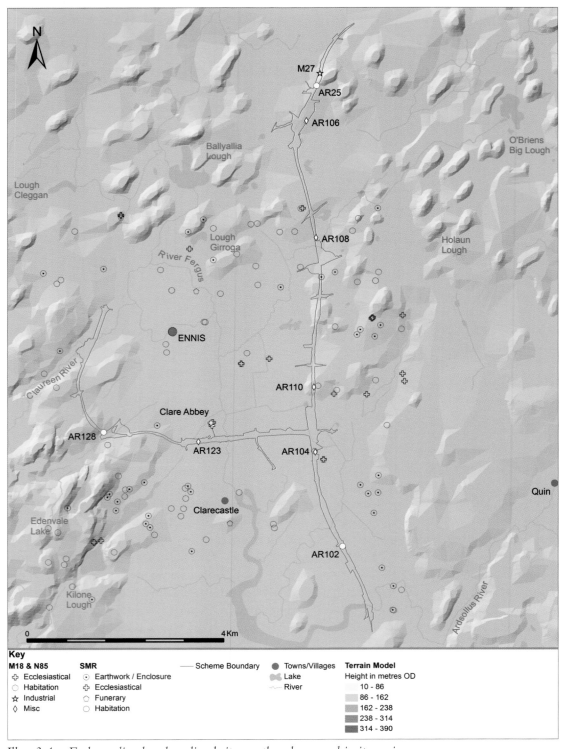

Illus. 3.1—Early medieval and medieval sites on the scheme and in its environs.

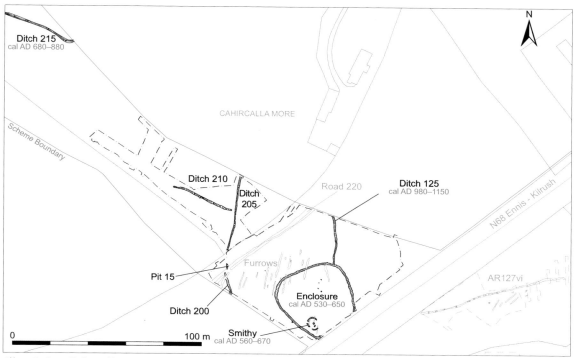

Illus. 3.2—Cahircalla More AR128. Enclosure with smithy and field system.

surviving width of 38 m. The ditch was U-shaped in profile, between 0.2 m and 0.8 m deep and 0.75 m to 1.35 m wide. The apparent absence of an entrance may be explained by truncation of the site in the south-east by the N68. Plough damage was extensive and particularly so in the north-east and may account for the absence of an associated bank.

In general, ditch fills were relatively sterile silts that had accumulated naturally, except in the south-west where the ditch was deepest and adjacent to the remains of a smithy. Here, ditch fills were mainly charcoal and artefact-rich silts. The relative sterility of many of the ditch fills suggests it was not deliberately infilled or used for waste disposal over its full circuit. A fragment of cattle bone from the primary ditch fill returned a radiocarbon date of AD 530–650 (Beta-211571); this represents the earliest date for the enclosure and associated activity on site. Artefacts from the ditch fills included a piece of a rotary quern-stone (04E0029:24) (Illus. 3.5), fragments of iron slag and a possible chisel made of iron (04E0029:79) (Illus. 3.6) (see Chapter 8). Animal bone, mainly of cattle and a single roe deer antler fragment, was also retrieved from the ditch. Cereal grains (oats and barley) were present in low densities in samples from the ditch and could represent windblown detritus as easily as scattered refuse.

The smithy

Within the southern corner of the enclosure there were foundations of a small structure, in the form of three short lengths of curvilinear gully (Illus. 3.7). This structure (120) survived due to the depth of overlying colluvium, which was greater here than over other parts of the enclosure, and so reduced the destructive effect of later ploughing. Oval in plan with internal dimensions of 6.3 m by 4.4 m, the gully segments were typically 0.65 m wide and 0.4 m deep with vertical sides and a flat base. Gully fills were typically dark with abundant charcoal, iron slag, fragments of teeth (cattle) and charred cereal grains including oats, barley and wheat in low densities. In contrast to the gullies, charred cereal grains were absent from the pits inside the structure. A sample of charred barley yielded a radiocarbon date of AD 560–670 (Beta-211572) and indicates that the enclosure and structure are contemporaneous.

Slag types, and their clustered distribution in features related to or near the structure, reveal that it functioned as a smithy. These mainly comprised hammerscales, microslags, and bulk slag indicative of smithing (see Chapter 8). Other supporting evidence includes pieces of vitrified hearth lining and *in situ* burning within pits (44 and 45) located

Illus. 3.3—Cahircalla More AR128. Aerial view of the enclosure and smithy.

inside the smithy. The pits were concave in profile, between 1.19 m and 1.41 m long, 0.15 m and 0.3 m deep, and up to 0.75 m wide. Pit fills were similar to those of the gully segments and produced considerable quantities of iron slag and some animal bone.

Some slag may have been produced by smelting and the recovery of a magnetic fragment of burnt stone, identified as iron-oxide hematite or iron ore, suggests limited smelting may have been undertaken on site. Bulk slags or pieces of smithing-hearth bottoms retrieved from the main enclosure ditch (100) illustrate that the smithy floor was cleaned of bulky waste material, which was then dumped into the nearby ditch. Iron shavings were also retrieved from the smithy and from Pit 21—a small pit outside the smithy but inside the enclosure. The shavings further illustrate that iron was worked on site as does the recovery of the possible chisel and an iron ring-pin from elsewhere on site.

Charcoal from the smithy gullies included hazel, hazel/alder, pomaceous fruitwood, ash, cherry/blackthorn, oak and yew. A similar array of taxa was represented in the main enclosure ditch, indicating the link between the activity within the smithy and the nearby ditch as a point of disposal.

Pits

Three further pits were identified within the enclosure—Pits 21, 25 and 29, with a fourth, Pit 26 located just outside the enclosure ditch in the south-west (Illus. 3.4). These were small pits, up to 0.7 m wide and 0.27 m deep. Pit 29 lacked artefacts or charred material. Pits 21 and 25 produced small pieces of iron, iron slag, burnt animal bone and charred cereal grains in low densities. The cereals found were barley with oats, rye and wheat also represented. Pit 26 appeared to have been dug deliberately to retain a broken quern or grinding stone (04E0029:45). Given, the presence of the quern, the occurrence of cereal grains in the pit fill is unsurprising. The range of inclusions

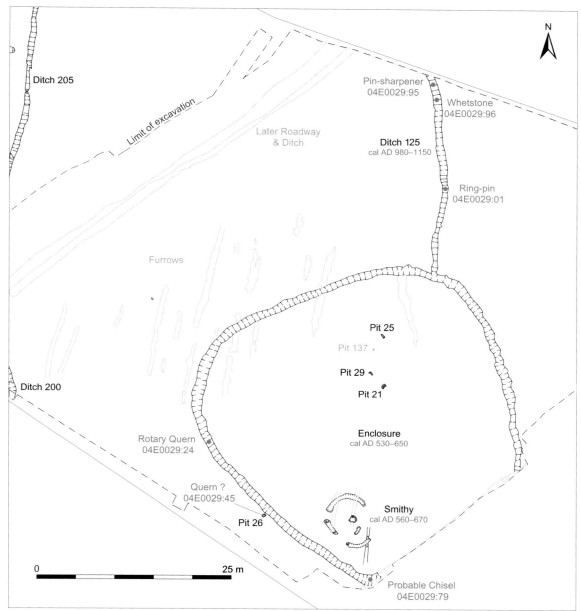

Illus. 3.4—Cahircalla More AR128. Detailed plan of enclosure and associated features.

referred to here is similar to that retrieved from dated early medieval features, suggesting the pits are broadly contemporary with this activity.

Field system

Elements of a field system were observed extending across an area about 200 m north–west of the enclosure (Illus. 3.2). The field system was represented by four ditches, at least one of which survived in

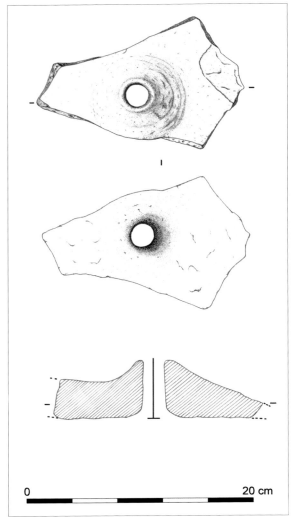

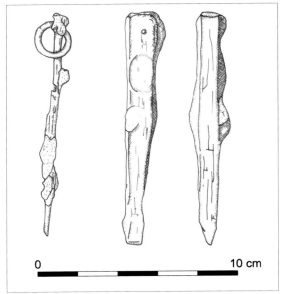

Illus. 3.6—Cahircalla More AR128. Ring-pin (04E0029:01) and possible iron chisel (04E0029:79).

two parts (200 and 205), and was truncated by a later, post-medieval road (220) (see Chapter 4). The ditches were roughly aligned north/south (125, 200 and 205) and north-west/south-east (210 and 215). They may have formed part of a larger system of broadly rectangular fields but additional test trenches did not find any further surviving elements within the lands acquired for the road scheme.

The ditches were generally U-shaped in profile. The surviving segments were up to 1.25 m wide and 0.67 m deep. Ditches 210 and 215

Illus. 3.5—Cahircalla More AR128. Rotary quernstone fragment (04E0029:24).

terminated abruptly at their north-western ends. A gap, 1.7 m wide, between Ditches 210 and 205 may represent a deliberate break or access point between fields. Ditches 200 and 205, and an elongated pit (15) located between them, were probably all vestigial remnants of the same north/south ditch.

The base of Pit 15 showed evidence of *in situ* burning. The primary fill was almost pure charcoal, with charred hazel, ash, pomaceous fruitwood, cherry/blackthorn and oak. The pit also contained abundant charred cereal grains of oats, barley, six-row barley, rye, wheat and weed seeds. (A similar array of taxa was identified in samples from the field system ditches.) The concentration of charcoal and cereal grains in this feature may have been a matter of chance as it seems to have formed part of the ditched field system, rather than a discrete feature within in, such as a simple field kiln.

The ditch fills were relatively sterile, and for the most part had accumulated naturally, which is consistent with ditches that formed part of a field system rather than those in close proximity to a habitation site. That said, three of the ditches yielded artefacts, animal bone and charred plant remains. The animal bone was mainly of cattle with bone fragments from sheep-sized animals also represented.

The earliest dated element of the field system was Ditch 215. Charred cereal grains from its fills returned a date of AD 680–880 (Beta-211573), which just overlaps with the radiocarbon date range for the smithy. At least two artefacts—a mini-anvil (04E0029:108) and a possible whetstone (04E0029:109)—were retrieved from this ditch, as well as some animal bone and several pieces of quartz (04E0029:110, 114–16) that may have been worked (see Chapter 8). Ditch 210 also yielded finds suggestive of an early medieval date, including iron slag and a mini-anvil stone (04E0029:99). In contrast, Ditches 200 and 205 lacked artefacts and neither of them was dated.

Ditch 125 was cut through the main enclosure ditch. It is also the latest of the radiocarbon-dated features on site, with charred cereal grains from its fill dated to AD 980–1150 (Beta-207730). Several pieces of struck chert, probably residual prehistoric material (04E0029:90-93, 100 and 107), were recovered from its fill and other finds included fragments of burnt animal and human bone, an oyster shell, a piece of slag, a whetstone (04E0029:96), a pin-sharpening stone (04E0029:95) and a ring-pin (04E0029:1) (Illus. 3.6).

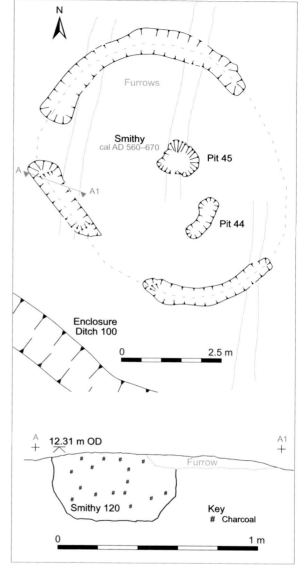

Illus. 3.7—Cahircalla More AR128. Plan of smithy and section drawing of wall-footing trench.

Conclusion

Excavations at Cahircalla More have produced evidence for a previously unknown early medieval settlement. The economy of the settlement was a mixed pastoral/tillage regime as evidenced by the associated field system, the identification of cereals and animal bone and the recovery of a range of craft and/or domestic objects typical of the period. The settlement was in an area where fuel wood from mixed woodland was available for the smithy and also to supply the needs of general domestic life. No doubt houses and other structures once stood within the enclosure but were destroyed by later ploughing and soil erosion. The settlement and the field system were established by the late sixth or early seventh century. When habitation ceased on site is unknown but dates from two of the field ditches point to activity in the late seventh to mid 12th centuries. It appears that the field system's lifespan extended beyond that of the enclosure or at least what is known about the enclosure. On the other hand, the recovery of early medieval objects and food waste in Ditches 215 and 125 suggests occupation of the hillside was still a feature of these centuries post-dating the primary period of the enclosure itself. (The focus of occupation may have moved or evidence of long-lived habitation of the enclosure has been destroyed.) Overall, it seems that the enclosure was still the focus of an active farmstead, though maintaining an earthwork around the homestead itself was no longer such a high priority as it had been. In this regard the present site seems to reflect the general change in Ireland, around the end of the first millennium and beyond, from an economy based predominantly on herding livestock to a more mixed farming economy.

Carrowdotia AR25: cashel[16]

Part of a previously known monument, enclosure (CL026-033), lay within the road-take at Carrowdotia AR25. The site is depicted on the first edition Ordnance Survey map of 1840 and occupies the side of a steep incline above a bog, which is now partly reclaimed (Illus. 3.8). Outcrops of limestone bedrock are visible and in places bedrock is overlain by gravel and patches of orange clay. Topsoil is thin or entirely absent. The limit of the excavation extended to the north and south of the enclosure encompassing an area of 7600 m². The excavated portion represents up to one third of the monument's original area and was limited to the part of the monument within the road-take.

Prior to excavation, trees and hazel scrub covered the site and plough ridges were evident, particularly in the northern end of the excavation area. The landowner recalled ploughing to grow vegetables in this area until the 1960s at least. The enclosure was 25 m in diameter and pre-excavation records suggest it comprised an earth and stone bank and lacked an enclosing ditch or evidence for internal features (Illus. 3.9 and 3.10). Relatively recent land division resulted in part of the enclosure wall being incorporated into a revised field system and a field wall was constructed across the monument sometime in the late 19th/early 20th centuries.

The enclosure wall
The base of the enclosure was built on a low, curvilinear gravel and clay bank (Illus. 3.11) that provided a level foundation for the wall. This foundation deposit was overlain by slumped stone and soil, 0.6 m deep and up to 6.35 m wide. The original width of this bank is unknown but was probably not much more than the wall subsequently erected on top. The outer, north-eastern edge of the bank had been truncated, probably due to post-medieval or later ploughing. In the south-west, part of a rotary quern-stone (03E1442:39), typical of the period, was recovered from topsoil overlying the bank. However, no other artefacts were recovered.

The wall was exposed for 18 m in length. It measured up to 2.55 m wide at the base and was 1.7 m high, narrowing from base to top. The wall was of drystone construction and comprised a rubble core, faced internally and externally with unworked large stones. The largest of these were placed at the base of the wall. There were no capstones in evidence and the upper surface of the

---

16 Carrowdotia, Co. Clare; barony Bunratty Upper; NGR 136850 182830; height 25 m OD; Excavation Licence No. 03E1442; SMR No. CL026-033. Excavation Director: Kate Taylor.

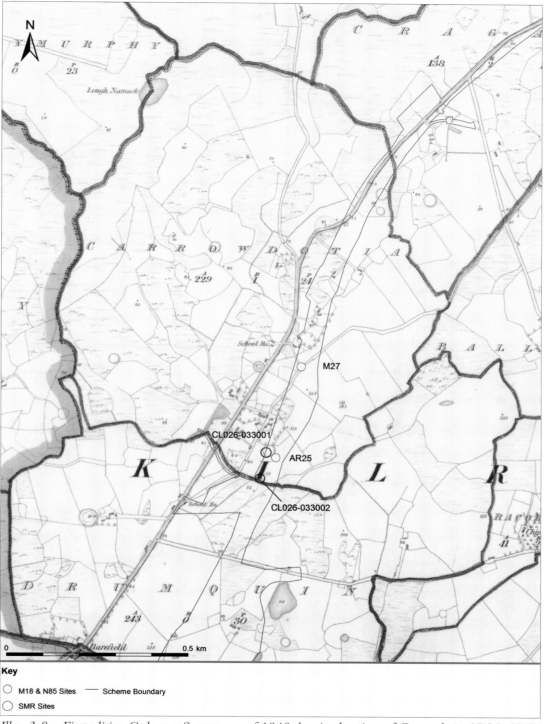

Illus. 3.8—First edition Ordnance Survey map of 1840 showing locations of Carrowdotia AR25, AR27 (=CL026-036-01 & CL026-036-02) and M27.

wall was simply the mounded top of the core deposit. Rubble, fallen from the wall, lay on the ground on either side of it. Root penetration and burrowing animals had caused significant damage. Once cleared, it was apparent the wall was largely linear but curved inwards towards the exposed ends. (This was particularly evident in the south.) This suggests the enclosure may have been sub-rectangular rather than sub-circular.

Enclosure interior

The interior of the enclosure was characterised by outcropping limestone bedrock, with a thin, patchy soil cover at best, and an uneven ground surface. A single feature (25), a steep-sided pit made by quarrying into bedrock, was identified at the western limit of the excavation within the enclosure (Illus. 3.9). Its location meant the pit was not fully exposed but the observed dimensions were 4 m by 1.3 m and 0.55 m deep. The primary pit fill was soil and gravel but against the pit's southern edge, under several large stones, was a small

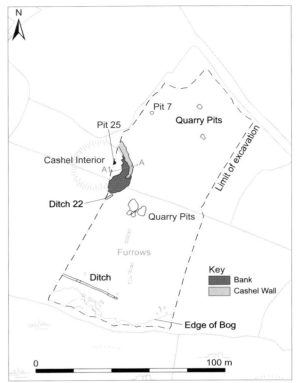

Illus. 3.9—Carrowdotia AR25. Plan showing cashel and later historic features.

deposit of charcoal-rich soil. Some small fragments of burnt clay were also recovered. Charcoal within the pit derived from hazel and pomaceous fruitwood. Hazel charcoal returned a radiocarbon date of AD 530–650 (Beta 211594) placing the pit fill in the early medieval period. Topsoil within

Illus. 3.10—Carrowdotia AR25. View of excavation with cashel in background, from south-east.

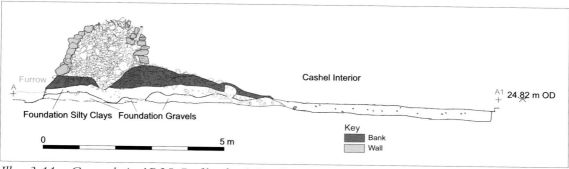

Illus. 3.11—Carrowdotia AR25. Profile of cashel wall and interior.

the enclosure, which sealed Pit 25, contained pieces of modern china, metal, clay tobacco pipe (03E1442:46–50) and animal bone, including horse and cattle teeth, and one human tooth. All represent post-medieval and modern finds unrelated to the construction and use of the enclosure.

External features

Running parallel to the enclosure bank at its outer edge in the south-west sector was a short and shallow ditch (22) (Illus. 3.9). Its full length is unknown as it extended beyond the limit of the excavation and there was no trace of it adjacent to the bank and wall located to the north. The ditch was at least 4 m long, 1 m wide and 0.4 m deep. It is relatively small and may simply have been a quarry ditch that served to provide construction material.

A small charcoal-filled pit (7) was recorded to the north of the enclosure (Illus. 3.9). The pit measured 0.8 m by 0.55 m and 0.12 m deep and had been damaged by ploughing. It contained ash and oak charcoal but cannot be unequivocally associated with the cashel.

A small, flat slate fragment (03E1442:29) was recovered from topsoil outside the enclosure. This was inscribed with a series of lines, some of which formed an arc and a triangle. The fragment may derive from a sundial or clock face and, although undated, sundials are known from eccelsiastical sites in Ireland from the early medieval period (Arnaldi 2000).

Conclusion

Until recently, the monument at Carrowdotia AR25 was recorded by the Archaeological Survey of Ireland as a stone-built enclosure. Excavation has confirmed its character and has, in addition, provided new evidence that allows the site to be interpreted as an early medieval cashel (CL026-033-01). The recovery of parts of a rotary quern-stone, albeit from a topsoil context overlying the bank, hints at the wider agricultural economic context of the site. The absence of evidence of buildings within the enclosure, and the relative paucity of finds, mean the character of the occupation of the site cannot be defined in detail. This might suggest the enclosure functioned as a stockyard or corral rather than a habitation site. However, it is not uncommon for excavated examples of cashels to lack extensive structural or habitation evidence. There are another three cashels recorded within Carrowdotia and several others are known from surrounding townlands.

Manusmore AR102: hearth/food preparation pit[17]

Close to the northern edge of the excavated area at Manusmore AR102 was an early medieval oval pit (27). The pit is significantly later than the prehistoric funerary activity identified at the site (see Chapter 2). The pit was distinguished from other pits on site as it contained large quantities of charred cereal grains, lacked evidence for cremated bone, and yielded a radiocarbon date of AD 690–900 (Beta-211586) (Illus. 2.14). The pit measured 0.84 m by 0.5 m and was 0.15 m deep, with gently sloping sides and a flattish base. There was evidence for *in situ* burning in its base—i.e. the underlying glacial till was heavily oxidised—suggesting the pit may have been a hearth, or possibly a simple grain-drying kiln.

Charred oats and barley grains formed the principal components of the assemblage retrieved from the pit with barley particularly abundant. A small number of six-row barley grains and chaff from wild oats were also recorded; the latter may indicate that the oats were present as contaminants of a main barley crop. Similarly, a small number of wheat grains and weed seeds recovered may represent 'volunteer weeds' from a previous cropping regime. The presence of the grains within the hearth may be the result of carelessness during food preparation or crop-processing. During this period, barley was the only cereal that was consistently used as a whole grain, either within soups and stews or toasted, and this assemblage would, therefore, be consistent with dietary refuse.

Carrowdotia M27: pits (iron-working)[18]

Carrowdotia M27 was situated at the extreme northern end of the road scheme. The area of excavation occupied a steep, north-west-facing incline. At the time of excavation the land was under pasture. Two stone-wall field boundaries with mature hedges were included within the site.

Immediately west of the excavation area, a previously unrecorded stone enclosure was identified during the initial walkover survey for the scheme, at EIS stage. This structure lay outside the road-take and was not included in the excavations. The southern arc of the enclosure is reasonably well defined as a heaped bank of small stones. The remainder is partly obscured by vegetation, though its interior is relatively clear. A later field wall and bank with mature ash trees bisect the enclosure. The corner of a field wall that extended into the excavation area was initially thought to form part of the same enclosure. Instead, it is related to a track depicted on the first edition Ordnance Survey map of 1840 (Illus. 3.8). The size and morphology of the enclosure suggest it may represent the remains of a small cashel—a monument type which typically dates to the second half of the first millennium AD.

Within the area of excavation extending over 2,880 m², multiple post-medieval archaeological features were identified and these are described in Chapter 4. Two pits, however, are likely to relate to the possible cashel described above (Illus. 3.12). Pit 1 was oval in plan; it measured 0.82 m by 0.65 m and was 0.2 m deep, with a steep-sided, concave profile. The upper of the pit's two fills was fairly rich in charcoal, while the lower was virtually sterile.

---

17 Manusmore, Co. Clare; barony Islands; NGR 137380 173160; height 13.6 m OD; Excavation Licence No. 04E0189. Excavation Director: Graham Hull.
18 Carrowdotia, Co. Clare; barony Bunratty Upper; NGR 136920 183090; height 25–35 m OD; Excavation Licence No. 03E1426. Excavation Director: Kate Taylor.

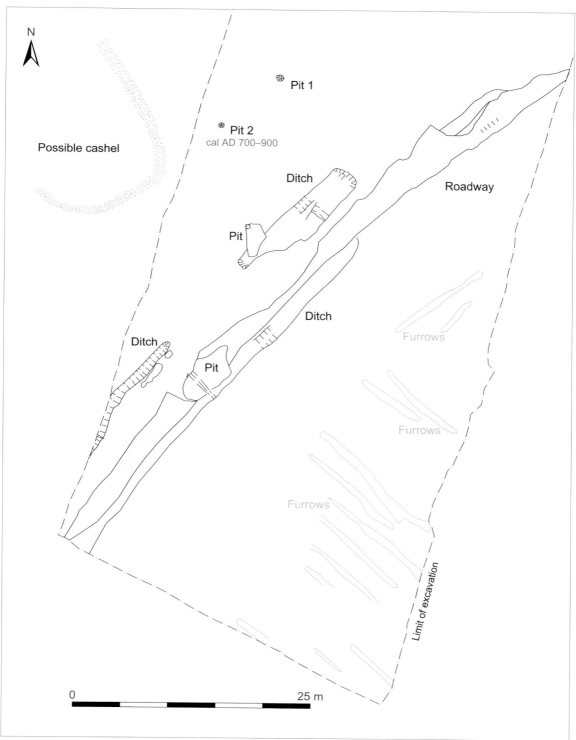

N

Possible cashel

Pit 1

Pit 2
cal AD 700–900

Ditch

Pit

Roadway

Ditch

Ditch

Pit

Furrows

Furrows

Furrows

Limit of excavation

0   25 m

Illus. 3.12—Carrowdotia M27. Site plan with location of possible cashel indicated.

Pit 2 was sub-circular in plan; it measured 0.6 m by 0.57 m and 0.2 m deep with steeply concave sides and a slightly rounded base. The pit sides were oxidised in part, indicating *in situ* burning. The lowest of the pit's three fills was almost entirely composed of charcoal—chiefly oak and ash but with alder, hazel and willow/poplar also occurring. The middle pit fill contained a moderate amount of iron slag. This showed an absence of diagnostic smelting slag though secondary smithing activity is implied by a tiny amount of flake hammerscale recovered. This microslag is the product of the ordinary hot-working and hammering of a piece of iron where fragments of the oxide/silicate skin flake off from the iron and fall to the ground. The small assemblage implies that iron-working took place as a one-off activity. Hazel charcoal from the basal fill of Pit 2 returned a radiocarbon date of AD 700–900 (Beta-211593).

Clareabbey AR123: pit and hearth cluster[19]

Excavations at Clareabbey AR123 recorded a cluster of relatively insubstantial features all of which had been truncated by modern plough furrows. Six small pits, a small hearth and a charcoal-rich deposit were identified within 15 m of each other, situated on gently sloping land, in a pasture field. Hazel charcoal from one of the pits returned a radiocarbon date of AD 790–990 (Beta-211559) suggesting an early medieval date for the activity represented.

The pits varied in size. The largest measured 1.03 m by 0.57 m and was 0.2 m deep. The others ranged in diameter from 0.24 m to 0.48 m and were between 0.07 m and 0.18 m deep. Pit fills were typically sandy silts with inclusions of charcoal and stone occurring in varying amounts. The hearth was circular in plan with a diameter of 0.3 m and was 0.1 m deep. Its base was defined by a charcoal-rich deposit with silty ash, and a heat-reddened or oxidised surface indicative of *in situ* burning.

Other than charcoal, no charred plant remains were retrieved from the pit or hearth deposits. Analysis revealed that alder, ash, hazel, pomaceous fruitwood and oak had been burned. Within one pit and the hearth one fragment of iron slag and a piece of vitrified clay (32 g) were present. The slag was undiagnostic of either iron-smelting or smithing. The vitrified clay represents a piece of vitrified hearth lining, which could have been produced by a domestic hearth. Neither find suggests any high-temperature activity, such as metal-working, was taking place on the site.

This cluster of archaeological features indicates low-level activity at this location in the eighth to 10th centuries AD. The activity was more than likely domestic in nature though a habitation or settlement with which it can be associated has yet to be identified. In a later period the townland would be dominated by the Augustinian foundation of Clare Abbey (see below).

Kilbreckan AR110: pit[20]

Investigations in Kilbreckan identified a single, seemingly isolated pit in which a fire had taken place. The site was located within well drained enclosed fields of pasture, on the summit of a small hill. An overgrown earthen ringfort (CL034-163) is situated 80 m to the south-west and

---

19 Clareabbey, Co. Clare; barony Islands; NGR 134444 175333; height 4.4 m OD; Excavation Licence No. 04E0019. Excavation Director: Graham Hull.
20 Kilbreckan, Co. Clare; barony Bunratty Upper; NGR 139807 176454; height 22 m OD; Excavation Licence No. 04E0056. Excavation Director: Markus Casey.

this, combined with the early medieval radiocarbon date returned for the pit, suggests the pit and ringfort may in some way be related.

The pit was oval in plan and measured 1.05 m by 1.02 m and was 0.27 m deep in the centre. It contained two fills: an upper fill of brown silt with charcoal and a primary fill of dark, sandy soil overlying a surface of partly oxidised glacial till suggestive of *in situ* burning. There were no artefacts, animal bone or plant macrofossils other than charcoal, mainly oak with cherry/blackthorn also occurring. The latter charcoal yielded a date of AD 1010–1180 (Beta-211579).

Elsewhere in the townland, on the line of a gas pipeline, an isolated though undated burnt spread was excavated. The pipeline excavations also yielded evidence for an undefined post-medieval structure (Grogan et al. 2007, 206–7). Without additional dates these activities cannot be directly related to one another but they each demonstrate low-key human occupation of the townland at various periods in the past.

Barefield AR106: charcoal production pit[21]

In a sheltered location in a pasture field, towards the bottom of a slope, investigations identified a single charcoal-rich pit. The field had undulating topography, outcropping bedrock, and in places was prone to flooding in winter. Topsoil cover varied from negligible up to 0.4 m deep and contained much modern pottery, glass and red brick fragments. The area of excavation extended over 356 m².

The pit was oval, shallow and aligned north/south (Illus. 3.13). It measured 4 m long, 1.6 m wide and had a maximum depth of 0.28 m, with a flat base. The base had undergone burning *in situ* and contained two layers of charcoal-rich, sandy soil, between 0.02 m and 0.1 m deep. These were separated by a horizon of ash and redeposited glacial till that had been deliberately laid down to allow a second fire to burn in the pit. This appears to have occurred almost immediately after the first fire had been damped down. Redeposited till was then used again to put out the second fire.

Oak was the predominant tree species

Illus. 3.13—Barefield AR106. Charcoal pit undergoing excavation.

represented within the pit, with willow/poplar and elm also occurring in small quantities. Elm charcoal returned a radiocarbon date of AD 1010–1180 (Beta-211577).

21 Barefield, Co. Clare; barony Bunratty Upper; NGR 136644 182089; height 2.7 m OD; Excavation Licence No. 04E0052. Excavation Director: Markus Casey.

The size and contents of the pit suggests it functioned as a charcoal-production pit or pit kiln. Oak was the preferred fuel in medieval charcoal pit kilns but the occurrence of multiple wood species is not uncommon (Kenny 2010, 108). The dump of redeposited till may have served to limit oxygen, thus creating the 'reducing' environment needed to make charcoal. A ringfort (CL026-079) is situated c. 200 m north-east of the excavaton site and while no direct connection can be made on present evidence, the ringfort attests to an established early medieval presence in the area.

Ballymacahill AR108: pits[22]

Three pits, similar in size, morphology and content, were excavated at this site, on the edge of a pasture field between mature hedgerows, in an area of outcropping limestone bedrock. These pits were identified during testing, but no other associated archaeological features were discovered and the pits represent the only evidence for medieval occupation of the townland.

Pit 1 was a shallow, oval feature, c. 1.2 m in diameter by 0.05 m deep, and was filled with brown silt and charcoal with some burnt stones. The base of the pit was discoloured by *in situ* burning. Pit 3 measured 2.55 m by 1.25 m and was 0.33 m deep, with a flat base. Its primary fill of brown silt, pebbles and charcoal was 0.19 m deep. This was sealed by a mix of redeposited glacial till and topsoil. Hazel charcoal from the pit returned a radiocarbon date of AD 1020–1220 (Beta-211578). Pit 6, the third pit, was situated immediately south of Pit 1 and measured 0.75 m by 1.35 m and was 0.23 m deep. It also had charcoal and burnt stone fragments in its fill.

The charcoal from these pits was mostly of oak but hazel, alder(?), ash and pomaceous fruitwood were also present. This suggests a preference for oak as fuel wood but also indicates the availability of other tree species in the vicinity. Other charred plant macrofossils or animal bone were absent and no artefacts were recovered.

The pits represent the remains of at least three fires perhaps related to charcoal production. The morphology, dominance of oak and occurrence of redeposited till in Pit 3 in particular supports this suggestion (Kenny 2010). Its date suggests the fires occurred sometime in the 11th to 13th centuries AD. Their presence hints at the possibility of nearby settlement though evidence of such a site has yet to be identified.

Carrowdotia AR27: site of enclosures and clearance cairns[23]

Excavations at Carrowdotia AR27 focused on the sites of two recorded monuments: CL026-036-01 and CL026-036-02. Both appear on the first edition Ordnance Survey map of 1840 as circular embanked enclosures (not illustrated), although neither is depicted on the second edition map of 1914, suggesting the enclosures were destroyed sometime between 1840 and 1914. The excavation was undertaken to record any evidence of the enclosures that might have survived. The excavation extended over an area of 4,144 m² and incorporated the site of the larger of the two enclosures (CL026-036-01) and part of the site of the smaller monument (CL026-036-02), as indicated by

22 Ballymacahill, Co. Clare; barony Bunratty Upper; NGR 136837 179632; height 9 m OD; Excavation Licence No. 04E0054. Excavation Director: Markus Casey.
23 Carrowdotia, Co. Clare; barony Bunratty Upper; NGR 137110 183590; height 24 m OD; Excavation Licence No. 03E1443. SMR Nos CL026-036-01 & CL026-036-02. Excavation Director: Kate Taylor.

map evidence. There was no visible surface expression of the enclosures prior to excavation. The terrain here is uneven and characterised by outcropping limestone bedrock. Soil cover is generally thin and in places no more than a mossy covering adhering to stone.

The shallow topsoil horizon and overburden (a layer of broken rock) were removed onto bedrock by machine (avoiding a modern driveway that traversed the site). The presence of bedrock so close to the field surface meant there were no cut features such as pits or ditches present. Instead, heaps or mounds of stones were visible under the thin covering of topsoil.

The excavations revealed six undated clearance cairns comprising small pieces of broken limestone bedrock, heaped in irregular oval mounds between 2 m and 6 m in length. No artefacts were recovered from any of the cairns. All six were north of the driveway and stratigraphically on top of overburden. A number of 19th- and 20th-century topsoil finds included glass and pottery fragments, and a coin dating to 1944.

The relationship of the cairns to the enclosures marked on the 1840 map remains unknown. The six cairns may derive from the rubble core of a robbed-out cashel wall but there is no other archaeological evidence to suggest that a cashel ever existed on the site, at least in the case of CL026-036-01, the larger of the two supposed enclosures. Local bedrock formations may provide an alternative explanation for the apparent existence of an enclosure at this location. The larger monument occupies a natural bowl-shaped depression formed by seriated bedrock terraces. This terrain, perhaps enhanced by clearance cairns, may have been erroneously interpreted by the mid 19th-century Ordnance Survey team as the remains of an enclosure. Hence, the six cairns are more likely to represent modern field clearance than the destruction of an earlier monument.

Clareabbey C020/A025: Augustinian Abbey[24]

Clare Abbey is an Augustinian foundation of 12th-century date, represented today by the well-preserved ruins of its church, cloister and conventual buildings (Illus. 3.14). The ruins occupy a tongue of high ground in the floodplain of the River Fergus. The river flows 200 m to the east and the Ennis to Limerick railway passes immediately to the west (Illus. 1.5). The lands around the Abbey are now in pasture, with some outcropping limestone bedrock, but when the Abbey was built, it was established on an island surrounded by marsh. In the post-medieval period river flood defences were constructed, chiefly earthen banks, that allowed greater access for agricultural use to reclaimed lands in the floodplain.

The layout of the Abbey is typical of medieval Augustinian establishments. The surviving ruins consist of a long, single-aisled church, subsequently divided into nave and chancel/choir by the erection of a tower. A cloister garth extends from the southern side of the church with a kitchen and refectory located at the opposite or south side of the garth (Illus. 3.15). Today, the ruined Abbey is a National Monument in State care.

The Abbey was dedicated to SS Peter and Paul. Gwynn & Gleeson (1962, 452) give the foundation date as AD 1189. This foundation date is listed in a 15th-century charter, though the charter itself has been shown to be a forgery designed to consolidate land claims (Flanagan 2005; MacMahon 1993).

---

24 Clareabbey, Co. Clare; barony Islands; NGR 134700 175730; height 6 m OD; Excavation Reg No. E2021 & E2022. Ministerial Consent: C020 and A025. SMR No. CL033-120. Excavation Director: Graham Hull.

Illus. 3.14—View of the Augustinian foundation of Clare Abbey, from south-east.

Nonetheless, the architectural remains support an early foundation date. They are predominantly Norman in date, though Westropp (1900a & b) described them as 15th-century work and probably there are elements of both periods present.

Following its dissolution in 1543, during the Reformation, the Abbey and its possessions were granted by Henry VIII to the O'Briens, Earls of Thomond and Barons of Inchiquin and the parish was administered from Killaloe (Power 2004, 162, 228). About 20 years later, John Nellan, the Protestant Archdeacon of Killaloe, complained to the English authorities that the Earl of Thomond and his brother, Sir Donald O'Brien of Ennistymon, were misusing the Abbey (Gallwey 1968, 65–73). Nicholas O'Nelan is listed as Abbot of Clare 70 years after dissolution while the Rev Dr De Burgho, Vicar-General of Killaloe, was its Abbot from 1647 to 1650 (MacMahon 1993). Despite this it is unclear if there were Augustinians in residence at the Abbey after dissolution, as was the case at the Franciscan abbey in Ennis where a small cohort of friars was tolerated by the O'Briens.

Depictions of the 17th to 19th centuries show the Abbey in advancing stages of ruin. A sketch by Thomas Dyneley, made in 1681, depicts a small chapel, with crosses on the gables, adjoining the east end of the Abbey church (reproduced in Ó Dálaigh 1998, 57). The sketch also shows the Abbey as unroofed, apart from the south-west portion where the kitchen had stood. By this time, the kitchen appears to have been converted into a house. An engraving made in 1783, from an original watercolour by Henry Pelham, records further changes: the chapel is no longer upstanding and the kitchen/house is unroofed. By the late 19th century, Wakeman's sketch (Illus. 3.16) and French's photographs of the Abbey in the Lawrence Collection show a more dilapidated, ivy-covered ruin

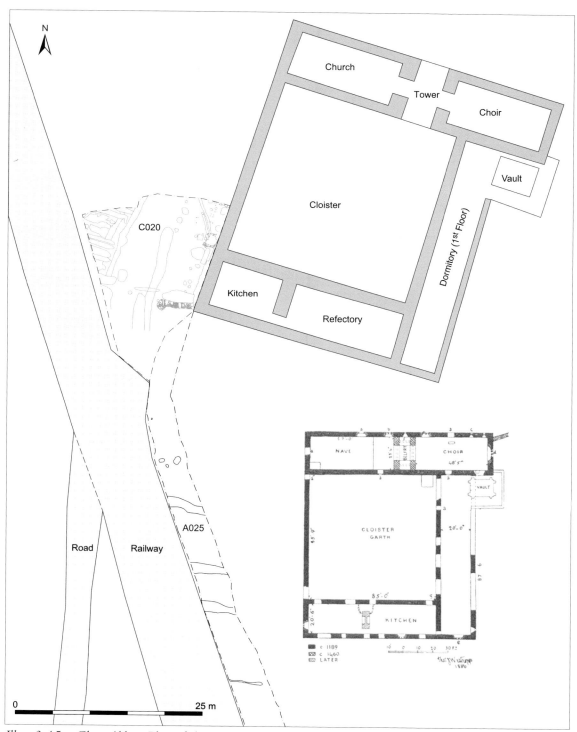

Illus. 3.15—Clare Abbey. Plan of the surviving building group showing the location of excavations in Areas C020 and A025 with (inset) a plan by Thomas J Westropp (1900a).

Illus. 3.16—Clare Abbey. A sketch by William Wakeman (1822–1900) (Royal Irish Academy 12.T.10[3]).

(http://catalogue.nli.ie/Record/L_CAB_06278). Throughout the post-medieval and early modern periods the Abbey continued in use as a burial ground and military objects recovered by the recent archaeological excavations suggest that it was garrisoned for a brief period in the 17th century (see below). The oldest legible tombs at the end of the 19th century were those of Charles Hallinan (1692), Owen O'Haugh (1726) and Denis Flinn (1755) (Gwynn & Gleeson 1962, 457) and the Abbey graveyard is still in use today.

Archaeological excavations at the Abbey

Excavations took place on the west side of the Abbey, as part of the investigations for the road scheme, to facilitate construction of a proposed improved access road and parking area for visitors. The excavations revealed evidence for all of the major phases in the history of the site, from the 11th to the 17th centuries.

Two excavation areas were opened immediately adjacent to the Abbey: Areas C020 and A025 (Illus. 3.15). Area C020 occupied a triangular plot, formerly a car park, defined by the west gable wall of the Abbey and the Ennis to Limerick railway. The total excavation area was 375 m². Area A025 was located south of C020 and comprised a narrow strip-trench parallel to the modern railway, 100 m long and with an area of 525 m². In each, all negative features (e.g. pits, drains) had been cut into glacial till and were sealed by topsoil, collapsed stone or tumble.

Area C020 (Illus. 3.17) contained a multiplicity of features including eight walls, two with construction cuts, two ditches, two drains, four pits, 34 post-holes and stake-holes, one cess-pit, a series of furrows and deposits related to railway construction. The majority represent features directly associated with the Abbey though some are of relatively recent origin. Seven cut features were identified in Area A025: one ditch, three gullies or furrows and three post-holes/pits.

A significant artefact assemblage was retrieved by the excavations. This included objects of stone, metal, pottery, glass, textile and iron slag with items dating from both the medieval and post-medieval phases of occupation of the Abbey (see Chapter 8). The excavations included use of a metal-detector with all cut features, and spoil examined for metal objects. Each excavation area yielded varying amounts of ecofacts, in particular animal bone, charred cereal grain and charcoal, which have provided valuable insights into the local food economy.

Three main phases of occupation of the Abbey have been identified: the earliest dates from the 11th/12th century and the latest dates to the 18th–20th centuries. Radiocarbon determinations

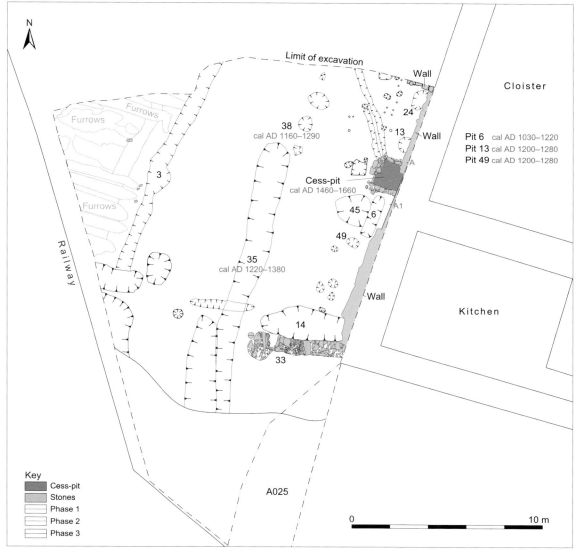

Illus. 3.17—Clare Abbey, Area C020. Plan of excavation area.

were obtained for select features within Area C020 but many features, including all those in Area A025, are dated by associated artefacts.

Phase I (11th to 14th century)

Rubbish pits In Area C020, two pits located at the foot of the kitchen gable wall are the earliest dated features on site (Illus. 3.17). Pit 45 measured 1.85 m by 1.6 m and was 0.35 m deep. It was truncated by a larger pit, Pit 6, which was 2.1 m by 0.8 m and 0.6 m deep (Illus. 3.18). Charred grains of wheat from Pit 6 returned a radiocarbon date of AD 1030–1220 (Beta-231531). It is unclear if the pits pre- or post-date the construction of the kitchen as their eastern edges appeared to either respect or be avoided by its gable wall. They may represent earlier occupation of the site—perhaps by an earlier church or monastery; or may simply represent temporary occupation or works associated with the construction of the Abbey, which may have continued over a number of decades. The pits held refuse, particularly food refuse. Charred cereal grains occurred in small quantities, including wheat, hulled barley and six-row barley. Charcoals from the pit included hazel,

Illus. 3.18—Clare Abbey, Area C020. Pit 6 following excavation.

oak and pomaceous fruitwood. Over 2,000 bones of eel, flounder and cod were retrieved from sieved soil samples. The dominance of eel bones reflects ease of access to the nearby River Fergus—where the Augustinians are likely to have controlled eel weirs—while the other fish species show that they had access to seafood also (see Chapter 6).

There were two other pits (13 and 24) that either pre-dated or coincided with the construction of the Abbey (Illus. 3.17). These pits extended beneath the outer foot of the cloister wall, though it is unclear if they related to an earlier building or represent temporary occupation, site clearance or other works prior to construction of the cloister wall. A pig bone from Pit 13 was dated to AD 1200–1280 (Beta-237217) (Illus. 1.7). A piece of Saintonge pottery, manufactured in western France, was recovered from the top of the same pit and provides a late 12th- to mid 13th-century date for infilling of the pit.

Post-holes Four post-holes situated to the west of the Abbey may represent the location of timber uprights corresponding with beam slots visible on the external face of the cloister wall (Illus. 3.19). These slots are massive, measuring 0.4 m wide by 0.3 m high and 0.45 m deep. The combination of slots and post-holes suggests that a wooden structure once abutted the outer face of the cloister

Illus. 3.19—Clare Abbey, Area C020. Outer (west) elevations of the cloister wall and kitchen gable, showing beam slots and putlock holes.

wall in this location. A pig bone from one of the post-holes (Pit 38) was radiocarbon-dated to AD 1160–1290 (Beta-237218) (Illus. 3.17).

Adjacent to the post-holes but closer to the cloister wall, and parallel to it, were two rows of post/stake-holes and three seemingly isolated stake-holes. These may relate to an insubstantial stone-wall remnant, perpendicular to the cloister wall, that was recorded at the northern limit of the excavation area. The wall and post/stake-hole rows appear to form a small rectangular outbuilding or lean-to construction at the outer face of the cloister wall.

Evidence for another structure is provided by a linear group of six post-holes parallel to the kitchen gable wall. A pig bone from one of these post-holes (49) yielded a radiocarbon date of AD 1200–1280 (Beta-237219). These post-holes may represent another lean-to building in this location or, alternatively, the location of wooden scaffolding poles erected during the construction of the tall kitchen gable wall. Putlock holes, i.e. holes in masonry for supporting transverse or horizontal scaffolding poles, are visible in the kitchen gable wall, corresponding roughly with the location of the post-holes (Illus. 3.19).

Ditches Two parallel ditches (3 and 35) were excavated in the centre of Area C020. Aligned north-east/south-west and 5 m apart they ran parallel to the west walls of the cloister and kitchen (Illus. 3.17). Relative to the density of archaeological features found across the rest of the site, the area between the ditches was largely devoid of features. This may be a product of truncation but, as this area corresponds with the location of a trackway depicted on the Ordnance Survey map of 1840, these features may represent flanking ditches along an early track or routeway—perhaps one that was established much earlier, in medieval times, giving public access to its church. Hazelnut shell from the fill of Ditch 35 returned a radiocarbon date of AD 1220–1380 (Beta-231533).

South of the Abbey, in Area A025, there was a well-defined, curving ditch in the centre of the excavation area, with a U-shaped profile, steep sides and a concave base (Illus. 3.15). It was 6 m wide, 0.65 m deep and at least 5 m long (i.e. it spanned the full width of the cutting) and had infilled with silt. Six different fills occurred, ranging in depth from 0.07 m to 0.28 m. They contained charcoal and charred plant macrofossils, albeit in low quantities, including wheat, hulled barley and six-row barley, with hazelnut shells, and weed seeds of vetch or tare also occurring. Charcoal included hazel, hazel/alder, oak, ash and pomaceous fruitwood.

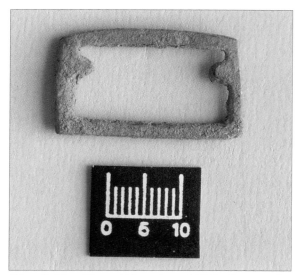

Illus. 3.20—Clare Abbey, Area A025. Copper-alloy belt hasp (E2022:59:2).

Artefacts recovered from the ditch fills included a horseshoe (E2022:57:3) dating to the 13th century or earlier; a copper-alloy belt hasp (E2022:59:2; Illus. 3.20) with parallels dating to the 14th/15th century, and a single body sherd of an earthenware vessel dated to the 18th/19th century (see Chapter 8). The finds, however, were not deposited in chronological order. The belt hasp was stratigraphically below the horseshoe and the pot sherd, which both derived from the same upper ditch fill. Evidently the ditch was backfilled sometime in the modern period but the belt hasp found in its lower fills suggests that it was originally of 14th/15th-century date or older.

Metal-working (Phase I/II)

Iron slag was retrieved from several features in both Areas C020 and A025 (see Chapter 8). Metal-working appears to have occurred at the Abbey in Phases I and II though the extent and the precise location where it took place is unknown. Three pits or large post-holes, located in the northern end of Area A025, included slag within their fills (Illus. 3.15). The largest measured 0.8 m by 0.66 and 0.49 m deep, and contained small amounts of burnt wheat and hazelnut, with ash and pomaceous fruitwood charcoal. One pit had small limestone pieces packed against the edges. Although slag occurs, the pit fills are characteristic of general site debris rather than specific metal-working features. The pits did not yield datable finds but their contents suggest they relate to either Phase I or Phase II.

Phase II (mid 16th century to late 17th century)

Cess-pit Some time in the 16th–17th centuries a rectangular, stone-lined pit was constructed against the external wall of the cloister (Illus. 3.17). The pit is likely to have functioned as a cess-pit but one into which

Illus. 3.21—Clare Abbey, Area C020. Pits underlying the cloister wall, cess-pit and drains.

kitchen slops were also dumped. It presumably served a latrine located within the cloister and its construction resulted in the removal of stones from the cloister wall foundation. The pit measured 1.5 m by 1.25 m and was 0.72 m deep, although the original masonry lining probably stood higher. An associated egress hole, 0.72 m by 0.73 m, was cut into the cloister wall, which enabled the flow of waste into the pit, from where it drained via a pair of linear gullies (Illus. 3.21 and 3.22). A radiocarbon date of AD 1460–1660 (Beta-233431) was obtained from a single hare vertebra retrieved from the basal fill of the pit. In the pit bottom, several fragments of a single, high-quality glass vessel (E2021:67:10) were recovered, dated to c. AD 1600 (see Chapter 8). The combined dating evidence and the insertion of a latrine into a formerly hallowed space (i.e. the cloister) suggest the cess-pit was constructed after the dissolution of the Abbey in AD 1543.

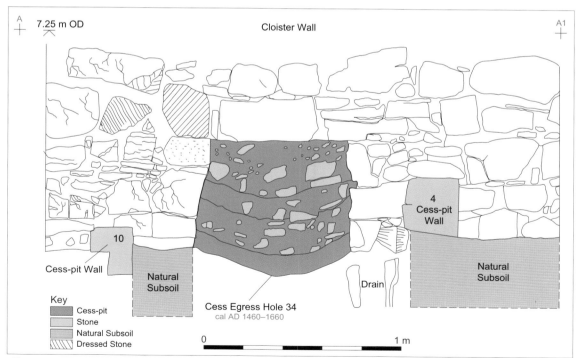

Illus. 3.22—Clare Abbey, Area C020. Egress hole for the cess-pit at the base of the cloister wall.

Other finds included nails, pins, a gun pellet, iron slag, window glass, a roof tile and pieces of linen (see Chapter 8). The latter occurred in small pieces and may have been used as toilet wipes. There were no coprolites recovered but the basal fill included cess-like material. Faunal remains were abundant with a range of domestic and wild species represented; these included sheep/goat, pig, dog, hare, black rat, woodmouse, chicken, goose, duck, woodcock, frog, as well as fish such as flounder, pike and eel (see Chapter 6). The cess-pit yielded more plant remains than other features on site. Cereal grains of wheat, barley and oats along with weed seeds and vetch or tare occurred within the cess. Charcoal was also present, mainly oak, pomaceous fruitwood and ash (see Chapter 7). The pit contents demonstrate that it was utilised both for cess (linen wipes) and for kitchen slops.

Secondary building A wall (33) and ditch (14) may represent a building appended to the outer wall of the Abbey at the south-west angle of the kitchen (Illus. 3.17). The wall and ditch did not intrude on the foundations of the kitchen and evidently post-dated it. A piece of a clay tobacco pipe dating from the 18th/19th century was retrieved from the upper fill of the ditch.

Rubble layer The cess-pit, the wall and ditch, and several of the earlier archaeological features located close to the Abbey on its west side, were sealed by a substantial layer of limestone rubble and sandstone roof tiles. This material probably derived from the kitchen or perhaps from the later extramural building represented by the wall and ditch described above. The rubble deposit contained several post-medieval artefacts and there was a noticeable absence of cut or dressed stone within the horizon. Given that the adjacent cloister would have been vaulted and pillared, the absence of architectural stone suggests these elements had been selectively robbed-out by the time the collapse occurred in the post-medieval period.

Illus. 3.23—Post-medieval finds from excavations at Clare Abbey: coin (E2021:51:3) and ring (E2021:39:6).

Illus. 3.24—Post-medieval finds from excavations at Clare Abbey: spur rowel (E2021:51:66) and rowel spur (E2021:59:41).

Military finds The nearby village of Clare (c. 1 km to the south), or Clarecastle as it would eventually be known, is located at a strategically important crossing of the River Fergus. In the 17th century the castle was home to successive military garrisons. It was occupied by Crown forces during the rebellion of 1641, by Cromwellian forces in the 1650s and again by Jacobite forces during the 'War of the two Kings' in 1688–91 (Power 2004). There is no documentary evidence that the Abbey was ever garrisoned, but it is unlikely that a large, defensible masonry building—and moreover one with a tower—would not have been exploited as a strong place and billet during one or more of these conflicts. This would account for the discovery of a number of artefacts of military character during the excavations described here (for details see Chapter 8), including cavalry spurs (parts), buckles, horse equipment and an example of the infamous 'gun money' coins minted by James II to fund his campaign in Ireland (Illus. 3.23 and 3.24).

Phase III (18th century to 20th century)

Cultivation furrows The main activity identified during this period relates to cultivation and the construction of the Ennis/Limerick railway. A series of shallow linear features, most likely the remains of pre-Famine cultivation furrows, was recorded in Area C020 (Illus. 3.17). A range of 18th- to 20th-century artefacts was retrieved from their fills. The old trackway that was defined by lateral ditches and map evidence (Phase I, above) appears to have been respected by these cultivation furrows, so that it would seem to have run between the Abbey and adjacent tillage land.

To the south, in Area A025, three more shallow furrows were revealed. They appeared to respect the line of the ditch described above (Phase I) (Illus. 3.15). These furrows were infilled with silts containing charcoal and occasional charred cereal grain. Wheat, six-row barley and hazelnut shell occurred along with oak, hazel and pomaceous fruitwood charcoal.

It is assumed that these furrows are early modern vintage as spade-dug tillage was at a peak at this time in the West of Ireland and, in any case, the lands around the Abbey were not drained for agricultural use until the 19th century. But as the two groups of furrows respected a trackway and ditch (in Areas C020 and A025, respectively), it is possible that they are in fact remnants of medieval cultivation in the immediate environs of the Abbey.

Railway construction In the south-west part of Area C020, a series of cut features, including two pits, a post-hole and a depression (Illus. 3.17), are attributed to the construction of the Ennis to Limerick railway in the mid 19th century. They truncated earlier medieval features, including the probable routeway.

Killow AR104: double ditches[25]

Killow AR104 was situated c. 150 m north-west of a medieval church (CL034-102). Both occupied dry ground flanking a bog with the excavation site situated on a drumlin that had also been the focus of prehistoric funerary and burnt mound activity (Chapter 2).

A set of double ditches curved around the east side of the drumlin and, if projected fully around its perimeter, would have enclosed an oblong area on the summit about 100 m long (Illus. 3.25). The ditches were very shallow and poorly defined, with fills of topsoil over silt and gravel. The gap between them varied from 0.4 m to 3.5 m. Hazel, ash and oak charcoal were retrieved from the ditch fills, but in such small quantities that they may simply represent windblown detritus. Animal bone from the fill of one ditch (Ditch 11) returned radiocarbon dates of AD 1280–1410

---

25 Killow, Co. Clare; barony Bunratty Upper; NGR 136822 175115; height 2.5–3.8 m OD; Excavation Licence No. 04E191. Excavation Director: Kate Taylor.

(Beta-211590) and AD 1430–1630 (Beta-213002). The dates suggest the ditches were constructed by the late 13th or 14th century and remained open until the 15th century or later. The ditches were too slight to have formed a defensive enclosure or homestead and, in any case, no associated archaeological features were identified inside them. They most likely represent a livestock paddock or some such enclosure on the summit of the drumlin.

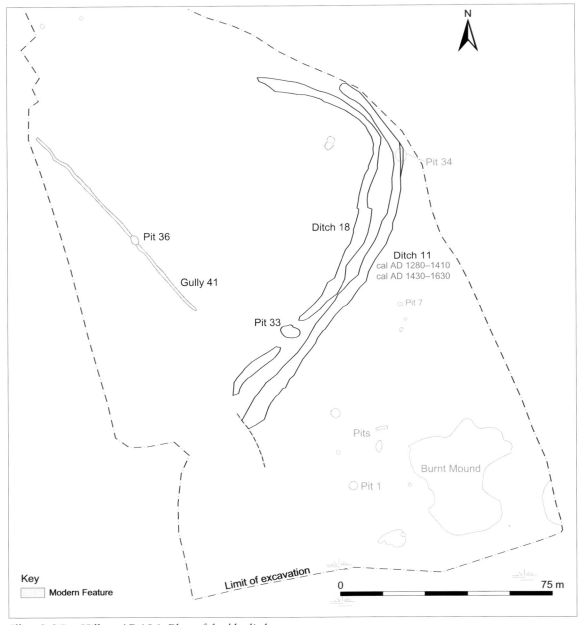

N

Pit 34

Ditch 18

Ditch 11
cal AD 1280–1410
cal AD 1430–1630

Pit 36

Gully 41

Pit 7

Pit 33

Pits

Burnt Mound

Pit 1

Limit of excavation

Key
Modern Feature

0   75 m

Illus. 3.25—Killow AR104. Plan of double ditches.

Medieval settlement in the Fergus Valley

Michelle Comber

Early medieval sites

Archaeological remains radiocarbon-dated to the early medieval period on this scheme include a cashel (Carrowdotia AR25), a ditched enclosure with field system (Cahircalla More AR128), isolated pits or hearths and pit groups with various possible purposes at several other sites (Carrowdotia M27, Manusmore AR102, Kilbreckan AR110, Clareabbey AR123, Barefield AR106, Ballymacahill AR108).

Pits

Seemingly isolated pits are something of a new 'monument type' in Irish archaeology. Such features were rarely identified in Ireland prior to the introduction of development-led excavations that typically investigate areas without extant surface remains, areas largely ignored in earlier excavations. Early medieval pits described as 'isolated' are usually features found some distance from any known enclosure or settlement of that period. They include rubbish pits, iron-working hearths and furnaces (e.g. Carrowdotia AR25), charcoal-production pits (e.g. Barefield AR106), and domestic/cooking fires (e.g. Manusmore AR102). These may represent the exploitation of natural resources that occurred away from the main settlements, or temporary stopping places by people moving across the landscape. It is also possible that they represent a stratum of previously unknown, unenclosed settlements, occupied by the poorest elements of society, those without the resources or need to build an enclosed settlement. These pits and pit clusters are a reminder that 'settlement' in the early medieval landscape was not confined to visible, permanent enclosures but included a wide range of other, perhaps seasonal, activities associated with livestock and crop management, and the exploitation of natural resources.

Iron-working

Archaeological evidence from Ireland suggests that iron-working occurred on the majority of early medieval settlements. The extent of that practice, however, appears to have varied, often in relation to site/occupant status. Most excavated 'classic' ringforts, for example, have produced evidence of a limited level of iron-working, with the occupying family capable of repairing and maintaining the iron implements they used on a daily basis. Larger, apparently wealthier, sites often saw more extensive iron-working, perhaps representing the activity of a specialist metalworker in both the repair and manufacture of iron implements.

A small number of excavated sites, such as Moynagh Lough *crannóg*, Co. Meath (Bradley 1991, 1993), may have been solely occupied by a group of craftsmen. The enclosure at Cahircalla More AR128 might be viewed in this way, with the only structure identified in the interior having been used as an iron-working smithy. The site also produced evidence of agricultural activity—a quern for grain processing, charred cereal grains, and an associated field system. Evidently, the occupants did not rely solely on iron-working for a livelihood but also farmed the adjoining land.

Early Irish documentary evidence also supports the existence of specialist iron-workers or 'smiths'. Both archaeological and documentary evidence suggests that such specialists may have been linked with higher-status settlements, perhaps through the patronage of upper-class occupants. It is uncertain whether or not such smiths operated on these sites on a temporary/seasonal or permanent basis. Some smiths may have had their own enclosed settlements, like Cahircalla More AR128, while still others may have been 'nomadic' (perhaps evident in the unenclosed iron-working hearths and associated features, e.g. Carrowdotia M27). The latter might have travelled from one place to another providing services to the communities they encountered, operating with the permission, and under the supervision, of the local master or chief smith, as suggested in the literary evidence of the period (Comber 2004, 12 & 2008, 18).

Cashels and ringforts

Ringforts are the most common field monument type in the country and the stone ringfort—cashel or caher—is especially common along the western seaboard of Ireland, and in other areas of plentiful rock outcrop. Most cashels are roughly circular with an average diameter of 20–25 m, and are defined by a drystone wall with no external ditch. Very few cashels have been excavated and even fewer in their entirety. The most famous excavated example is probably Cahercommaun in the Burren, Co. Clare (Hencken 1938). This, however, is far from an 'average' cashel, with its large diameter (115 m maximum), impressive cliff-top location, and three enclosing drystone walls. Another excavated cashel in the Burren, Caherconnell, is also larger and more impressive than the average cashel. Research excavations in 2007 and 2010 revealed a relatively late construction date for this cashel in the 10th century and settlement activity continuing into the 17th century (Comber & Hull 2010; Hull & Comber 2008). Therefore, despite their numbers, relatively little is known of typical early medieval cashels in County Clare.

If cashels functioned in a similar manner to the earthen ringfort, then most operated as enclosed farmsteads that housed a farming family and enclosed domestic, farming and craft/industrial activity. The cashel at Carrowdotia AR25 was a modest, univallate site (approximately 25 m in diameter), dated to the sixth or seventh century AD. The interior produced a single pit of unknown function and no evidence of domestic habitation. Whether this reflects a different or specialised use of the site (e.g. a livestock corral and not a dwelling place), or truncation of the site by later tillage, or simply the fact that only one third of the site was excavated, is uncertain.

Cahircalla More AR128 may have been an earthen ringfort, though only a steep-sided ditch, lacking any bank, was excavated. (The site was, however, heavily truncated by tillage in a later period.) Only one building was uncovered in the interior and that appears to have been used for iron-working. In Clare, and in the Burren in particular, there are many extensive early field systems peppered with ringforts and miscellaneous other enclosures of various sizes. From this evidence it seems that the early medieval landscape was an organised one, with spaces enclosed for many reasons—grazing, tillage, craft-working, herding/shepherding, status and political display, as well as for habitation.

Later medieval sites

Sites from this scheme that were dated to the later medieval period (post-AD 1200) include the remains of a double-ditched enclosure at Killow AR104 and features associated with the Augustinian Abbey at Clareabbey.

There is little that can be said of the two ditches partly enclosing the eastern side of a drumlin at Killow, other than they probably formed part of a 13th- to 15th-century field boundary. There is a ruined medieval church 150 m to the south-east and the ditches might represent farming on church lands.

The Augustinian house at Clare Abbey was established under the patronage of the O'Briens of north Munster as a highly visible demonstration of their piety, wealth and political power. This was particularly important in an era of increasing Anglo-Norman influence, and decreasing O'Brien power. The Augustinians (canons regular as opposed to the later mendicant Order of St Augustine) were one of the most powerful religious orders in the region, rivalled only by the Franciscans at places such as Ennis and Quin, which were also O'Brien endowments. The material evidence from the excavation at Clare Abbey suggests a wealthy household, with access to a very wide range of local food resources but also exotic, imported luxury goods. After its dissolution the Abbey was granted by the Crown to the O'Brien Earls of Thomond. Its history over the next 100 years is unclear and little appears to be known about the religious life of the Abbey until the mid 17th century. The parish appears to have been administered from Killaloe and it is unclear if the abbots named elsewhere resided at the Abbey. The excavation produced evidence for a military presence during one or other of the wars of the mid and late 17th century and it seems that its former resident clergy had long gone by that time.

The excavation also brought into focus some evidence for the changing fabric of the Abbey in the successive phases of its history. There are traces of the original construction methods (putlock holes, scaffolding pits) in both the standing remains and below ground. One or more lean-to buildings abutted the outer wall of the cloister on its west side, that farthest from the church; and the adaptation of the cloistral buildings for secular occupation in the post-Reformation period is represented in the excavated area by a well-built cess-pit with an outfall from the kitchen, punched through the base of the cloister wall.

4

POST-MEDIEVAL AND EARLY MODERN EXCAVATIONS

Nóra Bermingham, Graham Hull and Kate Taylor

Four of the sites excavated on the scheme are post-medieval/early modern in date and a further three sites had post-medieval elements (Illus. 4.1). All the sites occupy land that was ploughed during the lifetime of a given site and/or later. There are two industrial sites—brick kilns at Manusmore AR101 and Clareabbey AR120—but most sites are agricultural in nature and include a limekiln, ditches and quarry pits as well ubiquitous plough or spade-dug cultivation furrows. Two roadways with associated banks and ditches, a field boundary and a field system illustrate the evolution of the rural landscape in this period.

Site summaries

Manusmore AR101: brick kiln clamp[26]

The remains of a brick kiln clamp were discovered in this townland in a low-lying place dominated by reeds. (Locally it was reported that the field was once so wet that geese swam there.) Up to 0.15 m of topsoil overlay successive horizons of silt deposited over blue-grey clay at least 1.5 m in depth. The latter is typical of former post-glacial water bodies that have infilled with clays and the combination of clay, silt and vegetation is characteristic of a wetland zone flanked by higher ground. Ceramic drains laid in the field in 1905 were also uncovered during the excavation.

An excavation area of 225 m² was opened with the clamp situated at its centre. A series of eight, parallel, charcoal-rich linear slots was exposed. These were shallow, less than 0.05 m deep, and were orientated south-west/north-east. They were each 5 m long, 0.5 m wide and were separated by a regular interval of 0.5 m. The slots occupied a total area of 8 m by 5 m, which was overlain by a deposit of compacted brick fragments up to 0.1 m deep. A band of broken bricks bordered the south-west side of the charcoal-filled slots. The bricks formed an unmortared area of 6 m by 0.6 m and stood no more than one course high.

Fuel burned in the slots provided the heat to dry the bricks laid above in benches. Bricks manufactured at the kiln were hand-made, unfrogged (frogged bricks retain a depression on one brick face) and reddish-brown in colour. The bricks are uneven and vary in size though an average full-sized brick measures 215 mm by 102 mm by 63 mm. The kiln slots yielded fragments of fired clay, burnt peat and charcoal. Peat was the principal fuel though oak charcoal was also present.

---

26 Manusmore, Co. Clare; barony Islands; NGR 137530 172910; height 2 m OD; Excavation Licence No. 04E0188. Excavation Director: Graham Hull.

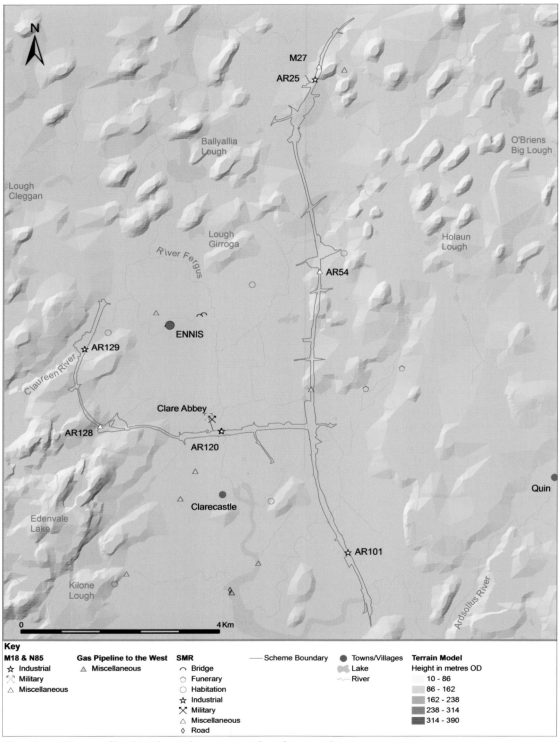

Illus. 4.1—Post-medieval/early modern sites on the scheme and in its environs.

Illus. 4.2—Manus House takes its name from the townland of Manusmore.

Manus House was a mansion house of later 18th/earlier 19th-century vintage located 300 m north-west of the brick kiln site. It was occupied by the Healy family, who were long-term tenants of the Wyndham estate from the 1820s. Brickwork at Manus House features bricks that are similar in size and shape to those found on the kiln site at Manusmore AR101 and they were probably manufactured there at the time of the construction of the house (Illus. 4.2).

Clareabbey AR120: three brick kiln clamps[27]

A group of brick kiln clamps was identified in a field bounded on the east side by the River Fergus and a flood-defence clay bund. The site occupied low-lying, wet pasture characterised by up to 0.6 m of alluvium over peat at least 1.5 m deep. Three principal areas of brick-making activity were identified: clamps A, B and C (Illus. 4.3). Each was situated directly on alluvium and sealed by a deposit of broken brick rubble and topsoil. Clamps A and B were single-use structures but three phases of kiln construction and use were evident at the northernmost kiln, Clamp C. Clamps B and C had been truncated by a back drain flanking the River Fergus flood bund. The bund and, presumably, the back drain are recorded in the first edition Ordnance Survey 1842, indicating that the brick clamps are at least older than the mid 19th century.

Clamp A

Clamp A was the best preserved of the three structures (Illus. 4.4) and comprised six rows or benches of unmortared brick orientated NNE/SSW. The benches were up to 4.7 m long, 0.45 m wide and

---

27 Clareabbey, Co. Clare; barony Islands; NGR 134970 175435; height 1.5 m OD; Excavation Licence No. 04E0027. Excavation Director: Kate Taylor.

two to three courses high. Between the benches, the fuel rows were defined by deposits of black, burnt peat up to 0.08 m deep. Brick air vents were visible at the ends of the fuel rows.

Clamp B

This structure was formed by 10 rows of brick benches, each typically 5.5 m to 6 m long, 0.5 m wide and orientated NNE/SSW. Burnt peat was evident between the benches.

Clamp C

This clamp demonstrated evidence of three phases of brick-making. The first phase comprised five fuel slots up to 0.2 m deep, 0.4 m wide and 6 m long aligned NNE/SSW. These slots were filled with burnt peat, the remains of

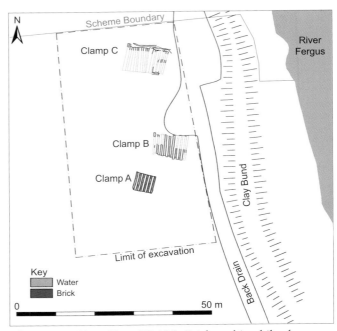

Illus. 4.3—Clareabbey AR120. Brick-making kiln clamps.

the fuel burned in the first phase. The filled slots were sealed and levelled by a layer of broken brick fragments and redeposited alluvium. Two more brick kilns were then constructed over the first clamp. These kilns were built next to each other although they were not necessarily contemporaneous. The western clamp had six benches covering an area of 6 m by 5.8 m while the adjacent kiln was

Illus. 4.4—Clareabbey AR120. View of Clamp A.

somewhat smaller covering an area of 6 m by 4.2 m. The benches of each kiln were 0.3 m to 0.45 m wide and retained the alignment of the earlier phase.

The bricks manufactured in these clamps were terracotta in colour and many retained surface impressions of grass. Some brick fragments had been burnt and were a greyish-brown colour. The bricks were uneven in size and varied from 227 mm by 100 mm by 65 mm to 235 mm by 110 mm by 70 mm. They also varied in weight from 2,619 g to 2,981 g.

The primary source of fuel for the kilns was peat. Burnt peat inclusive of charred heather stems was abundant at all three clamps. Charcoal was present but could not be identified to species. Pieces of fired clay were also common among the structures.

The number of kilns identified was five in total and this suggests brick manufacturing on an industrial or commercial scale. This contrasts with the brick clamp at Manusmore AR101, where the kiln seems to have been built specifically to supply construction materials for Manus House. The location of the clamps in Clareabbey, adjacent to the River Fergus, probably reflects use of the river for the transport of bulky materials and this kiln site may have supplied bricks to a wide market, beyond the immediate locality.

Carrowdotia AR25: quarry pits, field boundaries and furrows[28]

The early medieval cashel site at Carrowdotia AR25 (see Chapter 3) was very heavily modified by later changes in land-use. Relic cultivation ridges were aligned north-east/south-west across the site. Clearance cairns hugged the edges of the fields and also the wall of the earlier cashel. A single sherd of post-medieval pottery (03E1442:10) was recovered from one of the furrows but most of the artefacts from the ploughsoil were modern, including table wares, bottle glass, corroded pieces of iron, and fragments of clay tobacco pipe. There were several shallow quarry pits (up to 8 m wide and 1 m deep), backfilled with small limestone rubble and modern artefacts that included pottery, iron, clay tobacco pipes and glass sherds. The cashel itself was bisected by a field wall that did not appear on the first edition Ordnance Survey map of 1840 but does appear on a later edition of 1941. A field boundary at the southern end of the excavation area marks the townland boundary between Carrowdotia and Drumquin and replaced a wet-ditch, backfilled with rubble that had previously marked the townland boundary. None of these features is of any significance in itself but, together, they offer a glimpse of how the land surface can be aggressively worked and reworked from one period to the next, often resulting in the loss of evidence from the earliest periods.

Carrowdotia M27: road, ditches, furrows and pits[29]

Investigations at Carrowdotia M27 were instigated following the discovery of pits and other cut features adjacent to an unmarked enclosure, possibly a cashel (Illus. 3.12). The pits proved to be early medieval in date but the enclosure did not form part of the investigation as it lay outside the road-take. The majority of the other features identified were post-medieval or later in date and included

---

28 Carrowdotia, Co. Clare; barony Bunratty Upper; NGR 136850 182830; height 25 m OD; Excavation Licence No. 03E1442. SMR No. CL026-033. Excavation Director: Kate Taylor.

29 Carrowdotia, Co. Clare; barony Bunratty Upper; NGR 136920 183090; height 29 m OD; Excavation Licence No. 03E1426. Excavation Director: Kate Taylor.

a road and accompanying ditches, a series of later pits, a walled field boundary and evidence for tillage in the form of furrows of varying alignments.

The road is of particular interest because it was subsequently realigned, so that some of the original materials survive in this sector. It was represented by a series of mixed gravel and lime mortar surfaces, between 2 m and 4.5 m wide, with flanking ditches. It corresponds with a routeway depicted on the first edition Ordnance Survey map of 1840 (Illus. 3.8) but had fallen out of use by 1914 when the second edition Ordnance Survey map was published. The ceramic assemblage from the ditches associated with the road suggests that it was in use from the 17th to the 19th centuries.

Cahircalla More AR128: road, bank and ditch complex[30]

The first edition Ordnance Survey map of 1840 depicts a road running through the excavation area at Cahircalla More AR128. This road was superseded by the N68 Ennis to Kilrush road but traces of the earlier route (220) were recorded during excavations (Illus. 3.2). This earlier road was carried along a shallow terrace in the hillside up to 7 m wide. The terrace was levelled with compact layers of gravel and clay forming the road surface. This in turn was sealed by a later ploughsoil, bearing abundant fragments of pottery and glass. On the northern or upslope side a field boundary flanking the road consisted of a large earthen bank over 3 m wide and 2 m high. The bank was constructed from material thrown up in the construction of the road terrace and contained sherds of bottle glass. On the south side of the road there were remains of a flanking ditch, up to 1.3 m wide and 0.45 m deep. A similar ditch was revealed on the north side of the bank. Like the early road recorded at Carrowdotia M27, this feature is of interest because it affords a glimpse of early modern road-building techniques and materials on a sector that survived because the routeway was subsequently realigned as a modern, paved road.

Keelty AR129: limekiln[31]

A 19th-century limekiln, ancillary building and yard were recorded on a north-west-facing incline, overlooking the floodplain of the Claureen River. The kiln was not recorded on the first edition Ordnance Survey map of 1840 (Illus. 4.5), but is depicted as a ruin on a later edition, surveyed in 1894 and published in 1917. The complex was constructed on a scarp in a hillside comprised of glacial drift (gravel) and naturally outcropping limestone. At the foot of the scarp a road with drystone flanking walls linked the limekiln to the nearby road network.

The kiln

The limekiln was constructed of limestone blocks, roughly dressed and bonded with lime mortar. Mortared rubble walls partly enclosed the buildings and a metalled road served the kiln.

The kiln itself was rectangular in plan and measured 5.7 m by 6.6 m (Illus. 4.6). The front elevation (north-west) stood 4.7 m high (Illus. 4.7). The kiln had a flat upper surface with a centrally

---

30 Cahircalla More, Co. Clare; barony Bunratty Upper; NGR 132511 175537; height 15.6 m OD; Excavation Licence No. 04E0029. Excavation Director: Kate Taylor.
31 Keelty, Co. Clare; barony Islands; NGR 132192 177177; height 6–14 m OD; Excavation Licence No. 04E0025. Excavation Director: Graham Hull.

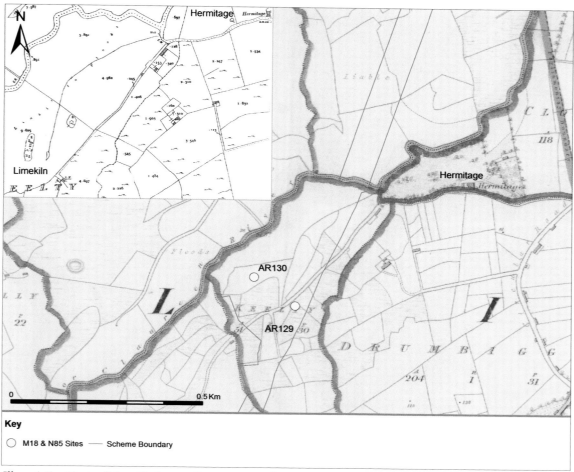

Illus. 4.5—First edition Ordnance Survey map of 1840 showing the townland of Keelty and location of Hermitage House with (inset) detail from the second edition map of 1894 (publ. 1917).

located circular flue or 'pot'. The flue was 2.2 m in diameter at the top and tapered downward to join a horizontal furnace chamber. (Thus the shape of the chimney and flue combined was reminiscent of the form of a clay tobacco pipe.) The mouth of the furnace was brick vaulted, with maximum dimensions of 2.2 m across and 2.1 m high. The bricks from the furnace were terracotta in colour, unfrogged and hand-made, with typical dimensions of 230 mm by 95 mm by 75 mm. The base of the furnace was made from limestone flags and the chimney was constructed from thin, mortared limestone blocks, reddened by heat.

A low parapet wall, 0.25 m high and 0.5 m wide, enclosed the flat roof of the kiln. A gap in the parapet on the south-western face was perhaps used as a drain. The roof of the kiln was linked to the hillside by a levelled, gravel dump that allowed access to the top of the flue. An overgrown track ran along the top of the hillside and would have facilitated loading the kiln with stone.

The kiln was half-sectioned (using a mechanical excavator) to examine its construction. It was built onto the natural limestone bedrock without cut foundations. The outer walls of the building formed a shell of mortared limestone blocks with the flue and chimney inserted. Sand and gravel

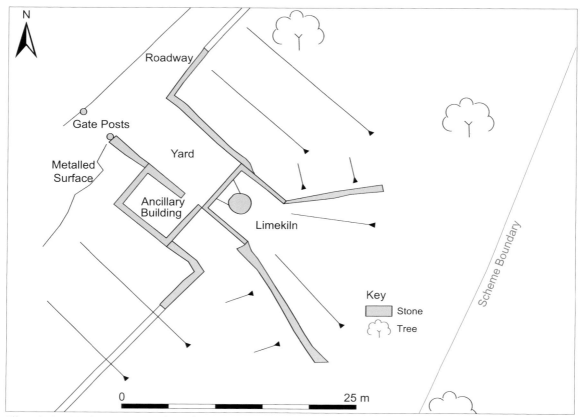

Illus. 4.6—Keelty AR129. Plan of kiln complex.

were added around the chimney and within the block shell. Banded tip-lines were evident within the sand and gravel fill. Dumps of earth and stone abutted the side and back walls of the building.

The kiln is a continous-type draw kiln into which both fuel and limestone were fed and burnt in the kiln bowl. The end product, quicklime, was drawn off at the base (Rynne 2006, 157). Lime was widely utilised as fertiliser and as mortar in the building industry.

Ancillary building

The ancillary building was a single-roomed, rectangular structure, west of the kiln, built from dressed, mortared limestone blocks (Illus. 4.6). The building measured 8 m by 3.7 m with walls 0.45 m thick that survived up to 3.9 m high. The north-west gable survived in part and appeared to be lit by a window. Debris found during excavation suggests the building had been roofed with slate. There was a doorway in the north-east wall, 0.8 m wide. Iron fastenings, perhaps to bar the door, were fixed into the stonework. The building lacked evidence for a surfaced floor. The structure may have served as a storeroom for fuel or for the quicklime product of the kiln.

Yard

The space in front of the kiln furnace formed a rectangular yard, 12 m by 6.5 m (Illus. 4.6). The yard was partly surfaced with rammed gravel and mortar and bounded by the ancillary building,

Illus. 4.7—Keelty AR129. Front (north-west) elevation of the kiln with (inset) glass ink bottle (04E0025:8).

low stone walls and a metalled roadway. The yard would have been where carts were loaded with the burnt lime product of the kiln.

Road

The metalled and walled roadway at the foot of the scarp below the kiln survives in the modern landscape over a distance of 500 m, approaching the site from north-east, but is now overgrown. At the limekiln, and at other points along the road, cut-stone gateposts once stood (Illus. 4.6), suggesting control of access to and from the kiln but also a degree of pride by the landowners that built the complex—so that embellishment as well as security were provided by the gateposts. On the first edition Ordnance Survey map the road extends beyond the kiln; by the edition of 1917 the road is depicted as terminating at the kiln.

Artefacts

A range of modern artefacts was recovered from demolition rubble adjacent to the kiln. The artefacts dated from the later 19th century or early 20th century and included transfer-applied 'china' table ware and bottle glass, a stamped clay tobacco-pipe bowl (04E0025:11), a piece of black glazed fire-brick stamped with the words 'COLTHURST &...' and 'PATENT.' (04E0025:13), and a glass inkpot (04E0025:8) which may have sat on a tally-clerk's desk (Illus. 4.7). Colthurst & Symons brickyard opened in Bridgwater, Somerset, England in the mid 1800s becoming one of the leading brick and tile manufactuers in and around the Bristol Channel. The fire-brick from Keelty is likely to have originated from this factory.

Conclusion

This complex of buildings, enclosing walls and road were clearly constructed in a single episode. While the buildings and walls were not keyed to each other, the integrated layout and identical construction techniques indicate a planned building event. The kiln was constructed sometime after 1840 and was a ruin by 1894. It is possible that the limekiln at Keelty was a commercial venture by the wealthy Keane family, who were big landowners in the locality throughout the 19th century. The Keane family had several houses in the locality. One of these, Hermitage House, was located at the head of the roadway leading to the kiln.

Knockanean AR54: field system[32]

In the course of the EIS for the scheme a circular stone enclosure was identified at Knockanean AR54 (Illus. 4.8). The enclosure was abutted by a series of field walls that formed three roughly rectangular fields framing its northern half. These various elements occupied an area of dense hazel scrub, on shallow topsoil overlying limestone bedrock.

Investigations focused on the enclosure, centrally placed within an excavation area of 1,000 m². The enclosure measured 23 m in diameter and defined an area of c. 350 m². Once cleared of vegetation, its wall stood up to 1.5 m high and 0.95 m wide, though it was generally lower. Stone tumble was evident on either face. The enclosure was identical in build to the field walls that abutted it, although two of these were clearly built after the enclosure had been completed (Illus. 4.9).

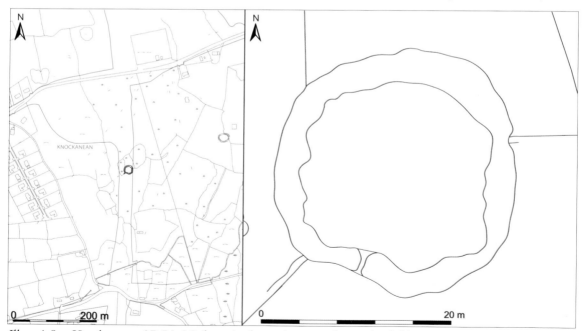

Illus. 4.8—Knockanean AR54. Modern circular enclosure within wider field system (based on the Ordnance Survey map).

32 Knockanean, Co. Clare; barony Bunratty Upper; NGR 136945 178800; height 22 m OD; Excavation Licence No. 04E0192. Excavation Director: Kate Taylor.

Illus. 4.9—Knockanean AR54. Composite photograph of the modern circular enclosure.

Excavations revealed that the circular enclosure had been built directly onto outcropping bedrock and was simply constructed using large unworked limestone boulders typically 0.3 m to 0.4 m in diameter. A narrow gap, 0.5 m wide, formed an entrance in the SSW. Cut features, either internal or external to the enclosure, were not present and there were no finds.

The similarity in construction between the circular enclosure and the abutting field walls suggests this group of structures represents part of a field system, probably of post-medieval or early modern date. The absence of other archaeological evidence and the relatively insubstantial nature of the circular enclosure—in contrast with the more massive walls of cashels and/or ringforts—supports this interpretation.

The site is depicted on the first edition Ordnance Survey map (1840) as a small sub-circular field within a patchwork of small fields. Nearby ringforts/cashels are indicated on the map by hachures and double lines. Knockanean AR54 was evidently not recognised as an archaeological monument in the mid 19th century survey and the excavation results confirm that judgement by the Ordnance Survey team.

Farming, transport and rural industry

Nóra Bermingham

In the archaeological record of the present road scheme, the post-medieval/early modern rural landscape is mainly represented by cultivation furrows and relict field boundaries that reflect the resurgence in tillage across Ireland in the 18th and 19th centuries; arable farming had all but been abandoned during the upheavals of the 17th century (Feehan 2003, 86, 93–9). From the mid 19th century ploughs were increasingly used, either in tandem with, or in place of spades as the chief means of cultivating soil (Bell & Watson 2008, 112–16). At Carrowdotia M27 both ploughing and the spade-dug ridges were represented. These need not be exclusive actions as the use of a plough to construct ridges is known, particularly on hilly ground or poorly drained soils (ibid.).

The need to protect crops and exclude or confine animals was probably a concern of farmers in every period of Irish history and prehistory, but the landscape did not become covered by a continuous network of field walls, hedgerows and embankments until the modern period. Post-medieval or early modern field boundaries were recorded at Cahircalla More AR127vii, Knockanean AR54 and Carrowdotia AR25. Field size typically reflects both the quality and the use of the farmland that is enclosed. For instance, the small regular fields around Knockanean AR54, where the soils are shallow and unsuitable for tillage, were probably paddocks for livestock and are typical of field systems on marginal lands in the West of Ireland.

The 18th and early 19th centuries in Ireland saw a tremendous growth in population and also an increasing trade in agricultural produce, industrial products and manufactured goods. Improvements in the rural road network can be seen as one response to this whether by private landowners or the Grand Juries that were responsible for local infrastucture. The short sectors of former roads recorded at Carrowdotia M27, Cahircalla More AR128 and Keelty AR129 provide a useful sample of road-building materials and construction techniques in the period. Generally, existing contours were followed but hillsides could be scarped to provide a level way. Flanking walls in drystone field rubble were common. Road surfaces were dressed with simple metalling of gravel and small stones or, less commonly, gravel and mortar. Side drains were also common it seems.

The products of limekilns were among the goods being transported on the rural road network in ever-increasing quantities (Feehan 2003, 99). Limekilns are the most numerous and widely distributed industrial monument within Ireland. The kiln products were chiefly used in construction (lime mortar) and as an agricultural fertiliser, but were also used in a very wide range of industrial processes, from leather tanning (to remove hair from hides) to iron-working (as a flux in blast furnaces) (Rynne 2006, 157).

The demands of the building trade were also met by brickworks such as those excavated in Manusmore AR101 and Clareabbey AR120. Throughout the post-medieval period bricks were manufactured by hand in kiln clamps. In larger urban centres, like Dublin and Cork, clamps were erected on sites called brickfields (ibid., 166). Kiln clamps were typically sited in proximity to sources of clay and water. Proximity to waterways facilitated their transportation. Bricks were made at Clareabbey AR120 on an industrial or commercial scale and were probably taken down the River Fergus. In contrast, some brick kilns were constructed to serve specific building projects and the example recorded at Manusmore AR101 probably supplied building material for nearby Manus House.

5
CREMATED REMAINS

Sian Anthony

Five sites provided the best evidence for cremation burial on the scheme: Manusmore AR100 and AR102, Killow AR104, Claureen AR131 and also a single pit at Cahircalla More AR128. Between them c. 2 kg of cremated bone was retrieved from pits and a single ring-ditch. With the exception of the example at Cahircalla More AR128 the pit cremations occurred in groups. These do not, however, represent discrete chronological clusters. At these sites, multiple phases of low-level cremation activity occurred over millennia.

Individual assemblages comprise a mix of human, animal and mammalian bone—the latter includes fragments that could not be securely identified as either human or animal. Two sites, Claureen AR131 and Cahircalla More AR128, contained exclusively human remains. The size of the assemblages and the time-span over which they range limit the analyses of the material and the potential for comparative studies. Here, each site assemblage is briefly presented with general comments on the contemporary context provided.

Methodology

The cremated remains were retrieved via wet-sieving with individual contexts subject to whole-earth recovery and then wet-sieved to a 2 mm fraction. All small pieces of bone were scanned rapidly, as fragments under <2 mm in size were abundant, resulting in a lack of recognisable pieces throughout the assemblage. Consequently, bones were not distinguished by size and percentage fragmentation was not calculated. As stated above, the overall and individual assemblage sizes limited the range of analyses undertaken. Reconstruction of demographic profiles, which can illustrate age and gender patterns, was not possible. Other analyses such as minimum number of individuals (MNI), minimum number of elements (MNE) or record of anatomical completeness were not warranted.

Human osteological analysis followed recommendations from McKinley (1994 & 2000) and Brickley & McKinley (2004) with animal identifications after Hillson (1992) and Getty (1975). Small amounts of cremated material were identified as mammalian only; some may be human but could not be readily identified as such.

Preservation

There was a high level of fragmentation across the assemblage with fragments of cremated human bone ranging between 2 mm and 10 mm in length (Table 5.1). Factors influencing fragmentation, including cremation, burial and natural processes have been outlined by Geber (2009). Analysis of fragmentation can indicate differences in ritual practice between sites and periods. However, greater quantities of bone and more closely dated material than is available here are required for worthwhile analysis.

Despite the high level of fragmentation, the majority of cremated fragments were relatively well preserved, although some deposits retained a slightly worn and chalky appearance; trabecular bone (spongy bone tissue) was poorly represented with general limb and skull pieces occurring more frequently. This is probably because of the easily identifiable nature of these pieces rather than any recognisable pattern in deposition (Neilson Marsh et al. 2000).

Overall, the small volume of cremated bone retrieved (c. 2 kg) may relate to preservation, particularly where sites had been ploughed resulting in a loss of material from the original deposit. However, in general, individual deposits are lightweight, suggesting recovered bone does not represent true or full cremation burial deposits but rather token burials, redeposited pyre debris or potentially cenotaph-type memorial deposits. Because the bone weight produced by the cremation of a single adult human corpse lies within the range of 1,000–3,600 g of bone (McKinley 2000, 404), the cremations discovered on the scheme are best interpreted in these ways.

Table 5.1—Cremated human remains from all excavated sites on the scheme.

Site name and date	Total frags	Total weight	Human	Animal	Mammal	Frag. size	Colour
Manusmore AR100 2500 BC–AD 250	1,194	1,484 g	245 g	789 g	450 g	<2–33 mm	Mainly white, some variable
Manusmore AR102 800–150 BC	445	164 g	141 g	—	23 g	<2–28 mm	Mainly white, some unburnt (non-human)
Killow AR104 1300–200 BC	231	167 g	55 g	46 g	66 g	<2–46 mm	Mainly white, some dark grey and variable
Claureen AR131 100 BC–AD 70	276	117 g	117 g	—	—	<2–23 mm	Mainly white, some grey
Cahircalla More AR128 undated	22	3 g	3 g	—	—	<2–15 mm	White
Total	**2,168**	**1,935 g**	**561 g**	**835 g**	**539 g**		
% Wt	—	100%	29%	43%	28%		

Pit burials

Manusmore AR100

The volume of cremated bone in the pits at Manusmore AR100 varied from a few specks to clearly identifiable and diagnostic pieces (Table 5.2). The deposits were made over two and a half millennia with the site dating from the Chalcolithic to the Late Iron Age. Both human and animal

Table 5.2—Cremated human and animal remains from pit burials.

Context	Colour	Frags	Weight	Maximum frag. size	Description
Manusmore AR100 (2500 BC–AD 250)					
Pit 24	White	43	530 g	33 mm	Rib, vertebrae and pelvis fragments (105 g); skull (62 g); unidentified skeletal element (363 g)
Pit 33	White	255	72 g	—	Pig teeth (15 g), mammal and human fragments (57 g)
Pit 36	Various	100	31 g	13 mm	Tooth and radius fragments
Pit 38/63	White	100	24 g	21 mm	Phalange/MP shaft, tooth fragments, skull, scapula and limb
Pit 50/62	White	100	23 g	25 mm	Limb, skull, pelvis, all very fragmented
Pit 97	White	17	<1 g	—	1 shaft, 2 flatter bones
Manusmore AR102 (800–150 BC)					
Pit 24	White	205	66 g	21 mm	Human skull, limb bones and fragments
Pit 35	White	31	11 g	25 mm	Human ulna and limb bones
Pit 72	Various	56	23 g	—	Mixed animal bone: 1 unburnt fragment, 1 pig tooth and fragments
Pit 76	Various	99	38 g	—	Human, phalange, metacarpal shafts, scapula, skull, limb bones and fragments
Pit 78	White	13	<1 g	11 mm	Human bone fragments
Pit 82	White	41	26 g	28 mm	Human humerus and fragments
Killow AR104 (1300–200 BC)					
Pit 7	White, dark grey	13	1 g	—	Mammal and possible human bone fragments. Burning varied
Pit 12	White	84 (14 human)	93 g (7 g human)	46 mm	Horse metacarpal; cattle-size phalange, bone and tooth fragments. Fragments of human bone
Pit 14	White/ Various	31	8 g	8 mm	Possible human bone fragments; sheep-sized limb bone and mixed animal bone fragments
Pit 15	White	12	2 g	23 mm	Human limb bone fragments
Pit 27	Various	41	15 g	37 mm	Human bone fragments; most cremated, some charred
Pit 34	White	4	<1 g	—	Human bone fragments
Cahircalla More AR128 (undated)					
Ditch 100 and Pit 137	White	22	3 g	15 mm	Vertebrae and fragments

bones were identified; five pits provided unequivocal evidence for the inclusion of human remains although only one of these pits, Pit 36, has been directly dated to AD 60–240 (Beta-207733). Pit 36 also represents the latest of those pits dated on site. The remaining pits, other than those where only flecks of burnt bone were preserved, contained mainly unidentifiable cremated mammal bone or mixed animal bone fragments with cattle, pig and sheep/goat represented.

The most complete cremated sample from Manusmore AR100 derived from Pit 24. There were no finds and the burial has not been directly dated. The cremated material weighed 530 g and included fragments of skull, vertebrae, ribs and maxillary tooth sockets. Several pieces of skull contained relatively open suture lines that may indicate a young adult, though exclusive use of this method of ageing individuals is problematic (Brickley & McKinley 2004).

Less than 1 g of cremated bone was retrieved from Pit 97 and other pits contained flecks or token quantities of burnt bone. The human remains in Pit 36 were distinct as some fragments were charred rather than cremated. This may have been deliberate if the intention was the partial cremation of the remains or may reflect a fire insufficiently tended to ensure complete destruction of the body.

Manusmore AR102

Six pits at the later Bronze Age/Iron Age site of Manusmore AR102 produced burnt mammal bone; of these five contained human remains and the sixth contained mixed animal bone (Table 5.2). The largest amount of cremated bone (66 g) was from Pit 24 and consisted of skull pieces including part of the occiput, a fragment of the petrous bone and occasional limb bones fragments. The earliest dated example, Pit 76, 780–410 BC (Beta-211587), produced 38 g of cremated bone and comprised the widest range of identified elements including a phalange, metacarpal shafts, scapula, skull pieces and limb bones (mostly upper limb pieces). The other pits yielded between <1 g and 26 g of cremated bone with fragments of ulna and humerus bones identified (Table 5.2). Pit 72 contained animal bone including pig but clearly identifiable human bone was absent.

Killow AR104

The bone assemblage from Killow AR104 included animal bone, a small amount of cremated human and possible human bone (Table 5.2). None of the fragments could be identified to skeletal element. As at other sites, human and animal bone occurred together and separately with a range of domestic animals represented including ovicaprids, cattle, horse and pig. Pits 7 and 34 returned radiocarbon dates of 750–390 BC (Beta-211589) and 390–180 BC (Beta-211592) respectively. In theory, at least, these date ranges may represent a single event, but they are more likely to represent two separate episodes of burial, in the later Bronze Age and in the Iron Age.

Cahircalla More AR128

The undated Pit 137 from Cahircalla More AR128 yielded a small quantity of cremated human bone (Table 5.2). The pit is thought to represent a probable cremation truncated by a later early medieval enclosure and field system (see Chapter 2). Small fragments of human bone were retrieved from the enclosure ditch (100) and are considered to be redeposited material of uncertain origin.

Ring-ditch/barrow

Claureen AR131

The bone assemblage from Claureen AR131 was retrieved from the fill of a small ring-ditch or barrow dated to the Late Iron Age, 100 BC–AD 70 (Beta-207732). Five deposits produced 117 g of cremated human bone, which includes pieces of skull, scapula and pelvis (Table 5.3). Many others were recognised as limb bone fragments though not as upper or lower limb. Almost all fragments were completely oxidised indicating high temperatures upon cremation.

Table 5.3—Cremated human remains from Claureen AR131.

Context	Colour	Frags	Weight	Maximum frag. size	Description
1	White, some grey	32	4 g	13 mm	Fragments
5	White	124	59 g	21 mm	Fragments, 9 skull inc frontal and 1 orbital, 1 radius fragment, 1 pelvis, 2 phalange shafts and limb bone fragments
10	White, some grey	50	16 g	23 mm	Upper limb and fragments
19	White	30	11 g	16 mm	Fragments, 1 upper limb, 1 rib, 1 tooth root
20	White, some grey	40	27 g	22 mm	Fragments, 1 ilium, large flatter pieces, 1 phalange fragment

Discussion

The cremations excavated on this scheme span a broad period of time and while no individual assemblage has returned substantial volumes of identifiable material, the assemblages as a whole provide insights into past funerary practices in the region. The earliest apparent funerary activity is at Manusmore AR100, which dates from the period c. 2500–2100 BC, though none of the pits with identified human remains have been directly dated to this phase. Cremation was commonly practised in this period and in the succeeding Bronze and Iron Ages (see Jones, Chapters 1 and 2). During these periods, cremated remains were deposited in isolation, in cemeteries or within monuments such as the ring-ditch at Claureen AR131. On this scheme, the cremations are evidently partial rather than full burials, of the sort frequently referred to as 'token' burials. Those with less than 1 g of burnt bone may even represent redeposited pyre debris.

The partial deposition of cremated human remains in these contexts, within pits in particular, is being increasingly identified in the archaeological record. Recent excavated examples of such seemingly meagre depositions are known from the M6 Ballinasloe to Galway scheme, where excavations in Treanbaun revealed later Bronze Age pits in which small quantities of cremated human bone occurred (Muñiz-Pérez et al. 2011; McKeon & O'Sullivan in press). Similarly, at Rathglass in east Galway, multiple middle and later Bronze Age pits contained significantly lower amounts of cremated bone than an average adult cremation would produce (McKeon & O'Sullivan in press). Later Iron Age cremations from ring-ditches at Ballyboy, in south Galway, were excavated on the M18 Gort Crusheen scheme, though here the amounts of cremated remains were more substantial (Geber 2012).

Over half the cremations excavated at the Bronze Age site of Derrybane 2, Co. Tipperary, weighed less than 100 g, prompting researchers to suggest that the partial deposition of cremated bone in pits may be one part of a complex ritual of primary and secondary funerary rites (Lynch et al. 2010). This may well have been the case at Manusmore AR100 and other sites (see Jones, Chapter 2) where identified human bone weights were typically below 30 g.

While the deposition of cremated remains was evidently partial, in general, the act of cremation itself appears to have been wholly successful at sites excavated on the present scheme. One measure of this success is the colour of the bones after burning. Most of the cremated fragments retrieved were white indicating high-temperature burning on the pyre. Temperatures in excess of 600°C are required to achieve this level of oxidisation which, as Geber (2009, 224) points out, is a fuel-rich and laborious process. Some lower temperatures are implied, however, in the recovery of charred pieces, such as at Manusmore AR100, and by small amounts of grey/white bone occurring on sites across the scheme. This reflects differential burning within individual pyres which, as stated above, could be a deliberate or accidental occurrence. It is presumed that the pyres were located near the pits where cremated bone was buried and patches of burnt glacial till at Manusmore AR100 and Killow AR104 may represent actual pyre locations.

At three sites, the cremated remains were not exclusively human. Animal bone, including horse, pig and cattle- and sheep-sized mammals occurred in pits either with or without cremated human bone. The combination of animal and human remains is not without parallel and may represent pyre goods such as food, charms, pets or the remains of funeral feasting (McKinley 2000, 416). Where there is an unequivocal human burial monument, i.e. the ring-ditch Claureen AR131, only human bone was present.

6
FAUNAL REMAINS

Sian Anthony and Matilda Holmes

Seven sites on the scheme produced individual faunal assemblages of varying size and condition: Carrowdotia AR25, Killow AR103 and AR104, Clareabbey AR122, Cahircalla Beg AR126, Cahircalla More AR128 and Clare Abbey (i.e. Clareabbey C020/A025). Typically, the sites yielded small quantities of bone with preservation fair to poor. No doubt soil conditions and water erosion contributed to the loss of bone from the record as did other taphonomic processes such as butchery and burning.

Bone was recovered by hand and via wet-sieving soil samples. The majority of fragments retrieved through sieving were less than 2 mm in size, and typically unidentifiable to species, but sieving proved to be very significant at Clare Abbey, where a wide range of bird, fish and small mammal species would otherwise have been unrepresented.

Faunal assemblages dating to the Chalcolithic, later Bronze Age, Iron Age, early medieval and medieval periods are described here. All post-medieval assemblages and any topsoil finds are described in the accompanying CD-Rom.

Methods

Species/element identification was after Schmidt (1972), Getty (1975), Hillson (1992), Bass (1995) and Cohen & Serjeantson (1996). Unidentifiable elements, where preservation allowed, were recorded in terms of the size of animal they might represent, e.g. large mammal = cattle/horse, medium = pig/sheep/goat/dog and small = rabbit/cat. Small amounts of burnt material were identified as mammalian only. This does not preclude the possibility that some may be human but could not be identified as such.

A simple fragment count was used to quantify each assemblage. All fragments were scanned with any newly broken elements rejoined and counted as one bone. There was an absence of measurable material within the assemblages. Although age-fusion and tooth wear analyses—which provide an estimate of an animal's age at the time of its death—were recorded (Amorosi 1989; Grant 1982; Silver 1969), there was an insufficient quantity of material for further analysis. Preservation was recorded in terms of general condition, burning, gnawing and the presence/absence of butchery or working marks.

Chalcolithic and later Bronze Age

Sian Anthony

A small assemblage of mammal bone, mainly derived from domestic mammals, was retrieved from four burnt mound sites. The bone fragments derive from mound, pit and trough deposits. In total, 195 fragments, weighing c. 472 g, were recovered from contexts dating from the third millennium BC to the early first millennium BC. Five bones, weighing 78 g, derive from the upper surface of the mound at Cahircalla Beg AR126. Saw marks indicate these are relatively recent origin and do not relate to the original use of the mound.

Most of the material retrieved was unidentifiable to species but of the identifiable elements, cattle, horse, pig and sheep/goat are represented. The occurrence of small amounts of animal bone from burnt mound sites, frequently burnt, is unexceptional, as is the predominance of domestic species within these contexts (Monk 2007). The earliest burnt mound site, Clareabbey AR122, included red deer. The occurrence of red deer, though less common than domesticates, is again unexceptional on burnt mound sites. The individual assemblages probably represent consumption waste—where the bone is burnt this suggests joints cooked on site or food waste thrown into a nearby fire.

Table 6.1—Summary of faunal species representation from burnt mound sites.

Townland and date	Context	Species/Element	Preservation	Maximum frag. size	No.	Weight
Clareabbey AR122 2430–2140 BC	45	Red deer metacarpal	Broken	—	1	22 g
	49	Mammal	Calcined	<1 mm	2	<1 g
Killow AR104 1280–1010 BC	Pit 1	Csz limb bones, s/g mandible	Some burnt	13 mm	2	16 g
	Pit 2	Csz and mammal	—	—	8	8 g
	Pit 5	Csz—maxilla, tooth and limb bone	—	—	15	243 g
	Pit 6	Mammal	Burnt	<1 mm	10	1 g
	Pit 8	Mammal	Burnt	<1 mm	27	1 g
	Pit 9	Horse tibia; Csz limb bones and fragments	Some burnt	—	15	84 g
	51	Mammal and cow	—	—	6	56 g
	60	Csz and mammal	Some burnt	18 mm	59	36 g
Cahircalla Beg AR126 1190–820 BC Unknown Post-med. or later	19	Mammal	—	<2 mm	10	<1 g
	23	Cow	—	—	1	9 g
	16	Pig, s/g skull with saw marks	—	—	4	69 g
Killow AR103 920–800 BC	51	Mammal	Calcined	17 mm	30	3 g
	52	Mammal	Calcined	<1 mm	10	2 g
				Total	**200**	**550 g**

Key: Csz = cattle-size. Ssz = sheep/goat size. S/g = sheep/goat.

Early medieval period

Sian Anthony

Two early medieval sites produced small assemblages of animal bone: the cashel at Carrowdotia AR25 and the early medieval enclosure and field system at Cahircalla More AR128. These included small amounts of cattle, red deer and sheep-sized animals (Table 6.2). Human elements represent redeposited cremated material (see Chapter 5). A single human tooth, a lower second molar of a young adult, was recovered from Carrowdotia AR25. The animal bone from the cashel excludes material retrieved from the topsoil but includes fragments recovered from a gravel layer within the cashel interior. All the material demonstrates the presence and exploitation of domestic mammals during the early medieval period. The occurrence of cattle, sheep and red deer in this context is to be expected.

Table 6.2—Summary of faunal material from early medieval sites.

Date	Context	Species and elements	Preservation	Maximum frag. size	Total	Weight
Cahircalla More AR128						
AD 550–650	Enclosure Ditch 100, Pits 21 and 5	Cow, red deer, Csz and mammal Limb bones and teeth fragments; deer antler (shed); cow teeth and mandible; cow pelvis in pieces	Burnt (n. 32)	10–18 mm	124	434 g
AD 560–670	Smithy 120 and Pit 45	Cow and mammal Teeth in pieces and misc. fragments	Burnt (n. 5)	<2 mm	7	24 g
AD 680–880	Field System Ditch 215	Cow and Ssz Scapula in pieces, limb bones, lower molar	Burnt (n. 1)	12 mm	3	68 g
AD 980–1150	Field System Ditch 125	Cow, Ssz, mammal, oyster and human Human, cow teeth, Ssz, limb bone and misc. fragments. Base shell	Burnt (n. 41)	11–13 mm	46	64 g
Carrowdotia AR25						
AD 530–650	92	Cow tooth			1	23 g
	95	Cow, human, Csz Tooth x 2 (cattle), x 1 (human), limb bone			4	20 g
				Total	**185**	**569 g**

Key: Csz = cattle-size. Ssz = sheep/goat size. S/g = sheep/goat.

Medieval and post-medieval periods

Matilda Holmes

The bone assemblages described here derive exclusively from the excavation of Area C020 at the Augustinian house at Clare Abbey. This material could be more closely dated than the assemblage retrieved from excavations in Area A025 at Clare Abbey, which was broadly dated to the medieval/post-medieval period. Both sites share a similar range of species with both domestic and wild fauna, including fish and bird. Neither assemblage was sufficiently large to warrant detailed investigation of animal husbandry preferences or economy. In both cases, there was limited evidence for butchery, burning and canid gnawing. The latter suggests some bones were available to dogs to chew prior to burial, although the majority were disposed of soon after use.

Animal bone assemblages from the 11th–14th and 16th–17th century phases of life at the Abbey are discussed below. All later material is described in a report on the accompanying CD-Rom. This includes a small number of human bones (nine) from disturbed burials, which had been redeposited in 18th/19th century contexts.

Phase I (11th–14th centuries)

This assemblage of 1,038 fragments (Table 6.3) was dominated by fish recovered from Pit 6, dated to AD 1030–1220 (Beta-231531). Cattle, sheep/goat and pig were also represented, though in very low numbers. Eel was the most common fish species indicating exploitation of local riverine fish stocks, presumably from the nearby River Fergus. Coastal links are reflected by the presence of fish of the cod family (gadoids).

Phase II (16th–17th centuries)

This phase is characterised by the wide range of species represented, particularly smaller wild fauna (Table 6.3). Comparatively few domestic species were recovered, and the main domesticates account for c. 11% of the assemblage. The majority comprised domestic birds (fowl and goose), wild birds (duck and woodcock), wild mammals (red deer and hare), molluscs (mussel and oyster) and fish (eel, flounder and pike). Background species were also recovered—rats, wood mice and frog—the latter indicating an environment with water nearby.

Most of the bones in this phase were recovered from sieved soil samples from the probable cess pit, dated to AD 1460–1660 (Beta-233431). This may explain the low ratio of the main domestic mammals to wild and bird species in this phase. The recovery of small bones in high numbers here demonstrates the fact that small bone representation is greatly enhanced by sieving. In general at Clare Abbey, nearly all bones from birds, small mammals, amphibians and fish were recovered from contexts subject to sieving. A number of sheep/goat and pig bones were also retrieved in this way.

The deposition of small bones within the cess-pit, typically from small-sized fauna, may have resulted from a number of processes, not least their inclusion in human waste (for example fish bones). Smaller-sized debris may have been deliberately selected for disposal into the pit—handier perhaps than dumping it with larger waste disposed of elsewhere. The recovery of a number of articulated bones from the cess pit, including four pieces of the partial skeleton of a baby chicken,

Table 6.3—Faunal species from Clare Abbey (Phases I and II).

Species	Phase I	Phase II
Cattle	35	12
Sheep/Goat	18	17
Pig	18	17
Dog	1	2
Rodent	—	55
Deer	—	1
Hare	—	3
Chicken	—	27
Goose	1	22
Duck	—	5
Wild bird	—	2
Amphibian	—	7
Mussel	—	2
Oyster	—	5
Eel	5	76
Pike	—	1
Flounder	—	1
Gadoid (cod family)	1	—
Fish	887	250
Total identified	**966**	**427**
Unidentified large mammal	18	16
Unidentified medium mammal	35	36
Unidentified small mammal	—	29
Unidentified mammal	19	54
Unidentified bird	—	81
Total identified and unidentified	**1,038**	**642**

15 fragments of two partial chicken skeletons and multiple duck legs, suggest the waste originated from nearby, probably the kitchen.

In general, the variety of wild and domestic mammals, birds, shellfish and fish from all phases at Clare Abbey reflect the high status of the site. A number of animals were most likely hunted from nearby woods (deer, hare and woodcock), and local rivers were an important source of fish, duck and probably geese. There is also some evidence for links with the coast in the presence of sea fish and the occurrence of mussels and oyster. A medieval abbey was a major manorial centre in its own right and enjoyed access to a variety of resources from its demesne lands and throughout its estates.

7
CHARCOAL

Simon Gannon

A glimpse into the nature of ancient woodlands and their exploitation by past populations can be obtained by the analysis of charcoal pieces retrieved from archaeological contexts such as pits, hearths and ditches. Charcoal analysis also allows us to look more closely at human behaviour and the use of fire in everyday life and death. Fuelled by wood, typically sourced locally and relatively easily, fires can be single or multi-purpose. Fires are set for a whole variety of purposes and the reason for the fire can determine the type of wood used, i.e. kindling, branch and/or logwood, and also the wood species selected. Here, the results of the analysis of over 6,000 individual pieces of charcoal from sites across the scheme are presented and discussed.

Methodology

Fragments selected for identification were at least 2 mm in radial cross-section; 100% of fragments this size and above were identified. Where samples contained an unusually large number of fragments the assemblage was sub-sampled. Grain direction of each fragment was identified with transverse, radial and/or tangential plains revealed where necessary. Identifications were made by microscope with magnification from x10 to x400 with reference to Schweingruber (1990), Hather (2000) and a comparative collection of charred samples. Shared anatomical characteristics prevent or impede certain taxa from being differentiated; e.g. members of the sub-family Pomoideae; the generas willow and poplar (family Salicaceae), and in cases of poorly preserved fragments of hazel and alder.

Results

The overall assemblage comprised 165 samples from 28 sites with a minimum of 6,441 fragments identified (Table 7.1). Only samples from securely dated contexts have been included within the analyses. This has resulted in a slightly reduced sample size with 35 samples from Manusmore AR100 excluded as they could not be securely assigned to a given phase within the site. In addition, analysis of charcoal from 18 samples from Clare Abbey (Clareabbey C020 and A025) was limited to taxa identification with no further quantification undertaken. These identifications were completed by Lucy Cramp.

Eleven taxa or wood types were identified, including alder (*Alnus glutinosa*), ash (*Fraxinus excelsior*), birch (*Betula* sp.), cherry/blackthorn (*Prunus* spp.), elm (*Ulmus glabra*), hazel (*Corylus avellana*), oak

(*Quercus petraea* and *Q. robur.*), rose/briar (*Rosa* spp.), willow/poplar (Salicaceae) and yew (*Taxus baccata*). In addition, pomaceous fruitwood (Pomoideae) also occurs, which can include up to 10 species such as hawthorn, apple, whitebeam and rowan. All of these taxa are native Irish flora with a complete absence of non-native tree taxa across the scheme. Many of these wood species favour upland drier soils, e.g. ash, oak, cherry and elm. In contrast, alder, birch and willow prefer wetter, poor soils while hazel and yew are tolerant of a wide range of conditions including marginal soils.

Table 7.1—Charcoal fragment counts from all sites and by period (LBA=later Bronze Age).

Site/Taxa	Alder	Ash	Birch	Cherry/ Blackthorn	Elm	Hazel	Hazel/Alder	Oak	Pomaceous fruitwood	Rose	Willow/ Poplar	Yew	Total
Early med.	9	315	4	33	4	311	42	548	550	0	44	349	2,209
Iron Age	4	614	0	124	15	509	22	844	176	0	22	25	2,355
LBA	22	176	5	128	6	243	59	67	376	0	15	20	1,117
Chalcolithic	12	378	0	48	2	49	121	22	23	1	2	102	760
Scheme total	47	1,483	9	333	27	1,112	244	1481	1,125	1	83	496	6,441

Oak (23%) and ash (23%) are the most commonly represented charcoal from the scheme with hazel and pomaceous fruitwood occurring in almost equal amount (16%). Yew (7%) and cherry/blackthorn (5%) are reasonably well represented compared with alder and willow/poplar (≤ 1% each) (Table 7.1; Illus. 7.1). Other taxa such as elm, birch and rose/briar occur though these are limited with, for example, a single instance of rose/briar from across the scheme. The overall values are broadly in keeping with those from other Irish archaeological sites, with certain taxa frequently prominent and others typically less well represented (c.f. WODAN Database 2011; Grogan et al. 2007, 27–69). It is worth noting, however, that variation can occur between individual sites with charcoal values sometimes higher for taxa less commonly recorded.

Chalcolithic

Four sites, Cahircalla Beg AR126, Cahircalla More AR127, Clareabbey AR122 and Manusmore AR100, date to the Chalcolithic. A fifth, Clareabbey AR124 straddles the Chalcolithic/Early Bronze Age and has been included here. The five sites yielded 16 samples containing a total of 760 identifiable charcoal fragments derived from 11 taxa.

Ash occurs most frequently as charcoal during this period, at 50%, and, with yew relatively high at 13%, best represent the large tree species. Conversely oak and elm are at low to negligible values. The prevalence of ash as charcoal may indicate its relative abundance in the local environment. Ash is able to re-establish more quickly than other large native tree species following land clearance and may have substituted for oak during phases of woodland regeneration (Peterken 1996). Yew may have particularly benefited from the decline in elm, where disease, primarily, caused its reduction in areas

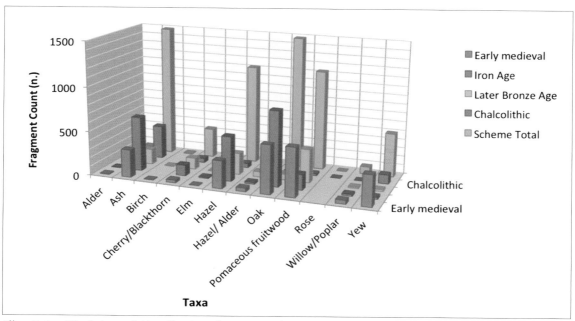

Illus. 7.1—Total charcoal identifications from across the scheme and by period.

not already cleared for farming. Pollen studies from Caheraphuca Lough, Co. Clare confirm episodes of land clearance and indicate that during some phases of this period yew may have found climate and post-elm decline conditions especially favourable (Molloy & O'Connell 2012).

Of the small tree/shrub taxa, hazel is well represented (16%). Cherry/blackthorn has low to mid level representation and there is minor representation of wetland taxa, alder and willow/poplar. The occurrence of rose/briar, representative of a wide range of common native shrubs, at Clareabbey AR122, may indicate the gathering of small-wood for fire kindling.

Later Bronze Age

Six later Bronze Age sites, Manusmore AR100, Killow AR103 and AR104, Clareabbey AR121, Cahircalla Beg AR126 and Cahircalla More AR127, yielded 1,117 identified charcoal pieces. The range of taxa represented is similar to the Chalcolithic although there is a change in the ratio of represented taxa, which is interesting given that three sites, Cahircalla Beg AR126, Cahircalla More AR127 and Manusmore AR100, are common to both periods.

There is a clear change in the choice of wood taxa occurring as charcoal between the Chalcolithic and the later Bronze Age. There is a substantial increase in the representation of small-wood producing species, particularly pomaceous fruitwood (34%) and hazel (22%) (Illus. 7.2), and a decrease in the large trees, ash (16%) and yew (2%), with oak increasing but still low. Birch appears for the first time, together with an increase in alder and willow/poplar, species typically drawn from marginal and wet areas. These changes may indicate reduced availability of first-choice wood from mature woodland and the necessity of firewood gathering from secondary sources. Pollen records from County Clare imply a phase of extensive woodland clearance occurred during the later Bronze Age (Molloy 2005

& 2012). Something similar may be reflected in the charcoal from this scheme.

Iron Age

Two of the five sites that yielded charcoal from Iron Age contexts have been previously represented in the Chalcolithic and later Bronze Age: Cahircalla Beg AR126 and Manusmore AR100. Killow AR104 is represented in the later Bronze Age and Iron Age with two sites, Manusmore AR102 and Claureen AR131, exclusive to the Iron Age. The

Illus. 7.2—Hazel woodland thriving on previously cleared land.

partial continuity in site location is not mirrored in the tree taxa exploited during the Iron Age. In sharp contrast to earlier periods, oak (36%) is commonest with ash (26%) and hazel (22%) also significant; pomaceous fruitwood (7%) is now a relatively minor component. The representation of cherry/blackthorn (5%) is relatively unchanged with other taxa, including yew, willow/poplar and alder, accounting for c. 3%. It is possible that oak was more available in the local environment. Pollen records from Mooghaun Lough, Co. Clare suggest that between 650 BC and 300 BC woodland regeneration, of oak and ash in particular, occurred during a period of sustained rather than intensive farming activity (Molloy 2005, 274–5). Similarly, at Caheraphuca, Co. Clare, south-west of Crusheen, a period of woodland regeneration suggests greatly reduced farming activity between c. 650 BC and 450 BC.

Early medieval period

Eight early medieval sites yielded charcoal with 2,209 pieces identified. With the exception of Manusmore AR102, the sites are not represented in earlier periods and include Carrowdotia M27, AR25 and AR27, Barefield AR106, Ballymacahill AR108, Kilbreckan AR110, Clareabbey AR123, and Cahircalla More AR128. Ten taxa occur, all of which appear in earlier periods, though there are significant changes in their representation from the Iron Age.

Oak (25%), hazel and ash (both at 14%) continue to be prominent in the charcoal record and there is a substantial increase in pomaceous fruitwood (25%). Low levels of willow/poplar, cherry/blackthorn, birch and alder occur, in total comprising c. 8%. Yew (16%) increases in value, with a return to representation achieved in the Chalcolithic (13%). The general picture is of access to mature woodland; large tree species and their common underwood species are well represented with little emphasis on species from marginal or wet areas. Pollen records for the period are varied and at Mooghaun from AD 300–600 renewed farming and woodland clearance are implied in the pollen sequence from the Lough (Molloy 2005, 275–7).

Later medieval period

Eighteen samples from the excavations at the Augustinian foundation of Clare Abbey (Clareabbey C020/A025) contained charcoal derived from oak, hazel and hazel/alder. Evidently, a more restricted range of taxa were either available or being selected in comparison with previous periods. The small sample hinders interpretation and the charcoal may represent little more than a one or two instances of fuel gathering.

Charcoal representation: burnt mounds and burial sites

All the prehistoric sites excavated on the scheme are either burnt mounds or probable cremation cemeteries. Many of the sites are broadly contemporary and some are linked spatially, e.g. Killow AR104 where the burnt mound and probable cremations occur in the same location. Comparing charcoal representation between site types may help to identify whether there was a relationship between particular activities, be they secular or ritual, and the choice of firewood.

Of the total charcoal fragments from burial sites 82% derive from just three taxa: ash, hazel and oak—representing no more than four species (Illus. 7.3). In contrast, 71% of charcoal fragments from burnt mounds (Illus. 7.4) come from up to 18 species, with the pomaceous group including up to 10 possible species. The greater range of species gathered for burnt mound fires, compared with the funerary fires, suggests two distinct approaches to fire preparation.

The tree taxa at the burial sites are dominated by the main wood providers: high calorie wood from oak and ash, with hazel providing a substantial part of the smaller wood and with other smaller and kindling wood taken from a diversity of small tree and shrub species. This range and ratio of taxa are more typical of planned fire-making and suggest a degree of selection. In addition, to successfully cremate human bodies the pyre would have been best served by selecting a considered mixture of large and small dry wood.

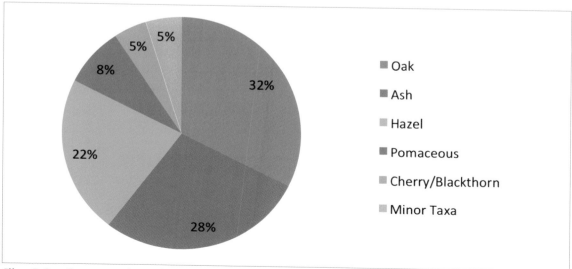

Illus. 7.3—Percentage charcoal representation from burial sites.

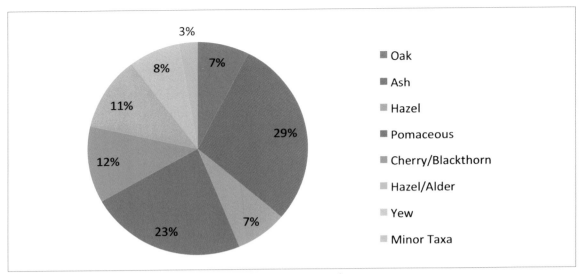

Illus. 7.4—Percentage charcoal representation from burnt mounds.

For the burnt mound fires, the broader species range suggests less preferential selection. The represented tree types mainly provide small-wood/brushwood. If burnt mound fires had been supplied from stored wood then a greater ratio of the more common firewood-providing taxa, especially larger wood, might be expected. In contrast, the evidence suggests relatively unplanned activity, with burnt mound fires set with wood gathered mostly from a variety of smaller trees and shrubs. Burnt mound fires once ablaze could have been maintained by repeated inputs of almost any type or condition of wood. Such wood probably did not require felling and could have been gathered and broken by hand, perhaps by the community on an ad hoc basis.

Discussion

Wood species in charcoal assemblages represent fuel choices made by past populations. These choices were influenced by a wide range of factors including species availability, ease of collection, the burning and perceived cultural attributes of individual taxa, and the purpose of the fire itself. The charcoal that survives, however, does not necessarily provide a complete record of fuel types selected for burning; some kinds of fuelwood, particularly kindling, can burn away completely, so that it is not represented in the archaeological material recovered from an excavated site.

Generally, a species will have been used for firewood if it was economic to do so and this may mean that the selection of firewood was secondary to other requirements. For example, trees felled for construction can provide substantial quantities of firewood as a by-product of building work, even though other, more numerous fuelwood species abound in the environment. Similarly, windfall branches from a given tree might be collected, because they are easily available, rather than the more 'desirable' fuelwood of another species still in the canopy. The most effective fire does, however, benefit from species selection and preparation, including, optimally, storage of dry wood. It is not known if any of the firewood used at sites on this scheme had in fact been stored.

As all wood species burn, so all can have value as fuelwood, although certain species may provide only kindling while others can supply logs. Generally, the most effective fires for most cooking/ heating purposes comprise several stages of construction starting with the driest, i.e. tinder, then kindling wood, including thin twigs and small thin branches, followed by thicker roundwood and, ideally, split wood. Finally, logwood is placed on the fire. Without achieving well-burning logwood, a fire will tend to burn out quickly and fail to take inputs of low quality, damp or large wood.

Mature ash and oak typically produce lengths of heavy wood from their branches and stems, suitable for fire logwood. These taxa are also easily cleft to produce split wood that can be both substantial and easy to light. Hazel is easily the best provider of mid-size and small roundwood. It keenly produces long straight rods as coppice in response to cutting. Hazel roundwood of 30 mm or more will not break by hand but has to be cut. Smaller wood and kindling can come from almost any species that easily gives up material, preferably dry, breakable by hand and in quantities close to the ground. For example, blackthorn and hawthorn tend to grow in low thorny thickets with thin, brittle branching. Blackthorn, in particular, may have been a highly sought-after firewood. Its wood is typically dry even in damp winter and its branches easily break and are often found, drying out, retained above ground by other thorny branches.

The charcoal fragment values for the scheme broadly reflect the commonest Irish tree species, with the most numerous charcoal taxa derived from dryland areas and taxa from wetland habitats occurring less frequently. This is the case across all periods represented on the scheme. Ash, hazel, oak and pomaceous fruitwoods are typically the best represented taxa within each period though individual representation, as shown above, can vary. Of the other taxa, the representation of yew is of interest. It is the third and fourth most commonly represented charcoal in the Chalcolithic and early medieval periods respectively: these are periods when yew is typically infrequent as charcoal or pollen in sample materials from other study areas. Yew has excellent firewood properties and on this scheme, in the early medieval period, is largely confined to one site, Cahircalla More AR128. This settlement included a smithy which had a high demand for good quality firewood and this may explain its increased representation here.

In summary, charcoal from the burnt mounds and funerary sites provides contrasting evidence for the use of fire and the selection of fuel. Building and maintaining funeral pyres requires more knowledge, skill and preparation than a simple fire burned to heat stones. In building the latter, the choice of firewood was less important, with fuel drawn from a broad range of wood species. In contrast, three high calorific wood types dominate the charcoal from the burial sites.

8
THE FINDS

Edward Bourke, Miriam Carroll, Michelle Comber, Maria FitzGerald, Steve Ford, Graham Hull, Lynne Keys, Tessa Machling, Clare McCutcheon, Declan Moore and Annette Quinn

Fourteen of the excavated sites produced finds—varying in type, material, preservation, quantity and date. The total number of individual finds was 858, of which the majority derived from post-medieval contexts, chiefly from the Augustinian house at Clare Abbey (Clareabbey C020/A025).

There were no finds made from the burnt mounds or burnt spreads. A wooden bowl from Killow AR104, found in close proximity to a burnt mound, was considerably later in date than the mound. Finds from the funerary sites included pottery, which was typically Bronze Age in date—blue and yellow glass beads and slag, including microslags—and lithics, mainly struck flakes and spalls, with a scraper being the only tool occurring.

There is greater diversity in the range of objects retrieved from early medieval and later contexts. Objects of stone, iron, copper alloy, glass and clay were retrieved from most historic sites though six sites yielded no finds. Many artefacts can be closely dated based on their material, form and function but there are others that provide broad date ranges for a given object and its deposition. Here, all the prehistoric, early medieval and medieval finds are described. Due to the quantity of material retrieved, however, only a selection of the most significant post-medieval finds are included in this chapter. Iron nails, pottery, particularly 18th-century or later sherds, clay and stone roof tiles, building materials, clay drain pipe, clay pipes, window and bottle glass are not described below. All finds, however, can be reviewed within the individual excavation reports on the accompanying CD-Rom.

Prehistoric pottery
Tessa Machling

Prehistoric pottery was recovered from two sites: the cremation cemetery site Manusmore AR100 and the early medieval enclosure Cahircalla More AR128. All is most likely later Bronze Age in date and, though poorly preserved, represents new material from this area of Ireland and as such is important in both a regional and national context.

In total, 73 sherds were retrieved and of these, 10 came from Cahircalla More AR128 (Table 8.1). Here, c. 1 g of pottery in tiny scraps had been inadvertently incorporated into an early medieval enclosure. Sherds from the cremation cemetery at Manusmore AR100 amounted to 80 g with more than 50% of sherds measuring less than 10 mm in diameter (Illus. 8.1).

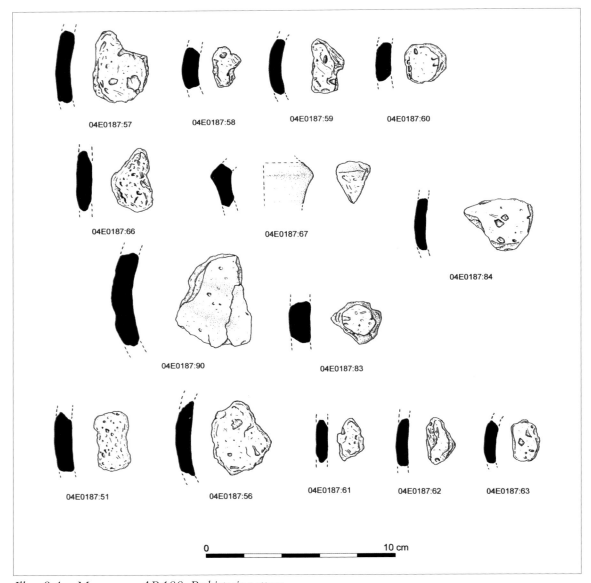

Illus. 8.1—Manusmore AR100. Prehistoric pottery.

Preservation

The sherds from each site were extremely abraded and none was decorated, burnt or re-fired. Surface treatment during manufacture in the form of wiping, possibly using organic material such as grass, was visible on one sherd from Manusmore AR100. It is probable that abrasion is responsible for the apparent lack of surface treatment and that other sherds may have shown comparable treatments prior to their erosion.

Analysis

From the cremation cemetery at Manusmore AR100 the surfaces and interiors of the sherds display large numbers of voids evidenced by the very low weight of the assemblage as a whole, with the majority of individual sherds weighing less than 1 g. Even the largest sherd, c. 50 mm in diameter, weighed only 6 g. The high representation of voids suggests leaching of fabric from the pottery either pre- or post-deposition. The poor quality of the sherds would suggest that, although aggravated by the post-depositional environment, some element of this leaching was initiated prior to deposition. The recovery of most sherds from within pits at Manusmore AR100 supports this theory of pre-depositional degradation.

Table 8.1—Catalogue of pottery from Manusmore AR100 and Cahircalla More AR128.

Site	Find no.	Fabric	Sherds (n.)	Weight	Diameter cross-section
Manusmore AR100					
Cremation cemetery	04E0187:29	V1	1	2 g	6 mm
	04E0187:48	V1	1	1 g	n/a
	04E0187:51	V1	1	4 g	9 mm
	04E0187:53–4	Variant	2	1 g	5 mm
	04E0187:56–63 and 04E0187:76	Indet.	4	<1 g	n/a
		V1	9	1 g	n/a
		Variant	10	25 g	9
	04E0187: 65–75	V1	10	12 g	n/a
		Variant	2	2 g	
	04E0187:78	V1	2	<1 g	n/a
	04E0187:80–84	Variant	5	12 g	1 mm
	04E0187:90–1	Indet.	c. 8	<1 g	
		Variant	8	17 g	11 mm
Cahircalla More AR128					
Enclosure	04E0029:17	V1	c. 10	1 g	n/a
Total			c. 73	81 g	

A single fabric type has been identified for all of the prehistoric pottery (Fabric VI), though a variation of it occurs within Manusmore AR100. A few sherds could not be assigned to a fabric group due their small size; however, it is unlikely that they represent anything other than the fabric or variation recorded. Fabric V1 is typically soft and irregularly fired with angular voids and inclusions of quartz sand, iron oxide, argillaceous material and mica. Occasionally, moderate to coarse-grade flint/chert is also present. The inclusions most likely derive from the source clay and the voids may represent particles of limestone or even bone (Cleary 2000) subsequently leached from the fabric. The sherds typically have a wall thickness of 6–9 mm and are generally much abraded on the surface.

A number of sherds display characteristics that suggest a variation on the fabric described above. The fabric of these sherds appeared to be finer with a wall thickness of 5–11 mm. They were slightly less abraded and include the largest sherd within the assemblage which displayed evidence of smoothing on the exterior of the pot.

The small size and severe abrasion of the sherds make it difficult to assign definite form types. All sherds, where identifiable, are body sherds with none showing any definitive form characteristics, although the large sherd from Manusmore AR100 suggests an urn form. The similarity of fabric makes it difficult to ascertain whether the assemblage from Manusmore represents more than one vessel. Macroscopic differences in wall thickness, firing and fabric suggests the sherds derive from multiple vessels that were broken, mixed up and abraded long before deposition.

If suitable resources can be found within 7 km to 10 km of a site, the pottery is said to be locally produced (Arnold 1985, 32–5). Clays that derive from beyond this limit can be regarded as non-local. In the present assemblage, the presence of common inclusion-types, such as limestone and quartz sand, mica and argillaceous material, could represent either a local or non-local source. The absence, however, of any diagnostic, non-local inclusions suggest the pottery was manufactured from local clays.

The fabric indicates Bronze Age origins for the pottery, almost certainly the later Bronze Age. Comparison with sites in the vicinity is hampered by a lack of comparable sites and the general paucity of pottery from this period. However, there are some similarities to other ceramics from south-west Ireland. In general, the fabrics compare well with the assemblages from the region. Excavations for example at Lough Gur, Co. Limerick (Ó Ríordáin 1954; Cleary 2000), Knockadoon Hill, Co. Limerick (Cleary 2000), the North Munster Project (Grogan 1995 & 1996) and at Clonfinlough, Co. Offaly (IAWU 1993) have all produced comparable coarsely gritted/voided fabrics.

The occurrence of abraded sherds with eroded fabrics resulting from pre-depositional processes is interesting. Probably the vessels that this pottery derived from were broken and exposed to erosive conditions long before they were placed in the cremation pits. It is also likely that the assemblage comprises disparate sherds from perhaps several vessels. Some pot sherds were retrieved from cremation deposits dated to between the 11th and eighth centuries BC. However, the dates are not directly applicable to the pottery as it is clear that the pottery was older than the burials in question.

The absence of larger and/or decorated sherds suggests an absence of significant 'ritual' pottery deposition, other than the token sherds that accompanied cremated bone in some pits, similar to the token bone deposits recorded at Manusmore AR100. The lack of burnt or re-fired sherds suggests that pottery was not included in cremation pyres but could have been deposited as an accessory. Alternatively, the pottery could be an accidental inclusion from relict sherd scatters in the general vicinity of the pits or pyres, with sherds being incidentally scooped into the pits with soil and hence accidentally buried.

Chipped stone tools and debitage
Steve Ford

Five prehistoric sites and the excavations at the Augustinian house at Clare Abbey produced lithic assemblages. The material was recovered by hand-collection and from sieved soil samples. The individual assemblages were typically small, comprising 273 items with a total weight of c. 2.5 kg. None of the sites produced large quantities of lithic finds and the individual assemblages did not merit metrical analysis or consideration of manufacturing technique, though it is assumed that a hard hammer was used. In addition, none of the items was chronologically distinctive but can be viewed as typical of the prehistoric contexts of their recovery. That lithics were present on prehistoric sites at a time when metal tools were also available is unexceptional (Ford et al. 1984), particularly in the case of funerary sites, a site type where lithics commonly occur as inclusions within cremation pits.

Raw material

The assemblage indicates a restricted range of material types with chert the commonest stone type, followed by quartz and flint (Table 8.2). A single item appeared to be of a fine-grained metamorphic or igneous rock but is otherwise unidentified. Typically, the chert items were not uniform in texture or colour, exhibiting black and grey colours and some variation in grain size. Of the two chert items recovered from Killow AR104, one was fine grained, partly cortical and patinated a whitish colour, and the other was grey/black in colour. The flint flake is from Clare Abbey (Area C020) and is brown flint with a large grey cherty inclusion. Here, quartz is typically represented by small lumps that lack flake scars or other indications that they had been worked.

Table 8.2—Stone types represented in the chipped stone assemblage, by site.

Site	Pieces (n.)	Flint	Chert	Quartz	Other
Manusmore AR100	86	22	67	–	–
Killow AR104	19	–	2	16	1
Cahircalla More AR128	25	–	8	17	–
Claureen AR131	19	–	–	19	–
Carrowdotia AR25	1	–	1	–	–
Clareabbey C020/A025	123	1	1	121	–
Total	273	23	80	163	1

Chert and flint would have been available locally as pebbles in glacial drift deposits that were deposited by moving ice sheets during periods of glaciation. Though as yet the distribution of both primary sources (i.e. *in situ* bedrock) and the complex pattern of drift geology in this region are not fully understood (Briggs 1988), glacial drift is the most likely source for the raw materials represented here.

Quartz, though it produces sharp edges, is a less tractable material than either flint or chert. Its selection as a raw material for tools is therefore problematic though it may be present locally in drift deposits (Knight 1991). The majority of the quartz from Clare Abbey, for example, was retrieved from modern contexts but six pieces derive from medieval or probable medieval features.

Lithic types

A restricted range of lithic types was recovered with most represented by tiny fragments, less than 5 mm in size (Table 8.3). These may represent spalls or retouch chips waste material broken from a larger piece of stone, in this context perhaps unrecovered lithic tools. Flint, chert and quartz, possible retouch chips, were represented. The recovery of a possible chert core and two chert lumps that display partial flake scars suggests lithic production occurred on or nearby the sites in question. Eighteen flakes, including two of quartz, were retrieved across the scheme with the best examples deriving from Manusmore AR100 and Cahircalla More AR128. The latter also yielded the only clearly retouched item from the scheme, a chert scraper (04E0029:90; Illus. 8.2). The scraper was broken, measured 37 mm by 17 mm by 6 mm and had been redeposited within an early medieval field system ditch (see Chapter 3).

Table 8.3—Summary composition of the chipped stone assemblage by site.

Site	Flake	Scraper	Spalls/ chips	Core?	Lump	Minute fragments
Manusmore AR100	4	—	26	—	3	53
Killow AR104	3	—	16	—	—	—
Cahircalla More AR128	8	1	14	1	1	—
Claureen AR131	—	—	—	—	—	19
Carrowdotia AR25	1	—	—	—	—	—
Clareabbey C020/A025	2	—	—	—	111	—

Both chert and flint were commonly used throughout prehistory in the manufacture of chipped stone tools. The use of quartz is less well documented though not unknown and indeed it is unclear here if the quartz pieces retrieved on the scheme actually represent manufacturing material. It is unclear how much of the quartz retrieved was flaked as, by and large, it does not exhibit conchoidal fractures yet can produce sharp edges (Knight 1991). The concentration in which quartz occurs, however, might suggest on-site production at these locations (e.g. 10 fragments were retrieved from a single pit at Manusmore AR100 and at Claureen AR131 the ring-ditch yielded 19 pieces).

Slag
Lynne Keys

Slag is a waste product of metal-working which, in the context of excavations on this scheme, relates to iron. An assemblage of material was collected and identified as slag by sieving soil samples from excavations across the scheme. The material was examined by eye and categorised on the basis of morphology, with a magnet used to test for hammerscale and other magnetic material. Each slag type from each individual context was weighed and details are given in Tables 8.4–8.6. Slag was retrieved from Iron Age, early medieval, medieval and post-medieval/modern contexts.

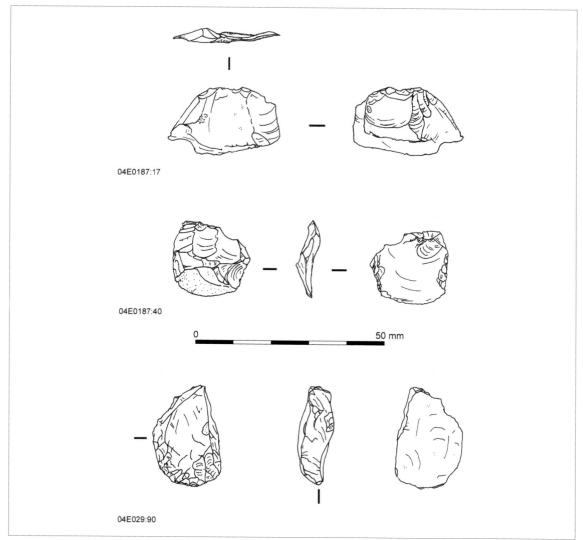

04E0187:17

04E0187:40

0   50 mm

04E029:90

Illus. 8.2—Manusmore AR100 (above). Flint flakes from Pit 43 and Pit 85. Cahircalla More AR128 (bottom). Scraper from Ditch 125.

Activities involving iron production can take two forms, smelting and smithing. Smelting is the manufacture of iron from ore and fuel in a smelting furnace. The resulting products are a spongy mass called an unconsolidated bloom, i.e. iron with a considerable amount of slag, which includes still-tap, run, dense or furnace slag. Tap slag, for example, is formed when liquid slag is allowed to flow out, continuously or intermittently, through a hole in the side of the furnace. This removal of the slag facilitates retrieval of the bloom after the smelting operation.

Smithing involves both primary and secondary smithing. The former involves hot working, by a smith using a hammer, of the bloom on a 'stringhearth' (usually near the smelting furnace) to remove excess slag. The bloom becomes a rough lump of iron ready for use. The slags from this process include smithing-hearth bottoms and microslags, in particular tiny smithing spheres. Smithing-hearth bottoms are the most characteristic bulk slags produced by smithing. They are produced by a high-temperature reaction between the iron being worked and the 'flux' used by the smith. The slag produced drips down to form the smithing-hearth bottom. When it cooled or when it grew to such a size that it might obstruct the tuyère (the ceramic cone or pipe through which the bellows air enters the hearth) it was removed. If left on the floor of a building, smithing-hearth bottoms would make movement around a dimly lit smithy hazardous so were usually thrown against the inside wall or outside into the nearest cut feature.

Secondary smithing is hot working, using a hammer, of one or more pieces of iron to create or repair an object. As well as bulk slags, such as smithing-hearth bottoms, this generates microslags including hammerscale flakes from ordinary hot working (making or repairing an object) or tiny spheres from high-temperature welding to join or fuse two pieces of iron. Other constituents within submitted samples included vitrified hearth lining, fired clay, fuel ash and cinder (Tables 8.4–8.6). These be the result of a variety of high-temperature activities including domestic hearths, accidental fires, and even cremations and cannot be taken in their own right to indicate iron-working.

Table 8.4—Catalogue of slag from prehistoric contexts, all Iron Age.

Site	Find no.	Slag type	Undiagnostic	Fuel ash
Manusmore AR102 Cremation cemetery	04E0189:1	Runs 20 g	—	—
	04E0189:2	—	2 g	—
	04E0189:6	—	—	20 g
	04E0189:8	—	10 g	—
Manusmore AR100 Cremation cemetery	04E0187:4	—	1 g	—
	04E0187:11	—	2 g	—
	04E0187:13	—	12 g	—
	04E0187:16	Microslag: 1 flake and 3 spheres	—	—
	04E0187:21	—	2 g	—
Claureen AR131 Ring-ditch/barrow	04E0026:21	—	< 1 g	—

Prehistoric slag

Three prehistoric sites yielded slag, with material retrieved from within cremation pits at Manusmore AR100 and AR102 and the ring-ditch Claureen AR131. None of the material, however, is clearly derived from metal-working. The slag from Claureen AR131 is considered intrusive and at Manusmore AR100 and AR102, the amount of slag represented is too small to suggest metal-working occurred. The slag types present (Table 8.4) could have been produced instead by the combustion of fuel and any naturally occurring silica present. If objects of metal were also burnt—personal ornaments worn by a cremated corpse for instance—this might contribute to the production of slag. Alternatively, if the slag derives from metal-working, it may have been inadvertently imported from elsewhere, as it is unlikely to have been produced on site.

Early medieval slag

Three early medieval sites also produced a range of types and quantities of slag: Carrowdotia M27, Clareabbey AR123 and Cahircalla More AR128 (Table 8.5). An 8th- or 9th-century pit from Carrowdotia M27, located adjacent to a cashel, produced a very small quantity of iron slag (540 g). While no diagnostic smelting slag was present, some secondary smithing activity, and hence iron-working, is implied by the tiny amount of flake hammerscale recovered. Specimens recovered from Clareabbey AR123 (32 g in total), however, do not necessarily reflect metal-working. The pieces retrieved include a fragment of slag, undiagnostic of either iron-smelting or smithing. The other material was a piece of vitrified hearth lining. Neither suggests any high-temperature industrial activity was taking place on the site.

These results contrast with discoveries made at Cahircalla More AR128, where a smithy was identified (see Chapter 3). Just over 16.6 kg of iron slag and related material was recovered from a small, oval building and ditch fills of a related enclosure and field system. The slag types, and their clustering in features related to or near the building, reveal that it had been used as a smithy. Some slag may have been produced by smelting—the production of iron in a furnace from an ore and a flux—but the pieces were too fragmentary to be definitive. It is possible the smith carried out limited smelting to produce iron for working. A small magnetic fragment of burnt stone in the ditch may be ore, but would require geological identification to confirm this.

Quantities of hammerscale and other microslags—tiny runs and dribbles—were found in the interior of the building interpreted as a smithy, in two pits, while quantities of similar material were recovered from the ring gully that probably held the wall-footing of the building. Many of the larger slag types had been broken up or were types which could not be securely assigned to either smelting or smithing activity. Since hammerscales are not visible to the naked eye when in the soil, they usually remain in the immediate area of smithing activity (around the anvil and between it and the hearth) when larger (bulk) slags are cleared out. No bulk slags such as smithing-hearth bottoms were found within the structure; these had been dumped outside in the part of the enclosure ditch nearest to the smithy.

The two pits inside the building contained iron slag and related debris: substantial amounts of broken slag, microslags and fragments of vitrified hearth lining. There was evidence of *in situ* burning in the base of one of the pits. The curvilinear gully defining the building also produced a substantial amount of slag (6.2 kg), including microslags and hammerscale. Iron shavings found here echo those found nearby in the enclosure ditch fill.

The enclosure ditch produced 3.2 kg of slag, including four smithing-hearth bottoms and tiny amount of hammerscale. It was here that a possible iron chisel (04E0029:79) was found. Two small pits within the enclosure contained some iron fragments, iron shavings (as found in the smithy), some tiny fragments of fired clay and undiagnostic slag. In one of the ditches of the nearby field system, a small quantity (744 g) of undiagnostic slag was recovered and within the ploughsoil two smithing-hearth bottoms were found, which probably originated in the smithy.

Table 8.5—Catalogue of slag from early medieval sites.

Site	Find no.	Slag type	Smithing bottom	Undiag.	Hearth lining	Iron
Carrowdotia M27 Pits (iron-working)	03E1426:1	Microslag 130 g. Some hammerscale flake	—	354 g	—	—
	03E1426:14	Microslag 56 g. Occasional hammerscale flake	—	—	—	—
Clareabbey AR123 Pits and hearth	04E0019:1	—	—	24 g	—	—
	04E0019:2	—	—	—	8 g	—
Cahircalla More AR128 Enclosure, smithy	04E0029:7	—	1,208 g	28 g	—	—
	04E0029:25	—	498 g	—	—	—
	04E0029:31	Flake and spheres	—	—	—	2 g
	04E0029:35	Flake, 1 large sphere	—	4 g	—	—
	04E0029:38	—	—	—	—	2 g
	04E0029:40	—	—	—	Present	Shavings
	04E0029:41	—	812 g	—	—	—
	04E0029:44	—	—	12 g	—	—
	04E0029:51	Microslag 24 g. Large hammerscale flake, some spheres	—	—	—	Shavings
	04E0029:52	Microslag 2 g	—	—	—	—
	04E0029:53	—	—	Iron rich 66 g	—	—
	04E0029:54	Microslag 2 g	—	—	44 g	—
	04E0029:55	Microslag 162 g. Hammerscale present	—	88 g	10 g ★	—
	04E0029:56	Run slag 434 g. Some broken hammerscale flake	—	3,442 g possibly smelting	356 g	—

Site	Find no.	Slag type	Smithing bottom	Undiag.	Hearth lining	Iron
Cahircalla More AR128 (cont.)	04E0029:57	Slag runs 50 g. Flake and some spheres 1 g	—	350 g	10 g ★	—
	04E0029:58	Tiny runs 40 g. Hammerscale present	—	—	—	—
	04E0029:80	—	1,862 g	—	—	
	04E0029:81	—	—	—	2 g ★	—
	04E0029:82	Tiny broken flake	—	528 g	30 g	—
	04E0029:83	Microslag 156 g. Large flakes, few spheres	—	176 g	129 g	—
	04E0029:84	Run 102 g. Flake, occasional spheres 6 g and flake trapped in slag	—	1,586 g	166 g	—
	04E0029:85	Microslag 824 g. Flake and large spheres 30 g	—	164 g	4 g	—
	04E0029:86	Run 192 g. Little and broken hammerscale	—	1,833 g (276 g iron rich) Possibly smelting.	172 g	—
	04E0029:87	Microslag 160 g. Hammerscale flake and spheres	—	—	—	—
	04E0029:94	—	—	1 g	—	—
	04E0029:102	—	—	740 g	—	—
	04E0029:103	—	—	4 g	—	—
Key: ★ = *fired clay*						

Later medieval slag

The only later medieval site to produce slag (c. 11 kg) was the excavation at the Augustinian house at Clare Abbey (Clareabbey C020/A025) (Table 8.6). Much derives from modern, 18th or 19th-century contexts and is listed in a report on the CD that accompanies this book, but the remainder (6.57 kg) dates from the 11th to 15th centuries. Diagnostic smelting slag (tap slag), smithing slag, chiefly hearth bottoms and hammerscale were recovered from Ditch 35 dated to AD 1220–1380 (Beta-231533). The amount of hammerscale retrieved was small, suggesting the smithing activity occurred elsewhere with the waste products dumped in the ditch. The location or extent of metal-working is unknown and this gap is further illustrated by the small quantity of slag retrieved from other contexts across the site.

Table 8.6—Catalogue of slag from medieval contexts at Clare Abbey.

Site	Find no.	Slag type	Smithing bottom	Undiag.	Hearth lining	Cinder
Clare Abbey (Area C020)	E2021:53:13–14	Run 17 g	—	1 g	—	—
	E2021:65:2 and 4	—	—	224 g	—	
	E2021:67:12–13	—	—	1 g	3 g ★	—
	E2021:74:4–5	Hammerscale: 1 sphere, 1 flake and other heat magnetised material 7 g	3,896 g	4,282 g	—	26 g
	E2021:93:4	—	—	Run 4 g	—	—
	E2021:157:2	—	—	1 g	—	—
	E2021:168:1–2	—	—	871 g Smelting?	1 g	—
	E2021:178:1	—	—	1 g	—	—
	E2021:194:2	—	—	81 g	—	—
	E2021:195:2–3	Tap slag 36 g	227 g?	74 g	—	—
	E2021:197:2–4	Runs 41 g	—	5 g	—	Run cinder 2 g
Clare Abbey (Area A025)	E2022:55:8	—	—	—	7 g	—
	E2022:56:9–10	—	583 g?	525.5 g	—	—
	E2022:57:11–12	—	1,467 g	92.5 g	—	—
	E2022:59:12	Tap slag 249 g	—	433 g	—	—

Key: ★ = fired clay

Wooden bowl

Graham Hull

Part of a wooden bowl (04E0191:1) was retrieved from the bog bordering a Bronze Age cremation cemetery at Killow AR104. The piece was extremely soft and degraded and was recovered in five larger and two smaller pieces. The bowl originally had a maximum external diameter of 225 mm and a maximum internal diameter of 205 mm. The surviving portion is 100 mm high and 10 mm thick. The surface of the bowl is undecorated and lacks obvious turning lines, indicative of lathe manufacture. There are, however, two carved ridges that may represent the beginning of a rim detail or perhaps the upper part of the bowl (Illus. 2.16 and 8.3).

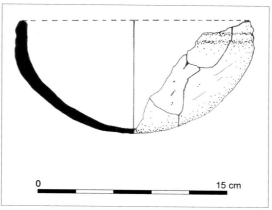

Illus. 8.3—Killow AR104. Wooden bowl (04E0191:1).

The bowl was made from *Fraxinus excelsior* (common ash or European ash; Lorna O Donnell identified the species). Ash is a native Irish species. It favours nutrient-rich soils and was probably available on the higher, dry ground adjacent to the bog, but this does not necessarily mean that the bowl was produced locally. A small sample of wood from the bowl has been dated to the Iron Age, 777–407 BC (UBA-6287).

Parallels

Of the few dozen prehistoric wooden bowls that have been discovered in Ireland or Scotland, most are from non-archaeological peat-digging in the north of Ireland. Earwood (1990) has demonstrated clear typological affinities between wooden bowls and cauldrons and these same vessel types made in bronze. Radiocarbon dating has shown that many of the wooden bowls were manufactured in the late prehistoric period. The bowl from Killow is similar in form to some of the other vessels from this period but incomplete survival means that there is no evidence of the handles that characterise those bowls. The lack of tool marks, on what are likely to be lathe-turned bowls, is typical and probably reflects high quality finishing by sanding or polishing the vessels. The choice of ash is unusual as other examples are mostly made from alder, including recently discovered pieces from a raised bog on a road scheme in Edercloon, Co. Longford (Moore 2007, 20–1). In common with the Edercloon examples, the Killow bowl was incomplete and fragmentary when deposited in the bog.

Given the lack of ceramic vessels in the Iron Age, wooden vessels must have played a significant role in daily life. Earwood (1990) believes that the fineness of manufacture of many of the wooden vessels indicates that they were not merely 'poor man's substitutes' for metal vessels but were highly prized alternatives.

A lathe-turned reproduction of the complete bowl has been made by New Jersey wood turner Mark Zdepski (Zdepski 2008) and is on exhibition at the Clare Museum, Ennis, Co. Clare. The reproduction is a beautiful object—as the original must once have been too—and bears testimony that the Iron Age craftsman who made the Killow example was motivated by aesthetic as well as functional concerns.

Glass beads

Graham Hull

The ring-ditch recorded at Claureen AR131 was dated to 100 BC–AD 70 (Beta-207732). The ditch produced three small glass beads (04E0026:1–3). The beads are perforated discs with rounded edges, flattened surfaces and straight perforations (Illus. 8.4). Both annular and globular examples occur (annular = height-to-diameter ratio of < 1:2; globular = height-to-diameter ratio of > 1:2) (Table 8.7).

Table 8.7—Catalogue of glass beads from the ring-ditch at Claureen AR131.

Find no.	Colour	Type	Dimensions (bead)	Dimensions (threading hole)
04E0026:1	Dark blue	Globular	Diam 4.5 mm, Th 2 mm	Diam 1 mm
04E0026:2	Yellow	Annular	Diam 3 mm, Th 1.5 mm	Diam 1 mm
04E0026:3	Yellow	Annular	Diam 2.5 mm, Th 1.55 mm	Diam 1 mm

The two yellow beads are small, opaque and annular in shape. This type of glass was produced by an admixture of lead, antimony and tin and the colour was probably chosen to imitate amber (Guido 1978). The blue glass bead is an undecorated globular example. The blue hue derives from cobalt, a colour that was relatively rare until the Roman period.

The recovery of glass beads in association with cremation burials dating from the Iron Age is increasingly common, though the number of beads recovered from individual sites does vary considerably. For example, excavation of a cremation cemetery at Kilmahuddrick, Co. Dublin (Doyle 2006), recovered part of an amber bead and a smaller, probable yellow glass bead. The beads were heat affected suggesting that they were with the body when cremated. The Kilmahuddrick beads are earlier than those from Claureen AR131, deriving from contexts radiocarbon-dated to 992–822 BC and 393–192 BC. Fourth to first century BC contexts in a ring-ditch at Knockcommane, Co. Limerick,

Illus. 8.4—Claureen AR131. Glass beads (04E0026:1–3).

produced nine blue glass beads and two pieces of fused glass (Molloy 2009, 165). Five of the beads were fused suggesting they had been laid as a string. Eleven beads, of similar size, colour and form to those from Claureen AR131 were recovered from a ring-barrow in Marhill, Co. Tipperary (Scully 2009). The beads derived from deposits dated to 40 BC–AD 130, a date broadly contemporary with Claureen AR131. Up to 50 tiny, yellow, glass beads were retrieved from an Iron Age ring-ditch with human cremation burial at Ferns, Wexford (Ryan 2000). Higher numbers, 80 yellow and blue glass beads, were retrieved from a centrally placed cremation burial within a ring-ditch at Ballydavis, Co. Laois (Keeley 1999).

Much closer to the present scheme, glass beads were also recovered from two ring-ditches excavated in Ballyboy, south Co. Galway (Delaney et al. 2012). The ring-ditches were dated, based on several calibrated radiocarbon dates, to the period between the second century BC and first century AD. There were nine glass beads and one amber bead in the ditch of Ballyboy 1 and 77 glass beads and 28 amber beads in the ditch of Ballyboy 2. The glass beads were either light blue-green or dark blue, with a small number of red/red-brown examples. Three glass beads were decorated with simple linear (red on blue) or cable twisted (brown-and-white on red) designs. Two beads—one glass and the other amber—were 'toggle' or dumbbell shaped but most were plain or annular (Carroll in Delaney et al. 2012).

Beads are clearly a feature of burials dating to the second half of the first millennium BC, whether deposited as individual items or as sets, perhaps stringed. The recovery of beads from Claureen AR131 further corroborates this practice of inserting grave goods with cremated remains during this period.

Bronze Age palstave axehead

Declan Moore

A Bronze Age palstave, a type of axehead, was discovered during the testing phase of the project by archaeologists from Moore Group. The object (03E1293:005) was retrieved from topsoil in the townland of Ballymacahill. An area of 150 m² was opened around the find-spot but other archaeological features were absent. Metal-detection of the spoil arising from the investigations did not identify any related objects (Licence No. 03R130). The field in which the palstave was found has been improved by mechanical means within the last 30 years and was used as a dump fairly recently. These activities may have destroyed or led to the removal of the axe from its original context.

Description

The palstave is a development of the flanged axe in which an axehead is hafted using flaps or flanges of metal at the edges of the tool to grip the haft above the blade (Waddell 1998, 186–90). Palstaves are characterised by a ledge-stop or bar ledge-stop that joins the flanges across the tool to form a continuous U shape. This jutting ledge of metal projects to the same height as the flanges and is sometimes undercut to form a pocket. Below the stop the blade is thicker than the expanse (or septum) between the flanges. Decorative motifs, which may also serve to strengthen the tool, can occur on the blade below the stop.

The axehead is a bronze object with overall dimensions of (L) 123 mm by (W) 51 mm by (Th) 31 mm. The flanges increase in depth from 3 mm at the butt to 11 mm at the stop and do not continue below the stop ledge. The septum is 5 mm thick. The stop ledge is concave with pockets 5 mm deep. A midrib extends 35 mm below the stop, tapering from 18 mm in width to 2 mm. The blade splays from 31 mm at the haft end to 51 mm at the cutting edge.

Prior to conservation, the surface of the palstave was corroded, the worst affected area being the cutting edge. Pitting from bronze disease occurred across the entire object and disturbed the original patina, which was fragile and in some areas completely undermined by powdery copper carbonates and lost. The flanges on both faces have been subject to physical loss and distortion, some of which appeared to be quite recent. On one face, the stop has been deformed slightly and a small piece had broken off (Illus. 8.5).

Illus. 8.5—Palstave axehead (03E1293: 005) found in Ballymacahill townland.

Discussion

Irish palstaves are classified broadly into four groups, A–D (Mount 1997; Waddell 1998, 186–90). The Ballymacahill palstave falls into the Group C category where flanges do not extend below the stop and the stop is often undercut. This group is subdivided into C1 where the flanges in side view form convex curves from stop to butt and C2 where the flanges have their highest point above the butt. The Ballymacahill palstave conforms to the first of these with the best surviving flange performing a slightly convex curve, rising from the butt to the highest point at the stop before this prominence tapers to the midrib. The stops are undercut by 5 mm.

Palstaves were the main wood-working tool of the later Bronze Age and were probably also valued as currency. They date from the Middle Bronze Age and occur in north-western France, The Netherlands, Germany, Britain and in Ireland, where several hundred examples are known (Eogan 2000, 15). The earliest Irish examples are associated with the Killymaddy metal-working phase dated to approximately 1500–1350 BC (Waddell 1998, 161–2). There is considerable variation in the form of the palstave which may represent attempts to improve hafting methods.

Considerable evidence of prehistoric activity was discovered elsewhere on the scheme, a few kilometres south of the palstave find-spot, but the Ballymacahill palstave was found in isolation from other archaeological features in an area that had been subjected to modern agricultural improvements.

As a consequence, its original context remains unknown. With the possible exception of a standing stone in nearby Carrowdotia townland, no Bronze Age monuments are known in the immediate area. Whether the palstave was a chance loss, deposited in an archaeological feature or buried as part of a hoard remains unknown.

Early and later medieval stone artefacts
Michelle Comber

Eleven stone artefacts were retrieved from three excavation sites on the scheme (two early medieval sites and one later medieval site). The assemblage comprises three quern-stones, four whetstones, three mini-anvils, a pin sharpener and a carved fragment (Table 8.8). All are of sandstone and most are fine grained in texture. They are all objects typically employed in domestic and craft-related activities. Some, at least, were used to sharpen points and blades, others possibly forming work surfaces for any number of craft or domestic cutting activities. It is not possible to closely date these objects, other than to say that they are not uncommon in the first millennium AD and beyond.

Table 8.8—Catalogue of stone artefacts from early and later medieval sites.

Site	Find no.	Type	Dimensions	Description
Carrowdotia AR25 Cashel, burnt spreads	03E1442:39	Rotary quern-stone	W/D 330 mm R 140 mm Th 55–70 mm Perf. 55 mm	Upper stone. Coarse sandstone with quartz inclusions. Low rise or collar around central perforation on upper surface. Flat grinding surface. Straight sided perforation
Cahircalla More AR128 Ditched enclosure, smithy, field system	04E0029:24	Rotary quern-stone	L 185 mm W 120 mm Th 17–55 mm Perf. 23–37 mm	Central fragment of upper stone with intact perforation. Stone thickens from surviving edge to central cone surrounding central perforation
	04E0029:45	Quern (?)	L 300 mm W 280 mm Th 105 mm	3 adjoining fragments. Small, shallow working surface upper surface
	04E0029:95	Pin-sharpening stone	L 107 mm W 78 mm Th 35 mm	Broken. Sub-rectangular with rectangular x-section, broad smooth faces and edge-wear hollows. U-sectioned groove (L 90 x W 3 mm x D 2 mm) tapering to point. Fine-grained sandstone

Site	Find no.	Type	Dimensions	Description
Cahircalla More AR128 (cont.)	04E0029:96	Whetstone	L 65 mm W 42 mm Th 2–19 mm	Broken. Sub-oval, with irregular section. Ends rounded. Central wear hollow on broad face. Opposite face – deep scratches (L 35 mm x W 1 mm x D 1 mm). Fine-grained sandstone
	04E0029:99	Mini-anvil (poss.)	L 130 mm W 110 mm Th 50 mm	Broken. Rectangular x-section. Flat faces with scratches of different length and depth. Fine-grained sandstone
	04E0029:108	Mini-anvil (poss.)	L 200 mm W 135 mm Th 50 mm	Broken. Rectangular section. Flat faces with scratches. Fine-grained sandstone
	04E0029:109	Whetstone (poss.)	L 75 mm W 43 mm Th 12–18 mm	Broken. Sub-rectangular with rectangular section. Wear facet on 1 edge. Grooved (L 20 mm x W 2 mm x D 1 mm). Opposite side worn but lacks hollows/facets. Notch on 1 edge. Fine-grained sandstone
Clare Abbey (C020) Augustinian abbey	E2021:51:59	Whetstone	L 45.2 mm W 15.5 mm Th 14.6 mm	Broken. Rectangular with square section. Rounded edges, smooth faces with wear marks, various depth and orientation
	E2021:77:34	Whetstone	L 61.7 mm W 23.6 mm Th 11.4 mm	Broken. Triangular with rectangular section. Tapers to a broad point at intact end. Haphazard scratches and gouges on multiple surfaces
	E2021:158:4	Carved fragment	H 17.6 mm W 22 mm Th 8.7 mm Perf. 1.6 mm	Sub- triangular with irregular section. Rectangular perforated recess carved into finely smoothed surface. Perforation circular. Sandstone

Quern-stones

The cashel at Carrowdotia AR25 yielded two conjoining fragments of the upper stone of a rotary quern (03E1442:39) (Illus. 8.6). This is one of the smaller examples of a rotary quern from the early medieval period (Comber 2000). A fragment of the upper stone of a small, lightweight rotary quern was retrieved at Cahircalla More AR128 (04E0029:24) (Illus. 3.5). The difference in thickness and perforation size between the two quern-stones suggests they were used for grinding different materials.

A second artefact described as a quern, possibly a saddle quern (04E0029:45) was retrieved from

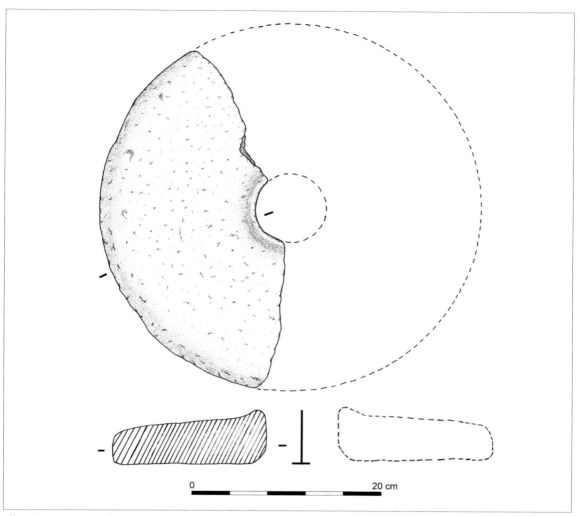

Illus. 8.6—Carrowdotia AR25. Upper stone of rotary quern-stone (03E1442:39).

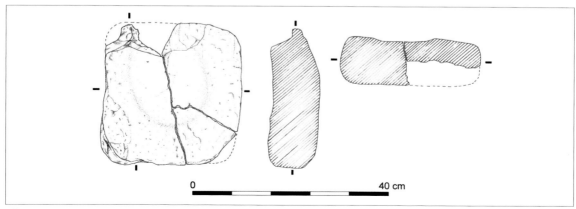

Illus. 8.7—Cahircalla More AR128. Quern (?) (04E0029:45).

141

Cahircalla More AR128 (Illus. 8.7). Clearly not part of a rotary quern, the object is not part of a typical saddle quern either. Its working surface, which was produced through grinding, is relatively small and shallow when compared with corn-grinding querns or classic bowl-shaped mortars. It is more likely that this stone was used for grinding some other material, possibly in a craft-working or domestic context. There is no obvious reason to ascribe it to prehistory.

Whetstones

Whetstones are typically hand-held and portable. They are common finds on archaeological excavations and hundreds have been recovered from ringforts and cashels. A wide range of shapes and sizes is known, with only one attempt having been made to classify them: four different groups of whetstones and five different forms of wear, each representing different sharpening tasks, have been identified (O'Connor 1991).

Two artefacts identified as possible whetstones are from Cahircalla More AR128. One is wedge-shaped in plan (04E0029:109), thus fitting into one of O'Connor's categories. It has a possible wear facet on one edge, between the scratched face and side. The second possible whetstone (04E0029:96) consists of a fragment of a larger piece and has a central wear hollow, created by drawing an implement, such as a chisel, back and forth over a relatively small area of the stone, on one broad face. The intact end is rounded, as are the edges of the broken end, perhaps reflecting its continued use after breaking.

The whetstones from Clare Abbey (E2021:51:59, E2021:77:34) are the latest examples found on the scheme being post-medieval or early modern in date. Each was originally longer though both were still relatively small and portable and, when complete, they would have fallen within the typical size range of hand-held whetstones identified by O'Connor (ibid.). Their overall shapes and patterns of wear are unexceptional. The combination of smooth surfaces, haphazard scratches and gouges visible on multiple surfaces suggests they each formed part of longer whetstones used for sharpening blade edges by rubbing the stone along the blade.

Pin-sharpening stone

A fragment of a pin sharpener (04E0029:95) was retrieved from Cahircalla More AR128 (Illus. 8.8). Hollows in the stone were probably created by sharpening a fine, narrow blade, such as a knife. A distinct groove on one face was used to sharpen, for example, an awl, pin or knife point.

Mini-anvils

Two other stone artefacts from Cahircalla More AR128 (04E0029:99 and 04E0029:108) seem less like whetstones and more like mini-anvils or work surfaces. The pieces are rather large and heavy to have operated as hand-held whetstones. Their faces are flat and level, marked by frequent shallow scratches, but do not exhibit wear hollows or facets. Despite this, both would have provided ideal flat working surfaces, perhaps for metal-work or some other craft.

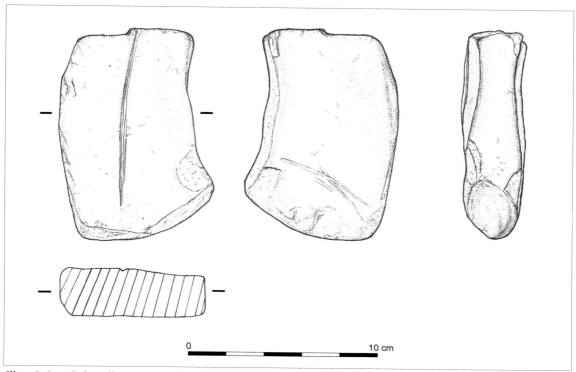

Illus. 8.8—Cahircalla More AR128. Pin sharpener (04E0029:95).

Architectural fragments

An architectural fragment was retrieved from Clare Abbey (E2021:158:4). It was finely carved sandstone and originally formed part of a rectangular tablet or block with a rectangular recess. It could originate from a small fixture such as a church water font.

Early medieval metal artefacts
Michelle Comber

The enclosure at Cahircalla More AR128 was the only early medieval site to produce metal finds (Table 8.9). Six metal pieces were retrieved including a simple ring-pin (04E0029:01) and a possible chisel (04E0029:79). The other pieces are small, fragmentary pieces of iron (04E0029:118), possibly waste material, that were retrieved from a pit within the smithy.

Ring-pin

The ring-pin consists of a copper-alloy ring attached to an iron pin (Illus. 3.6 and 8.9). It was retrieved from a ditch in a field system associated with the enclosure (Illus. 3.4). The pin-head is a simple loop or bend of the top of the pin shaft. The rest of the shaft is in two pieces, though almost the entire

Illus. 8.9—Cahircalla More AR128. Ring pin (04E0029:1).

original length appears to be represented. The iron shaft was originally sub-rectangular or sub-circular in section, and tapers to a point. The copper-alloy ring is complete and well preserved. It is circular or sub-circular in section with ends that abut to form a complete ring. There is no decoration apparent on the artefact. The iron shaft is badly corroded and bears heavy mineral accretions.

Ring-pins are a relatively common find on sites dating from the second half of the first millennium AD. The simplest form consists of a straight shank, with the top looped over to facilitate ring attachment. This is the form most commonly seen in iron, though the present example is unusual in that it consists of both iron and copper alloy. The Cahircalla More example fits perfectly with the general size range of these pins.

Table 8.9—Catalogue of selected metal finds from early medieval contexts from Cahircalla More AR128.

Find no.	Type and material	Context	Dimensions	Description
04E0029:01	Ring-pin, iron and copper alloy	Ditch 125	Ring: Diam 22 mm, Th 3.5 mm Pin-head: W 6 mm; hole: Diam 5 mm Pin: L 120 mm	Iron shaft (with heavy accretions); copper-alloy ring Undecorated
04E0029:79	Chisel (poss.), iron	Ditch 100	L 120 mm W 16 mm, Th 11 mm; 'blade' W 9 mm, Th 1–2 mm	Rectangular section, tapers to broad, flat blade. Perforated shaft?
04E0029:118	4 frags, iron	Smithy Pit 44	Largest piece: L 3 mm, W 6–11 mm, Th <1 mm	Broken pieces of iron, possibly scrap or waste fragments

Possible chisel

A rectangular iron implement, tapering to a broad flat blade, was recovered from the enclosure ditch (Ditch 100). There is a small circular perforation 9 mm from the broader end of the piece. (X-ray confirms that this extended through the object.) In shape, this piece resembles a chisel (Illus. 3.6). The chisel is neither socketed nor tanged—as is common for chisels of the first millennium AD and earlier—and the perforation suggests, instead, a handle attached by a metal pin, a long rivet or a nail. A number of excavated early medieval sites have produced iron chisels. The closest in size to this example come from ringforts at Garryduff, Co. Cork (O'Kelly 1962, 46), and Carraig Aille II, Co. Limerick (Ó Ríordáin 1949, 79–81). Both are socketed and roughly 30 mm longer than the Cahircalla More artefact, though of a similar width. The shape of the Carraig Aille chisel closely resembles this present example in that the width of the 'blade' is less than that of the opposite end. Many of the other iron chisels from the period have expanded blades.

Medieval and post-medieval metal artefacts

Miriam Carroll and Annette Quinn

Twenty-three metal objects are included in this assemblage (Table 8.10). All of them come from the Augustinian house at Clare Abbey (C020/A025). The artefact range includes small implements, dress accessories, horse-related accessories, nails and a possible gun pellet. The objects date, variously, from the 13th to the 18th centuries. The entire metal assemblage from Clare Abbey amounts to 138 items, including 66 nails, but as most of this material is modern it is not all described here. (For a full list see the Final Report on the CD that accompanies this book.)

Table 8.10—Catalogue of selected medieval and post-medieval artefacts from Clare Abbey.

Find no.	Type and material	Date	Dimensions	Description
E2022:55:2	Awl (poss.), iron	Medieval or later	L 56.5 mm W 4.8 mm Th. 3.8 mm	Incomplete. Rectangular section. Tapers both end. Widens one end, opposing narrower end for attachment to handle
E2022:55:3	Needle/pin shaft, iron	Medieval or later	L 27.6 mm Diam (shaft) 1.8 mm	Incomplete. Circular section. Poss. fragment pin/needle shank, head and point missing
E2022:56:3	Horseshoe nail, iron	13th/14th cent.	L 47.1 mm W (head) 15.5 mm Th (shaft) 4.2 mm	Complete. Eared nail
E2022:57:3	Horseshoe, iron	13th/14th cent.	L 128.6 mm W 31.9 mm Th 8.9 mm	Incomplete. Corroded fragment of branch with 1 nail. 2 rectangular nail holes
E2022:57:4	Horseshoe nail, iron	13th/14th cent.	L 37 mm W (head) 14.1 mm Th (head) 9.3 mm	Complete. Expanded, poss. eared head. Shaft bent, with poss. spiral clench. Corroded
E2022:59:2	Belt hasp, copper alloy	14th/15th cent.	L 15.4 mm W 25.8 mm Th 1.3 mm	Complete. Rectangular frame. Small inner projection/bar on either side

Find no.	Type and material	Date	Dimensions	Description
E2021:39:5	Buckle, iron	Medieval or later	L 49.8 mm W 35.4 mm Th 5.4 mm	Incomplete. D-shaped buckle, broken. Frame rectangular x-section. Pin rectangular x-section tapers to blunt point
E2021:39:6	Ring, copper alloy	Unstratified	Diam 27.7 mm W 3.1 mm Th 2.7 mm	Complete. Annular ring. Lozenge-shaped section
E2021:39:13	Spur attachment, leather	16th cent. or later	L 36.7 mm W 15.2 mm Th 2.9 mm Diam (ring) 1.3 mm	Complete. Lozenge-shaped, looped terminal with ring attached. 2 rivets extant
E2021:51:66	Spur rowel, copper alloy	16th cent. or later	Diam 55.7 mm	Complete. Well preserved star rowel, 8 widely spaced points, triangular-oval section. Roughly central oval perforation for attachment to spur
E2021:53:6	Horseshoe nail, iron	13th/14th cent.	L 21.1 mm W (head) 11.5 mm (shaft) 5.5 mm Th (head) 8.2 mm (shaft) 3.2 mm	Incomplete. Rectangular shouldered head. Shaft broken midway
E2021:53:2	Horseshoe nail, iron	13th/14th cent.	L 36 mm W (head) 13.4 mm (shaft) 5 mm Th (head) 11 mm (shaft) 4.1 mm	Complete. Rectangular expanded head, poss. shouldered with clenching at tip
E2021:53:3	Horseshoe nail, iron	13th/14th cent.	L 30.3 mm W (head) 14.3 mm Th (shaft) 3 mm	Complete. Eared nail with spiral clench
E2021:54:4	Buckle frame fragment, iron	Unknown (19th-cent. context)	L 34.2 mm W 33.4 mm Th 5 mm	Incomplete. Fragment poss. rectangular buckle frame. Corroded
E2021:59:41	Rowel spur, iron	Post-medieval	L 133.5 mm (neck including rowel) 6.5 mm W 48.4 mm Th (neck) 10 mm (side) 5.1 mm	Incomplete. Straight neck. D-sectioned sides at angle with neck to pass under wearer's ankle. Single ring terminal on 1 side, opposing side broken. Neck oval section, tapers to 7 star rowel attached by rivet. Relatively sharp points, rectangular section

Find no.	Type and material	Date	Dimensions	Description
E2021:60:2	Buckle pin (poss.)	Unknown (18th/19th-cent. context)	L 61.1 mm W 6.4 mm Th 4.3 mm	Incomplete. Rectangular section, tapers to slightly rounded point
E2021:67:15	Wire fragments, copper alloy	15th–17th cent.	Diam 3.3 mm Th 0.6 mm	Incomplete. Numerous fragments, some portions looped and twisted. Function unknown
E2021:67:19	Buckle pin (poss.), copper alloy?	15th–17th cent.	L 40.3 mm Diam 2.8 mm	Incomplete. In 2 pieces. Poss. folded/rolled metal. Tapers to rounded tip
E2021:67:20	Wound-wire headed pin, copper alloy	15th–17th cent.	L 20.2 mm Diam (head) 1.1 mm (shank) 0.4 mm	Complete. Fine pin, spherical head. Shank bent towards tip, circular section
E2021:67:21	Pin fragment, copper alloy	15th/17th-cent.	L 22 mm Diam (head) 2 mm (shank) 0.8 mm	Incomplete. Fragmented. Shank circular section. Poss. solid head
E2021:67:24	Gun pellet (poss.), Lead?	15th/17th-cent.	Diam 4.2 mm	Complete. Small spherical, slightly flattened on 1 side
E2021:50:3	Coin, copper alloy	AD 1691	Diam 26.3 mm Th 1.2 mm Wt 5.2 g	Complete. James II halfpenny. Obverse shows bust facing left. Legend IACOBVS·II·GRATIA· Reverse Hibernia facing left with left hand resting on harp and right hand raised holding cross. Legend HIBERNIA 1691. Reversed 'N' in Hibernia
E2021:74:3	Horseshoe nail, iron	13th/14th-cent.	L 40.4 mm W (head) 13.2 mm (shaft) 5 mm Th (head) 8.1 mm (shaft) 4.6 mm	Complete. Expanded head with ears. Corroded

Buckles

One buckle (E2021:39:5) (Illus. 8.10), a buckle frame fragment (E2021:54:4) and two possible buckle pin fragments (E2021:67:19 and E2021:60:2) were recovered from the excavations at Clare Abbey. The size and form of buckles used in the medieval and post-medieval periods varied widely and also had a variety of functions. The smaller forms were used on men's and women's clothing and also as stirrup buckles. In the post-medieval period, small buckles were also used on shoes. Larger examples may have been used as part of horse equipment although it is known that large buckles were also used with swords and occasionally for men's and women's waist belts (Egan & Pritchard 2002, 50). The size of the almost complete buckle E2021:39:5 suggests it was originally used on a belt as it is probably too small to have been used as horse equipment and is too large to have been used on a shoe. Belt buckles are often indistinguishable from light ornamental horse-harness buckles (Hume 1969, 86), however, the wide variety of D-shaped buckles from Winchester and elsewhere in Britain (Goodall 1990a, 526) suggests in general that this form was an all-purpose type.

Belt hasp

A belt hasp (E2022:59:2; Illus. 3.20) was recovered from an undated context. The term hasp refers to an item that joins one strap to another without using a pin and eye, as a buckle does. Hasps of this type take many forms; however, similar examples to that from Clare Abbey have

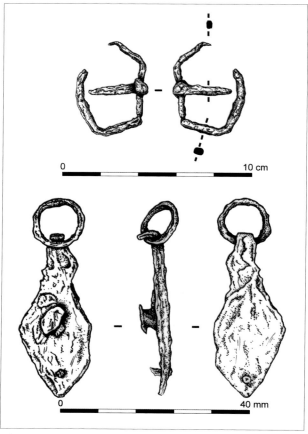

Illus. 8.10—Clare Abbey. Belt buckle (E2021:39:5) and spur attachment (E2021:39:13).

been recovered from 14th- and 15th-century contexts in Winchester (Hinton 1990, 540, fig. 143). This type consists of a simple, almost rectangular frame with two internal bars or projections. The two bars prevented the strap to which the frame was sewn from sliding; the remainder of the frame took a metal clip terminating another strap.

Needles/pins

One wound-wire-headed pin (E2021:67:20), a fragmented pin (E2021:67:21) and four needle/pin shafts that lacked diagnostic heads or eyes (E2021:58:19–21 and E2022:55:3) were retrieved. The wound-wire-headed pin is complete and was recovered from a 15th- to 17th-century context. Such pins were used in Ireland and England throughout the medieval period and became abundant in the archaeological record during the 14th century and subsequently. The heads of wound-wire pins were made by twisting a length of wire around the shank in either a Z- or S-direction (Egan & Pritchard 2002). Two twists were usual and suggest a uniformity of head wire length employed throughout the industry. A wound-wire-headed pin was recovered from a post-medieval context in Waterford City (Scully 1997, 453, fig. 15:5:5) and a number from medieval and post-medieval contexts in Cork City

(Carroll & Quinn 2003, 274–5, fig. 5:9:2–6). Such pins had a variety of functions including fastening clothes, fixing women's head-dresses and pinning papers.

Tools

A possible awl (E2022:55:2) was recovered from an undated context. Awls are a common tool found in medieval contexts and are generally thought to have been used for leather-working. Larger examples may also have been used in wood-working. Awls have been recovered from 11th/12th-century contexts in Waterford (Scully 1997, 469–72) and 13th/14th-century contexts in Cork (Carroll & Quinn 2003, 266–68).

Horse equipment

This assemblage includes one horseshoe fragment (E2022:57:3) and six horseshoe nails (Table 8.10), all of which derived from 13th/14th-century contexts. While horseshoes have a long history of use from the medieval period to the present, several indicators can suggest the date. In the 13th century horseshoes had broad webs (20–30 mm) and countersunk nail holes that held nails with eared, expanded heads (Goodall 1990b, 1056). They also frequently had three nail holes per branch. The later forms, from the 14th century to the present, had rectangular nail holes and fewer calkins, i.e. projections formed by turning down the heels of the horseshoe to provide a better foothold on soft ground. After the 13th century the holes were generally no longer countersunk and the shoe consequently had a plain outline (Scully 1997, 474). Although the horseshoe fragment was corroded, an X-ray suggests countersunk rectangular holes.

Horseshoe nails are distinctive from other nail types in that their heads are specifically shaped and expanded for the purpose of both securing the horseshoe to the hoof and in some cases to project beyond the surface of the shoe. Seven eared horseshoe nails occur with two displaying the distinctive 'spiral clenching' at the nail tip (E2022:57:4 and E2021:53:3). Eared nails sat in the countersunk slot of the shoe while the function of the spiral clench may have facilitated the tightening of loose nails. Similar examples are known from 13th/14th-century contexts in London (Clark 2004, 87) and an example of an unclenched horseshoe nail with an expanded head was recovered from the excavations at Clontuskert Priory, Co. Galway (Fanning 1976, 140, fig.14:75).

Spurs and spur accessories

Find E2021:59:41 is a well preserved, although incomplete, rowel spur (Illus. 3.24). The rowel spur first appeared in the 13th century when it was in use with the earlier prick spur. The rowel spur replaced the latter and by the second quarter of the 14th century most spurs had rowels (Clark 2004, 124–48). Spurs would frequently have been wet while in use, which would have resulted in the corroding together of similar metals. This in turn would have restricted the movement of rowels and may have resulted in the use of rowels made from metals other than iron. The rowel spur from this excavation has a small iron rowel though a copper-alloy rowel (E2021:51:66) was also recovered.

By the 15th century the necks of spurs were becoming increasingly longer and this in part reflected a fashion trend to lengthen and point items such as the toes of shoes and boots. The spur from this assemblage has a relatively long neck, which suggests it may be of 16th-century or later date. The spur sides also suggest a late medieval or later date as they project down into a moderate curve, which would have placed the spur under the wearer's ankle, but are not strongly curved. By the end of the 15th century, for example, many spur sides were (horizontally) fairly straight while earlier examples displayed deep curves. The extant terminal at the end of the spur side consists of a single ring, which would have held an attachment for spur leathers or a buckle.

The rowel (E2021:51:66) comprises a well-preserved star of eight, widely spaced points. The latter are triangular-oval in section and a central perforation allowed attachment to a spur neck. Detached spur rowels are difficult to date closely (Ellis 1990, 1038) and simple star rowels with varying number of points have been used on spurs from the introduction of rowels in the 13th century until modern times (Ellis 2004). A spur leather attachment (E2021:39:13) (Illus. 8.10) completes the group of spur related objects from Clare Abbey. These objects held leathers either by rivets, as in this example, or by a hook which pierced the end of the leather. The leathers were then passed around the spur terminals by its looped terminal or a ring.

Coin: James II halfpenny

One coin dating to the late 17th century was recovered from a 20th-century context at Clare Abbey (Table 8.10). The coin consists of a James II halfpenny, minted in Limerick when the city was under siege by the army of William III in 1691 (Illus. 3.23). Under the reign of James II a mint was established at the Deanery in Limerick in May of 1690, under Commissioner Walter Plunkett (Colgan 2003, 149). The Duchess press was sent to Limerick with a set of obverse and reverse dies and punches that are distinguishable from the coins struck at Dublin from the same year. A proclamation of June 1690 called for all large shillings and half-crowns struck before May of the same year to be replaced by new smaller coins in an attempt to make supplies of metal go further. Small shillings were struck in Dublin in May and June of 1690 and also at Limerick in April, May and September, however, the decision to reduce the size of coinage further diminished public confidence in James's brass money. Political and military events then came to a head with the Battle of the Boyne, which saw William III defeat James II's army in July 1690. The majority of James's forces withdrew to Limerick, however, William pursued them and laid siege to the city. The War of the Kings continued into 1691 when the second siege of Limerick occurred and heralded the final stage in the history of James II's emergency coinage. Behind the walls of Limerick the Duchess press re-coined large and small shillings into halfpennies and farthings to meet the needs of the besieged city. The coins known as 'Hibernias' feature a portrait of James II on the obverse and the figure of Hibernia on the reverse and are the first coins to feature the figure of Hibernia. The halfpenny, as seen on the Clare Abbey example, has a reversed 'N' in the word Hibernia.

Miscellaneous objects

Items that may have been used in a domestic context include a ring (E2021:39:6) (Illus. 3.23) that could also have been part of horse equipment. Additional items not readily classifiable due to their fragmentary state, or which are undiagnostic, include copper-alloy wire fragments (E2021:67:15) and a possible gun pellet (E2021:67:24). Both were retrieved from the cess-pit at the outer face of the cloister wall at Clare Abbey.

Medieval and post-medieval pottery

Clare McCutcheon

A total of 81 sherds, all from Clare Abbey (Area C020), were studied. Following identification and some reassembly, this was reduced to 71 sherds. Most of this is early modern but a significant amount is post-medieval and there are two medieval sherds (Table 8.11). Pottery types dating from the 18th/19th centuries are not described here but are included on the CD-Rom that accompanies this book. They include glazed red earthenware, pearlware, black glazed ware, transfer printed ware, stoneware and chinaware.

A single sherd of Ham Green B and one of Saintonge mottled green glazed were retrieved from two possible stone clearance sockets. Each pottery type is likely to be found on almost every Anglo-Norman site in Ireland. Ham Green pottery is an import from Bristol and is named after the location where the ware was produced (Barton 1963; Ponsford 1991). Two hand-built glazed wares were produced: Ham Green A dating to c. AD 1120–1160 and Ham Green B dating to c. AD 1175–1250 as well as a cooking ware which appears to have been contemporary with both glazed wares.

Table 8.11—Catalogue of medieval and post-medieval pottery sherds from Clare Abbey.

Find no.	Fabric type	Sherds	MVR	Form	Date	Description
E2021:71:2	Saintonge green glazed	1	1	Jug	13th/14th cent.	Body sherd
E2021:85:2	Ham Green B	1	1	Jug	Late 12th to mid 13th cent.	Body sherd
E2021:55:66, 77 E2021:57:2 E2021: 58:4, 7, 10	North Devon gravel free	6	1	Pancheon	17th cent.	Base, body, rim sherds
E2021:36:2 E2021:51:16, 17 E2021:55:55 E2021:58:3, 8, 71, 72 E2021:60:4 E2021: 77:8 E2021: 81:2	North Devon gravel tempered	10	2	Pancheon, bowl	17th cent.	Base, body, rim, handle sherds
E2021:55:61-65	Donyatt	4	1	Dish	17th cent.	Rim and body sherds

Key: MVR = minimum vessels represented

Saintonge ware was produced in the Saintonge region of south-west France and was imported into Ireland and Britain as a by-product of the extensive wine trade (Chapelot 1983; Deroeux et al. 1994). The fabric of all the Saintonge wares is generally the same, a fine white micaceous fabric with occasional quartz. The mottled green glaze results from the addition of copper filings to the clear lead

Illus. 8.11—Clare Abbey. Post-medieval pottery: North Devon and (lower left) Donyatt sherds.

glaze. While the term Saintonge ware is used for these vessels, it may be that some of them, particularly this variation, have come from the Cognac area some kilometres east of Saintes.

The vessels represented by sherds of North Devon ware (Illus. 8.11) were produced in the Bideford and Barnstaple areas of North Devon from the late 15th century. A large-scale export trade to Ireland developed in the mid 17th century and continued to a lesser extent in the 18th century (Grant 1983). A basic fine earthenware is used in all cases, with the addition of a distinctive gravel temper for the heavier vessels. The *sgraffito* vessels were covered with a white clay slip, through which a design was scratched, appearing brown in a yellow overall glaze on firing. Donyatt wares were made in Somerset and are closely associated with the North Devon wares. The bowl from Clare Abbey was in a typical red clay, covered with a white slip, and then wet *sgraffito* decorated (Illus. 8.11).

Textiles
Maria FitzGerald

Four small textile fragments were recovered from the primary fill of the 15th- to 17th-century cess-pit, at the outer face of the cloister wall at Clare Abbey (Area C020) (Table 8.12). Analyses of the finds suggest the textiles date to c. AD 1600.

Table 8.12—Catalogue of textile fragments from Clare Abbey (Area C020).

Find no.	Date	Dimensions	Description
E2021:67:11(a)	c. AD 1600	9 x 4 mm	16/16 tpcm, warp medium Z-spun (0.45 mm), weft loose Z-spun (0.35 mm). Fragment doubled over, may represent remains of hemmed edge, no thread survives. Oval-shaped needle holes
E2021:67:11(b)	c. AD 1600	5 x 3 mm	Buff-coloured, Z/Z tabby weave, 18/18 tpcm, warp medium Z-spun (0.45 mm), weft loose Z-spun (0.35 mm)
E2021:67:11(c)	c. AD 1600	8 x 3 mm	Buff-coloured, Z/Z tabby weave, 17/17 tpcm, warp medium Z-spun (0.45 mm), weft loose Z-spun (0.4 mm)
E2021:67:11(d)	c. AD 1600	6 x 3 mm	Buff-coloured, Z/Z tabby weave, 18/18 tpcm, warp medium Z-spun (0.5 mm), weft loose Z-spun (0.4 mm)

All four fragments appear to have originally derived from the same cloth. The fabric is woven in the simplest tabby-weave structure, and is of medium-to-fine weave with approximately 18/18 threads per cm recorded. The fibre was examined under high magnification and appears to have been made from a vegetable fibre source (probably flax).

The cloth was woven from loose to medium Z-spun yarns in both systems. The fragmentary nature of the textiles and the absence of selvedges (the edges of a finished woven piece) and weaving errors mean it is not possible to distinguish warp from weft. However, the yarn in one system is slighter finer (0.35 mm) than the other (0.45 mm) and is likely to have been used for the weft. As a rule, the warp needed to be more robust as it was fixed to the loom and sustained much more friction from the action of the heddles (one of a set of parallel cords or wires in a loom used to separate and guide the warp threads and make a path for the shuttle). The textile from Clare Abbey is a pale buff colour and the yarns have a golden lustrous appearance. The fragments appear to have come from an undyed cloth.

All of the textile fragments preserve oval-shaped needle holes but no thread survives. The thread was likely to have been formed from a different fibre type that was less resistant to decay. These fragments may have originally come from a hemmed textile edge.

During the later medieval period, textiles were an extremely important element of material culture and were used extensively for soft furnishings as well as clothing. In addition to cloth woven in urban centres, the wealthy upper and middle classes in Ireland would have had access to imported cloth and clothing items in luxurious fabrics such as silk and velvet with gold trimmings. The occupants of the Abbey post-dissolution appear to have been materially wealthy, as attested by the imported pottery and glass found on the site, so they may have been purchasing their cloth from urban centres such as Limerick and Cork. Throughout the 17th century, linen cloth was both imported from and exported to England, with important linen-weaving centres in Dublin and Youghal. During the late 17th century Acts of Parliament were passed to allow plain Irish linen to be imported to England without duty (Dunlevy 1989, 90). The fabric from Clare Abbey is a simple, undyed, plain-weave cloth, so there is nothing to suggest that the fabric was not of Irish origin.

Abbeys were traditionally centres of textile work during the medieval period, particularly for embroidery and sewing, so the limited area of the excavation may account for the lack of production evidence. Also, most of the tools used in the preparation of fibres, in spinning and in weaving were made from wood and would not have survived in this context.

The fragmentary nature of the textile makes it difficult to ascertain its original function. The fragments recorded here ultimately became discarded scraps for use in the latrine but the fineness of the weave suggests that it was originally used in fine clothing. Undyed linen cloth, like that from Clare Abbey, was traditionally worn in medieval Ireland for tunics or other garments worn next to the skin and the cloth may have come from an undershirt or chemise, a headdress or from fine hose.

Glass vessel
Edward Bourke

A decorated glass beaker was found in the cess-pit at the outer face of the cloister wall at Clare Abbey (C020) (Table 8.13). The beaker is a tall vessel decorated with red, white and black *vetro a fili* (glass with threads), marvered trails, marvered into a lightly ribbed (vertical) mould (Illus. 8.12). (A marver is a tool used to shape molten glass.)

Table 8.13—Glass beaker from Clare Abbey (C020).

Find no.	Type and material	Date	Dimensions	Description
E2021:67:10 E2021:67:26–32	Glass beaker	AD 1600–40	H 154.7 mm Rim diam. 105 mm Th 0.4–1.5 mm	28 rim and body sherds, 21 co-join. Simple thickened rim. Missing base ring and base

This beaker can be described as *façon de Venise* ('in the manner of Venice'). While glass beakers were common in the medieval period this product type did not begin to arrive until the late 15th century (Tyson 2000, 97). The type is defined as a cylindrical beaker with coloured trailing, usually white or blue, dating to the period AD 1550–1650 (Wilmott 2002, 40). Though traditionally regarded as products of Venice, these vessels are common in the Low Countries from where they are more likely to have come. A precise parallel for this vessel is held within the collections of the Museum of Decorative Arts in Prague, and is provenanced to The Netherlands, c. AD 1600 (Drahotová 1983, 57). While glass vessels are not common on Irish ecclesiastical sites of the period, a *façon de Venise* glass 'tazza' (a shallow saucer-like dish, mounted on a stem and foot or on a foot alone) came from a similar context at Kells Priory, Co. Kilkenny (Bourke 2007). The context here at Clare Abbey is from a cess-pit adjacent to the cloister, and from below a clay tobacco pipe dating to the 1640s, suggesting a date somewhere between AD 1600 and 1640 for this vessel.

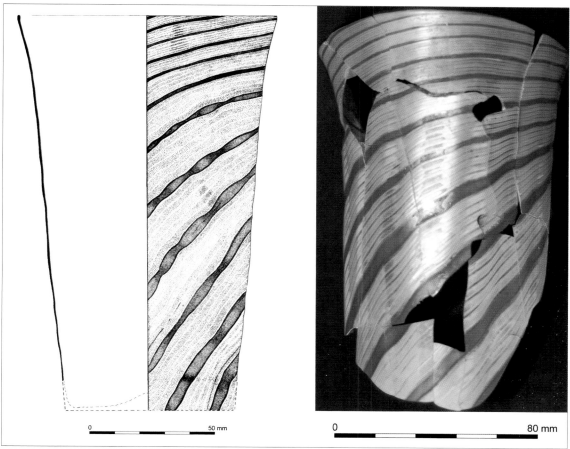

Illus. 8.12—Clare Abbey. Façon de Venise *glass vessel, c. 1550–1650 (E2021:67:10): profile (left) and reconstructed fragments.*

9
FOUR MILLENNIA IN THE FERGUS VALLEY: A CONCLUSION

Nóra Bermingham, Graham Hull and Kate Taylor

The Fergus Valley, the central valley of Clare itself, encompasses bog, estuary, town and field—and at one time extensive woodland. These elements, draped over the gross topography of the landscape, have more or less been constants in every chapter of this book. But while the landscape has been a fundamental pre-condition for all human life in the Fergus Valley, this has not been a one-way relationship. Past human communities have altered the landscape too. Woodlands were cleared and bogs drained; fields tilled, hillsides scarred by quarrying for building materials; roads laid out and towns and villages raised up. The river, the biggest organising principle in the landscape, was a source of food, water, transport and perhaps the final resting place of valley inhabitants in the Bronze Age. Although these excavations are not the only ones to have taken place in south-east Clare and the Fergus Valley they have succeeded in illuminating the lives of those who lived on and off the land and have provided an undisputed contribution to the archaeology of Clare, the region and the country.

Prehistory: burnt stone and cremated bone

Two forms of prehistoric archaeology are represented on the scheme—burnt mounds and cemeteries. Other forms, such as settlement or industrial sites, were not recorded on the scheme. Despite this the excavated sites reveal a great deal about the world inhabited by past populations.

Burnt mounds are domestic site types where cooking, bathing, brewing and dyeing could have taken place. Their primary purpose was to heat water but what purpose the hot water served remains uncertain, though cooking remains the favoured interpretation among many archaeologists. The burnt mounds on this scheme have not provided direct evidence for any of the activities already listed; the occurrence of a small quantity of animal bone at three sites suggests food was prepared and consumed, but this is by no means conclusive. The burnt mounds were also unproductive in terms of plant remains other than charcoal. In contrast to the funerary sites, there was no charred cereal grain retrieved from any of the burnt mounds or burnt spreads on the scheme. This is a feature of the burnt mound sites that were apparently used only once, as well as those with repeated phases of deposition. Given the absence of evidence for anything other than heating water it may be that related activities took place nearby, off-site, or that such activities left little physical trace of having occurred in the first place.

The burnt mounds excavated on the scheme added significantly to the number of these sites recorded within the study area. The distribution of the known and new sites is closely linked to the presence of water. Of the excavated examples, all were sited to take advantage of accessible groundwater and were located in marginal environments such as the edges of bogs, or within a river or stream floodplain. Pits/troughs dug at these locations infilled easily as natural pressure forced water upwards to the surface where it collected in the pit or trough. However, not all sites had pits or troughs, which suggests water was also heated in portable containers of wood or leather.

Heating large quantities of water required easy access to firewood and stone. The sandstone and limestone cobbles that were heated, and later discarded, were more than likely extracted from the underlying glacial till in and around a given site. The charcoal remains from the scheme demonstrate that a wide range of wood taxa—including oak, ash, hazel, pomaceous fruitwood, cherry/blackthorn and alder—was burned and that the wood was probably gathered, rather than felled or taken from stored wood supplies. It would appear that expediency and economy were as important in completing mundane tasks, such as heating water, in the past as they are today. In contrast, a higher level of selection and/or preparation is implied in the charcoal remains recovered from the funerary sites. Most of the charcoal identified derives from oak and ash, trees that can provide good burning branch and logwood suitable for firing and maintaining funeral pyres.

The success of a cremation was an integral part of the treatment of the dead and was probably one part of a complex and highly ritualised sequence of funerary actions. The cremation cemeteries excavated on this scheme were positioned on high ground with expansive views that took in the rivers Ardsollus and Fergus. The cremations interred at the cemeteries were token deposits, representative offerings of the individuals who had passed. It has been suggested (see Jones, Chapter 2) that the greater part of the cremated bone was deposited into the Ardsollus or the Fergus with the river(s) carrying the souls of the dead away from the land of the living. Location was key to the repeated selection of these places as burial sites, the landscape itself providing the the monumental setting needed to remind people where their ancestors had been laid to rest.

The people whose lives and deaths were marked by the cremation burials were more than likely farmers. Assessment of charred cereal grains, retrieved from funerary contexts at Killow and Manusmore suggest the cultivation of wheat, bread wheat, barley, six-row barley and oats. Where cereal grains occur in relative abundance, this may represent a deliberate deposit, incorporated into the funeral pyre or the burial pit itself. Small amounts of grains, in contrast, were more than likely accidental inclusions. A probable cremation pit at Killow returned the greatest variety with all five cereals represented within a single pit. The diversity suggests a preference for mixed cereal cultivation during the Iron Age. It may be that a more restricted range of cereals was cultivated when cremations were interred at Manusmore. At each site only two varieties were represented—wheat and barley at Manusmore AR100 and barley and oats at Manusmore AR102. The comparison is tentative, however, as more detailed and numerous data are typically required when making either inter-site or inter-period comparisons.

This is also the case with the faunal remains retrieved from both burnt mounds and funerary sites. The numbers of bones involved are small but nonetheless demonstrate that cattle, pig, horse and sheep/goat were farmed and red deer exploited. Domestic animals require supplies of food and water. In the case of most of the animals represented this means access to pasture, which was typically achieved via woodland clearance. We have already seen how pollen records from Clare suggest woodland clearance took place from as early as the Chalcolithic. The preponderance of charcoal from ash trees during this period may be explained by its vigour as a coloniser following land clearance. Similarly, the charcoal records of the later Bronze Age are dominated by smaller tree species. This is a period of major woodland clearance and increased arable and pastoral farming. There is good replicability between the charcoal results from the scheme and the pollen record from other studies, in the region and nationally. Both sources of evidence suggest that the Iron Age was a period of woodland regeneration with a corresponding decline in farming.

The artefacts recovered from the prehistoric sites, although not numerous, are significant finds. In some cases, the objects were an integral part of the burial rite and in others they simply represent objects lost or discarded. Some of the cremations at Manusmore AR100 were interred with broken pieces of later Bronze Age pottery. These were more than likely deliberate inclusions, in the form of a grave good or offering. Similarly, three glass beads from the ring-ditch at Claureen were inserted into the burial monument alongside the cremated human remains. Lithics too may in some cases have been deliberately interred, although the evidence here is less convincing than from other burial sites—mainly because the number, range and quality of lithics found are limited. The representation of microslag from burials at two sites in Manusmore is also interesting. The slag need not have arisen from metal-working activities: any high-temperature activity, such as a funeral pyre, could have resulted in the formation of slag. Intriguingly, any metal objects placed within the pyre could have been reduced to slag, which raises the possibility of grave goods lost or transformed during the act of cremation itself.

The finest prehistoric objects retrieved on the scheme are the Bronze Age palstave axehead from Ballymacahill and the Iron Age wooden bowl from Killow. As such, the bowl may represent a ritual wetland deposit. This was by no means an unusual practice during the Iron Age as the recovery of stray artefacts, hoards and human remains from bogs, rivers and lakes attests. The palstave axehead from Ballymacahill was a stray find. It too may represent a ritual deposit although equally it could just have been lost or buried for safe-keeping. Tools such as the palstave were used to fell and chop timber, perhaps even timber used to fuel the funeral pyres of the cremations interred far to the south of the object's find-spot.

Historic settlement, industry and the Church

The historic archaeological record on the scheme dates from the sixth to the 19th century. In contrast to the prehistoric narrative, evidence for settlement and landscape organisation, industry and craft feature strongly in the record of these later centuries. In the main, the farming communities of early medieval Ireland inhabited enclosed, mostly defended farmsteads such as ringforts and cashels. The excavation at Cahircalla More recorded an unusual example a farmstead that was also the home of a smith. The smithy stood within the enclosure and, based on the artefact assemblage, it is evident that the enclosure was the focus of metal-working, possibly other sorts of craftwork and farming. The farmstead enclosure did not occupy an 'open' landscape but was the focal point of a web of adjoining ditches, forming an extensive field system in its immediate environs. Within these fields, the occupants grew a range of cereal crops, including barley and six-row barley, oats, rye and wheat, and appear to have farmed cattle, and probably sheep and/or goats.

In contrast to the strongly defined spatial organisation of the farmstead at Cahircalla More, unenclosed individual pits, hearths and pit clusters of early medieval date were recorded at several locations elsewhere along the scheme. Possibly these represent unenclosed or temporary habitation, perhaps by nomadic or transient people moving across the landscape. It is more likely, however, that they represent the use of all of the landscape by a settled population, moving out beyond their enclosed fields, perhaps to take their herds into areas of rough grazing, or to camp for a few days around a slow-burning charcoal clamp at the woodland's edge, or simply on foraging excursions.

There are around 170 sites in the statutory Record of Monuments and Places classified as either enclosure or earthworks within the study area. Of these, the majority are undated and cannot be assigned a specific function or purpose. What number may represent early medieval settlement forms is unknown and hence the elevation of Carrowdotia AR25 from the generic classification of enclosure to cashel is significant for the interpretation of unexcavated enclosures in the region. Its probable sixth/seventh-century date places it relatively early within the overall time-span for cashel construction in Ireland.

As stated above, the rural and agricultural-based economy of the early medieval period is exemplified by the range of artefacts and food remains retrieved from sites across the scheme. This remains a feature of the succeeding medieval and post-medieval periods but equally, during these periods, the world beyond the farmstead is brought into greater focus by our investigations. Excavations at Clare Abbey have shown that the Abbey was a religious and economic hub from at least the 12th century, drawing resources from the adjacent river, and presumably from farmland elsewhere on its estates, located beyond the wet, peaty environs of the Abbey itself. The River Fergus supplied the Abbey with fish and eels and, no doubt, also served as an important corridor for transport and commerce. The cod and oysters consumed there may have been brought upriver to the Abbey. Its occupants in the 16th century were supplementing their diet with flounder, pike and eel, with game birds such as woodcock, and with domestic fowl including chickens, geese and ducks. Charred cereal grains of wheat, and of hulled and six-row barley were found at the site. It is not known where, or to what extent, cereals may have been processed at the Abbey, but it does appear that a range of cereals of probable local origin was available. The occurrence of frog is of interest. Common frog, the only species of frog found in Ireland, was until recently considered an introduced species. This is based on a late 17th-century account of the transfer of frogs from England to Dublin. Genetic research, however, suggests that the frog survived in a glacial refuge in the south-west and that the current population may be derivatives of these survivors combined with natural colonisation and introductions from Western Europe (Teacher et al. 2009).

After the Reformation and its consequent dissolution, the Augustinians' house at Clare Abbey and its possessions were granted by the Crown to the O'Briens, Earls of Thomond. It is not clear from the sources we have consulted whether the O'Briens allowed the canons to remain in residence—a privilege they allowed some of the Franciscans at Ennis for instance, or whether, conversely, the whole of the establishment became secularised in these years. What is clear from our excavated evidence is that the Abbey was still a wealthy household in the late 16th and 17th centuries. This is indicated by the imported pottery and glass and, in particular, the *façon de Venise* drinking glass—a luxury object by any standard. The vessel itself was probably imported from the Low Countries. Trading links with south-west England are reflected in pottery types from North Devon and Somerset. Scraps of a fine linen cloth also indicate access to market goods. These were evidently toilet wipes, deposited in a cess-pit around AD 1600, but came originally from a fine garment, possibly an undergarment. The cloth was most likely of Irish manufacture. The cloth, the imported pottery and perhaps the glass would have come from urban markets—in Cork, Limerick or even Ennis.

Whoever saw wealth at the Abbey at this time may have lived to see war too. Nearby Clare Castle was occupied by Crown forces during the rebellion of 1641, by Cromwellian forces in the 1650s and again by Jacobite forces during the 'War of the two Kings' in 1688–91. It seems unlikely that a large, masonry building like the Abbey would not have been garrisoned too during one or more of these conflicts. This would explain the artefacts of military character recovered by the excavations there, including cavalry spurs (parts), buckles, horse equipment and an example of the infamous 'gun money' coins minted by James II to fund his campaign in Ireland.

In the succeeding century the focus of the archaeological record on the scheme shifts to the wider rural landscape. Low-key, mundane activities related to cultivation (furrows), land management, maintenance and access (field boundaries, quarry pits and roadways) characterise the post-medieval and later archaeological record. Manufacturing industries—processing lime for agriculture or construction, and brick-making—were important to the local economy. This work took place within the sphere of influence of the landlords living at, for example, Manus House, Manusmore and Hermitage House; and the Keanes of Hermitage House probably commissioned the limekiln at Keelty. No doubt, as ever in the past, the River Fergus provided a means to transport the products of these industries.

Appendix 1: Radiocarbon dates from all excavated sites

All radiocarbon dates are based on the Accelerator Mass Spectrometry (AMS) method and have been calibrated using OxCal v4.1.7 (Bronk Ramsey 2009) with atmospheric data based on Reimer et al. (2009).

Lab. code	Sample/Context	Yrs BP	δ13C	Calibrated date ranges
Ballymacahill AR108: pits				
Beta-211578	Hazel charcoal (*Corylus* sp.) from fill 4, Pit 3	910 ± 40	-26.7 ‰	AD 1040–1180 (1σ) AD 1020–1220 (2σ)
Barefield AR106: charcoal production pit				
Beta-211577	Elm (*Ulmus* sp.) charcoal from fill 7, Pit A	950 ± 40	-24.1 ‰	AD 1020–1160 (1σ) AD 1010–1180 (2σ)
Cahircalla Beg AR126: burnt mound				
Beta-207728	Ash (*Fraxinus* sp.) charcoal from burnt mound deposit 22	3930 ± 40	-26.2 ‰	2470–2400 BC and 2380–2360 BC (1σ) 2550–2540 BC and 2490–2300 BC (2σ)
Beta-207729	Ash (*Fraxinus* sp.) charcoal from burnt mound deposit 16	2770 ± 40	-23.6 ‰	940–850 BC (1σ) 1000–820 BC (2σ)
Beta-211561	Hazel (*Corylus* sp.) charcoal from burnt mound deposit 17	2770 ± 40	-26.7 ‰	940–850 BC (1σ) 1000–820 BC (2σ)
Beta-211562	Hazel (*Corylus* sp.) charcoal from burnt mound deposit 18	2870 ± 40	-25.5 ‰	1100–990 BC (1σ) 1140–920 BC (2σ)
Beta-211563	Hazel (*Corylus* sp.) charcoal from burnt mound deposit 20	2860 ± 40	-26.1 ‰	1060–970 BC (1σ) 1130–920 BC (2σ)
Beta-211564	Hazel (*Corylus* sp.) charcoal from burnt mound deposit 21	3100 ± 40	-25.9 ‰	1410–1360 BC and 1360–1320 BC (1σ) 1440–1280 BC (2σ)
Beta-211565	Hazel (*Corylus* sp.) charcoal from burnt mound deposit 19	2880 ± 40	-25.7 ‰	1110–1000 BC (1σ) 1190–930 BC (2σ)
Cahircalla More AR127: burnt spreads, field boundary and furrows				
Beta-207731	Ash (*Fraxinus* sp.) charcoal from burnt spread (v)	3790 ± 40	-26.1 ‰	2290–2140 BC (1σ) 2330–2130 BC and 2080–2060 BC (2σ)
Beta-207735	Charred hazelnut from burnt spread (iii)	3490 ± 40	-26.3 ‰	1880–1750 BC (1σ) 1910–1700 BC (2σ)
Beta-211566	Charred hazelnut from burnt spread (i)	3870 ± 40	-25.7 ‰	2450–2290 BC (1σ) 2470–2210 BC (2σ)
Beta-211567	Hazel (*Corylus* sp.) charcoal from burnt spread (ii)	2830 ± 40	-27.8 ‰	1020–920 BC (1σ) 1100–900 BC (2σ)

Lab. code	Sample/Context	Yrs BP	δ13C	Calibrated date ranges
Beta-211568	Hazel (*Corylus* sp.) charcoal from burnt spread (iv)	3840 ± 40	-27.7 ‰	2340–2210 BC (1σ) 2450–2190 BC and 2170–2150 BC (2σ)
Beta-211569	Hazel (*Corylus* sp.) charcoal from burnt spread (vii)	3760 ± 40	-26.8 ‰	2210–2130 BC (1σ) 2290–2040 BC (2σ)
Beta-211570	Charred hazelnut from burnt spread (viii)	3570 ± 40	-28.9 ‰	1950–1880 BC (1σ) 2020–1770 BC (2σ)
Cahircalla More AR128: enclosure, smithy and field system				
Beta-207730	Charred cereal from fill 199, Ditch 125	1000 ± 40	-24.3 ‰	AD 1000–1030 (1σ) AD 980–1060 and AD 1080–1150 (2σ)
Beta-211571	Cattle limb bone from fill 91, enclosure Ditch 100	1470 ± 40	-21.7 ‰	AD 560–640 (1σ) AD 530–650 (2σ)
Beta-211572	Charred cereal from fill 192, Smithy 120	1430 ± 40	-23.9 ‰	AD 610–650 (1σ) AD 560–670 (2σ)
Beta-211573	Charred cereal from fill 380, Ditch 210	1250 ± 40	-26.9 ‰	AD 700–790 (1σ) AD 680–880 (2σ)
Carrowdotia AR25: cashel, burnt spreads, quarry pits, field boundaries and furrows				
Beta-211594	Hazel (*Corylus* sp.) charcoal from fill 99, Pit 25	1480 ± 40	-23.6 ‰	AD 550–630 (1σ) AD 530–650 (2σ)
Carrowdotia M27: road, ditches, furrows and pits				
Beta-211593	Hazel (*Corylus* sp.) charcoal from fill 57, Pit 2	1210 ± 40	-26.5 ‰	AD 770–880 (1σ) AD 700–900 (2σ)
Clareabbey AR121: burnt mounds				
Beta-211574	Hazel (*Corylus* sp.) charcoal from burnt mound 1	2770 ± 40	-26.3 ‰	940–850 BC (1σ) 1000–820 BC (2σ)
Clareabbey AR122: burnt spread and pits				
Beta-211575	Hazel (*Corylus* sp.) charcoal from fill 37, Pit 41	3430 ± 40	-27.6 ‰	1760–1690 BC (1σ) 1870–1630 BC (2σ)
Beta-211576	Hazel/alder (*Corylus* sp./*Alnus*) charcoal from fill 49, Pit 46	3820 ± 40	-26.6 ‰	2310–2200 BC (1σ) 2430–2140 BC (2σ)
Clareabbey AR123: pit and hearth cluster				
Beta-211559	Hazel (*Corylus* sp.) charcoal from fill 22, Pit 23	1140 ± 40	-27.7 ‰	AD 880–970 (1σ) AD 790–990 (2σ)
Clareabbey AR124: burnt mound				
Beta-211560	Hazel/alder (*Corylus* sp./*Alnus* sp.) from fill 4, Pit/trough 5	3700 ± 40	-26.2 ‰	2140–2030 BC (1σ) 2200–1960 BC (2σ)
Clareabbey C020: Augustinian abbey				
Beta-231531	Charred wheat (*Triticum* sp.) from fill 65, Pit 6	910 ± 40	-25.2 ‰	AD 1040–1170 (1σ) AD 1030–1220 (2σ)

Lab. code	Sample/Context	Yrs BP	δ13C	Calibrated date ranges
Beta-231532	Charred wheat (*Triticum* sp.) from cess-pit, fill 67	10 ± 40	-23.2 ‰	AD 1960–1960+ (1σ) AD 1890–1910 and AD 1950–1960+ (2σ)
Beta-231533	Hazelnut shell from fill 74, Ditch 35	720 ± 50	-24.2 ‰	AD 1260–1290 (1σ) AD 1220–1310 and AD 1360–1380 (2σ)
Beta-233431	Hare (*Lepus* sp.) vertebra from cess-pit, fill 67	270 ± 40	-21.7 ‰	AD 1490–1640 (1σ) AD 1460–1660 (2σ)
Beta-237217	Pig (*Sus* sp.) bone from fill 71, Pit 13	720 ± 40	-21.3 ‰	AD 1220–1270 (1σ) AD 1200–1280 (2σ)
Beta-237218	Pig (*Sus* sp.) bone from fill 157, post-hole 38	790 ± 50	-21.4 ‰	AD 1210–1270 (1σ) AD 1160–1290 (2σ)
Beta-237219	Pig (*Sus* sp.) bone from fill 166, post-hole 49	720 ± 40	-21.2 ‰	AD 1220–1270 (1σ) AD 1200–1280 (2σ)

Claureen AR131: ring-ditch/barrow

Beta-207732	Ash (*Fraxinus* sp.) charcoal from fill 14, cut 10	2010 ± 40	-24.1 ‰	50 BC–AD 40 (1σ) 100 BC–AD 70 (2σ)

Kilbreckan AR110: hearth

Beta-211579	Cherry (*Prunus* sp.) charcoal from basal fill of Pit 3	950 ± 40	-23.9 ‰	AD 1020–1160 (1σ) AD 1010–1180 (2σ)

Killow AR103: burnt mound

Beta-211588	Charcoal hazelnut from burnt mound 51	2710 ± 40	-25.3 ‰	900–820 BC (1σ) 920–800 BC (2σ)

Killow AR104: burnt mound, pits, cremations (probable), double ditches

Beta-211589	Charred hazelnut from fill 58, Pit 7	2390 ± 40	-24.3 ‰	430–400 BC (1σ) 750–700 BC and 540–390 BC (2σ)
Beta-211590	Cattle-sized limb bone from fill 76, Ditch 11	640 ± 40	-23.7 ‰	AD 1290–1320 and AD 1340–1390 (1σ) AD 1280–1410 (2σ)
Beta-211591	Hazel (*Corylus* sp.) charcoal from burnt mound 51	2940 ± 40	-25.9 ‰	1210–1060 BC (1σ) 1280–1010 BC (2σ)
Beta-211592	Hazel (*Corylus* sp.) charcoal from fill 150, Pit 34	2220 ± 40	-25.9 ‰	370–200 BC (1σ) 390–180 BC (2σ)
Beta-213002	Cattle-sized limb bone from fill 80, Ditch 11	400 ± 40	-23.8 ‰	AD 1440–1500 (1σ) AD 1430–1530 and AD 1560–1630 (2σ)
UBA-6287	Ash (*Fraxinus* sp.) wood from wooden bowl 04E0191:1	2461 ± 32	-28.5 ‰	764–513 BC (1σ) 777–407 BC (2σ)

Lab. code	Sample/Context	Yrs BP	δ13C	Calibrated date ranges
Manusmore AR100: cremation cemetery				
Beta-207733	Hazel (*Corylus* sp.) charcoal from fill 19, Pit 36	1870 ± 40	–26.9 ‰	AD 90–220 (1σ) AD 60–240 (2σ)
Beta-211580	Hazel (*Corylus* sp.) charcoal from fill 11, Pit 27	2960 ± 40	–26.0 ‰	1260–1110 BC (1σ) 1300–1030 BC (2σ)
Beta-211581	Charred hazelnut from fill 53, Pit 54	2240 ± 40	–26.3 ‰	380–350 BC and 310–210 BC (1σ) 390–190 BC (2σ)
Beta-211582	Hazel (*Corylus* sp.) charcoal from fill 87, Pit 85	3840 ± 40	–25.8 ‰	2340–2210 BC (1σ) 2450–2190 BC and 2170–2150 BC (2σ)
Beta-211583	Charred barley (*Hordeum* sp.) from fill 115, Pit 114	2820 ± 40	–24.7 ‰	1010–920 BC (1σ) 1060–880 BC (2σ)
Beta-211584	Hazel (*Corylus* sp.) charcoal from fill 99, Pit 98	2590 ± 40	–25.0 ‰	800–780 BC (1σ) 820–770 BC (2σ)
Manusmore AR102: cremation cemetery, hearth/food preparation pit				
Beta-207734	Hazel (*Corylus* sp.) charcoal from fill 81, Pit 82	2350 ± 40	–23.0 ‰	410–390 BC (1σ) 500–460 BC and 430–380 BC (2σ)
Beta-211585	Hazel (*Corylus* sp.) charcoal from fill 12, Pit 11	2190 ± 40	–26.5 ‰	360–280 BC (1σ) 380–160 BC (2σ)
Beta-211586	Charred barley (*Hordeum* sp.) from fill 28, Pit 27	1220 ± 40	–22.3 ‰	AD 770–880 (1σ) AD 690–900 (2σ)
Beta-211587	Pomoideae charcoal from fill 75, Pit 76	2460 ± 40	–25.4 ‰	760–620 BC and 590–420 BC (1σ) 780–410 BC (2σ)

BIBLIOGRAPHY

Aalen, F H A 1997 'The Irish rural landscape: synthesis of habitat and history' *in* F H A Aalen, K Whelan, & M Stout (eds), *Atlas of the Irish Rural Landscape*, 4–40. Cork University Press, Cork.

Aalen, F H A & Whelan, K 1997 'Fields', *in* F H A Aalen, K Whelan, & M Stout (eds), *Atlas of the Irish Rural Landscape*, 134–44. Cork University Press, Cork.

Amorosi, T 1989 *A Postcranial Guide to Domestic Neo-natal and Juvenile Mammals*. British Archaeological Reports International Series 533. Oxford.

Armstrong, E 1917 'The great Clare find of 1854', *Journal of the Royal Society of Antiquaries of Ireland*, Vol. 47, 21–36.

Arnaldi, M 2000 *The Ancient Sundials of Ireland*. British Sundial Society, London.

Arnold, D E 1985 *Ceramic Theory and Cultural Process*. Cambridge University Press, Cambridge.

ASI 2008 *Archaeological Survey of Ireland Inventory of Archaeological Monuments*. http://www.archaeology.ie

Babtie Pettit 2000 *N18 Road Improvements Dromoland to Crusheen (Including the Ennis Bypass). Environmental Impact Statement*. Clare County Council.

Barfield, L & Hodder, M 1987 'Burnt mounds as saunas and the prehistory of bathing', *Antiquity*, Vol. 61, 370–9.

Barry, T P 2000 'An introduction to dispersed and nucleated medieval rural settlement in Ireland', *Ruralia* III, Supplement 14, 6–11.

Barton, K J 1963 'The medieval pottery kiln at Ham Green, Bristol', *Transactions of the Bristol & Gloucestershire Archaeological Society*, Vol. 82, 95–126.

Bass, W M 1995 *Human Osteology*. Missouri Archaeology Society, Columbia.

Becker, B H 1881 *Disturbed Ireland: being the letters written during the winter of 1880–81*. Macmillan, London.

Bell, J & Watson, M 2008 *A History of Irish Farming, 1750–1950*. Four Courts Press, Dublin.

Bourke, E 2007 'The glass artefacts', *in* M Clyne, *Kells Priory, Co. Kilkenny: Archaeological Excavations by T. Fanning and M. Clyne,* 441–45. Archaeological Monograph Series 3, Stationery Office, Dublin.

Bradley, J 1991 'Excavations at Moynagh Lough, Co. Meath', *Journal of the Royal Society of Antiquaries of Ireland*, Vol. 121, 5–26.

Bradley, J 1993 'Moynagh Lough: an insular workshop of the second quarter of the 8th century', *in* R M Spearman & J Higgitt (eds), *The Age of Migrating Ideas*, 74–81. National Museum, Edinburgh.

Brady Shipman Martin 2000 *N18 Dromolond-Crusheen Road Project (Ennis Bypass). Landscape Impact Report*. Clare County Council.

Breen, T & Hull, G 2002 'AR49, Ballygirreen ring–ditch', *in* I Bennet (ed.), *Excavations 2000,* 15–16. Wordwell, Bray.

Brickley, M & McKinley, J (eds) 2004 *Guidelines to the Standards for Recording Human Remains.* IFA Paper No.7, BABAO & IFA, Reading.

Briggs, C S 1988 'Stone resources and implements in prehistoric Ireland: a review', *Ulster Journal of Archaeology,* Vol. 51, 5–20.

Brindley, A L 2007 *The Dating of Food Vessels and Urns in Ireland.* Bronze Age Studies 7. Department of Archaeology, National University of Ireland Galway, Galway.

Brindley, A L, Lanting, J N & Mook, W G 1990 'Radiocarbon dates from Irish fulachta fiadh and other burnt mounds', *The Journal of Irish Archaeology,* Vol. 5 (1989–90), 25–33.

Bronk Ramsey, C 2009 'Bayesian analysis of radiocarbon dates', *Radiocarbon,* Vol. 51, No. 1, 337–60.

Burke, B 1912 *Genealogical and Heraldic History of the Landed Gentry of Ireland.* Harrison & Sons, London.

Byrne, F J 2001 *Irish Kings and High-Kings.* Four Courts Press, Dublin.

Carroll, M & Quinn, A 2003 'Ferrous and non-ferrous artefacts', *in* R M Cleary & M F Hurley (eds), *Excavations in Cork City 1984–2000,* 257–98. Cork City Council, Cork.

Census 1851 (publ. 1852) *Census of Ireland, Area, Houses and Population, Province of Munster, County of Clare.* Dublin.

Census 1911 (publ. 1912) *Census of Ireland, Area, Houses and Population, Province of Munster, County of Clare.* Dublin.

Census of Population of Ireland 1966 (publ. 1967) Dublin.

Census of Population of Ireland 1986 *Local Population Report No. 23, County Clare 1989.* Dublin.

Chapelot, J 1983 'The Saintonge pottery industry in the later middle ages', *in* P Davey & R Hodges (eds), *Ceramics and Trade,* 49–53. University of Sheffield, Sheffield.

Clark, J 2004 *The Medieval Horse and its Equipment.* Museum of London, London.

Cleary, R M 2000 'The potter's craft in prehistoric Ireland with specific reference to Lough Gur, Co. Limerick', *in* A Desmond, G Johnson, M McCarthy, J Sheehan & E Shee Twohig (eds), *New Agendas in Irish Prehistory,* 119–34. Wordwell, Bray.

Cohen, A & Serjeantson, D 1996 *A Manual for the Identification of Bird Bones from Archaeological Sites.* Archetype Publications, London.

Colgan, E 2003 *For Want of Good Money, the Story of Ireland's Coinage.* Wordwell, Bray.

Collins, T & Coyne, F 2003 'Fire and water—Early Mesolithic cremations at Castleconnell, Co. Limerick', *Archaeology Ireland,* Vol. 17, No. 2, 24–7.

Comber, M 2000 *The Economy of the Ringfort in Early Historic Ireland.* Unpublished PhD thesis, NUI Galway, Galway.

Comber, M 2004 *Non-ferrous Metal-working in Early Historic Ireland.* British Archaeological Reports, International Series 1296, Oxford.

Comber, M 2008 *The Economy of the Ringfort and Contemporary Settlement in Early Medieval Ireland.* British Archaeological Reports, International Series 1773, Oxford.

Comber, M & Hull, G 2010 'Excavations at Caherconnell cashel, the Burren, Co. Clare: implications for cashel chronology and Gaelic settlement', *Proceedings of the Royal Irish Academy,* Vol. 110C, 133–72.

Condit, T & O'Sullivan, A 1996 'Formoyle Beg hillfort and later prehistoric frontier landscapes in east Clare', *The Other Clare,* Vol. 20, 39–45.

Condit, T & O'Sullivan, A 1999 'Landscapes of movement and control: interpreting prehistoric hillforts and fording-places on the River Shannon', *Discovery Programme Reports* 5, 25–39. Royal Irish Academy/Discovery Programme, Dublin.

Corlett, C 2009 'The Cloghoge and Inchavore valleys, Co. Wicklow', *Archaeology Ireland*, Vol. 23, No. 89, 26–9.

Crabtree, K 1982 'Evidence for the Burren's forest cover', *in* M Bell & S Limbrey (eds), *Archaeological Aspects of Woodland Ecology*. British Archaeological Reports International Series 146, 105–13. British Archaeological Reports, Oxford.

Cross May, S, Murray, C, Ó Néill, J & Stevens, P 2005a 'Catalogue of wetland sites', *in* M Gowen, J Ó Néill & M Philips, T*he Lisheen Mine Archaeological Project 1996–8*, 223–82. Wordwell, Bray.

Cross May, S, Murray, C, Ó Néill, J & Stevens, P 2005b 'Wetland structures: typologies and parallels' *in* M Gowen, J Ó Néill & M Philips, *The Lisheen Mine Archaeological Project 1996–8*, 209–22. Wordwell, Bray.

Cunningham, B 2008 'Continuity and change: Donnchadh O'Brien, fourth Earl of Thomond (d. 1624), and the anglicisation of the Thomond Lordship', *in* M Lynch & P Nugent (eds), C*lare History and Society*, 61–78. Geography Publications, Dublin.

D'Auria, L & O'Flaherty E (eds) 2005 *Changing Names. The dynamic world of Irish placenames and their meanings*. Ballyvaughan.

Dáil Éireann *Volume 89, 7 April 1943, Committee on Finance, District of Fergus Drainage Bill 1943, Second Stage*. Oireachtas na hÉireann.

de Valera, R & Ó Nualláin, S 1961 *Survey of the Megalithic Tombs of Ireland, Volume I, County Clare*. The Stationery Office, Dublin.

Delaney, F & Tierney, J 2011 'Burnt mounds in the Bronze Age landscape', *in* F Delaney & J Tierney, *In the Lowlands of South Galway. Archaeological excavations on the N18 Oranmore to Gort national road scheme*. NRA Scheme Monograph 7, 33–44. National Roads Authority, Dublin.

Delaney, S 2011 'M18 Gort to Crusheen road scheme. Summary of the final archaeological results', *The Other Clare*, Vol. 35, 56–65.

Delaney, S, Bayley, D, Lyne, E, McNamara, S, Nunan, J & Molloy, K 2012 *Borderlands. Archaeological investigations along the route of the M18 Gort to Crusheen road scheme*. NRA Scheme Monograph 9, National Roads Authority, Dublin.

Deroeux, D, Dufournier, D & Herteig, A E 1994 'French medieval ceramics from the Bryggen excavations in Bergen, Norway', *The Bryggen Papers*, 161–208. Supplementary Series No. 5, Bergen.

Doyle, I 2006 'Excavation of a prehistoric ring-barrow at Kilmahuddrick, Clondalkin, Dublin 22', *Journal of Irish Archaeology*, Vol 14, 43–77.

Drahotová, O 1983 *European Glass*. Peerage Books, London.

Dunlevy, M 1989 *Dress in Ireland*. Batsford Ltd, London.

Earthsound Archaeological Geophysics 2003 *Site AR22, N18 Road Improvements Dromoland to Crusheen (including Ennis Bypass), Ballyduff, Barefield, County Clare*. Archaeological Geophysical Survey, Licence No. 03R008. Unpublished technical report for Clare County Council.

Earwood, C 1990 'Radiocarbon dating of late prehistoric wooden vessels', *Journal of Irish Archaeology*, Vol. 5 (1989–90), 37–44.

Egan, G & Pritchard, F 2002 *Dress Accessories*. Museum of London, London.

Ellis, B M A 1990 'Spurs', *in* M Biddle, *Object and Economy in Medieval Winchester*, 1037–41. Oxford University Press, Oxford.

Ellis, B M A 2004 'Spurs and spur fittings', *in* J Clarke (ed.), *The Medieval Horse and its Equipment*, 124–56. Museum of London, London.

Eogan, G 2000 *The Socketed Bronze Axes in Ireland*. Prähistorisce Bronzefunde Abt. 9, Bd. 22. Steiner, Stuttgart.

Fanning, T 1976 'Excavations at Clontuskert Priory, Co. Galway', *Proceedings of the Royal Irish Academy*, Vol. 76C, 97–169.

Feehan, J 2003 *Farming in Ireland. History, heritage and environment*. Faculty of Agriculture, UCD, Dublin.

Finch, T 1971 *Soils of County Clare. National Soil Survey of Ireland. Soil Survey Bulletin 23*. An Foras Talúntais, Dublin.

Flanagan, M 2005 *Irish Royal Charters. Text and context*. Oxford University Press, Oxford.

Ford, S, Bradley, R J, Hawkes, J & Fisher, P 1984 'Flint working in the metal age', *Oxford Journal of Archaeology*, Vol. 3, 157–73.

Frost, J 1893a *The History and Topography of the County of Clare*. Sealy, Bryers & Walker, Dublin.

Frost, J 1893b 'Appendix VII – Irish local names explained', *in* J Frost, *The History and Topography of the County of Clare*. Sealy, Bryers & Walker, Dublin.

Gallwey, H D (ed) 1968 'A commentary on the nobility and gentry of Thomond, circa 1567', *The Irish Genealogist*, Vol. 4, No. 1, 65–73.

Geber, J 2009 'The human remains', *in* M McQuade, B Molloy & C Moriarty, *In the Shadow of the Galtees. Archaeological excavations along the N8 Cashel to Mitchelstown road scheme*. NRA Scheme Monograph 4, 209–40. National Roads Authority, Dublin.

Geber, J 2012 'Human remains', *in* S Delaney, D Bayley, E Lyne, S McNamara, J Nunan, & K Molloy, *Borderlands. Archaeological investigations along the route of the M18 Gort to Crusheen road scheme*, 128–29. NRA Scheme Monograph 9, National Roads Authority, Dublin.

Getty, R 1975 *Sisson's and Grossman's the Anatomy of the Domestic Animals*. Vol. 1, 5th Edition. W B Saunders Company, Philadelphia, USA.

Gillespie, R 2006 *Seventeenth Century Ireland. Making Ireland modern*. New Gill History of Ireland 3. Gill & MacMillan, Dublin.

Goodall, I H 1990a 'Iron buckles and belt-fittings', *in* M Biddle, *Object and Economy in Medieval Winchester*, 526–38. Oxford University Press, Oxford.

Goodall, I H 1990b 'Horseshoes', *in* M Biddle, *Object and Economy in Medieval Winchester*, 1054–67. Oxford University Press, Oxford.

Grant, A 1982 'The use of toothwear as a guide to the age of domestic ungulates', *in* B Wilson, C Grigson, & S Payne, *Ageing and Sexing Animal Bones from Archaeological Sites*, 91–108. British Archaeological Reports, British Series 109. Oxford.

Grant, A 1983 *North Devon Pottery. The seventeenth century*. University of Exeter, Exeter.

Grogan, E 1995 'Excavations at Mooghaun South, 1993', *Discovery Programme Reports 2,* 57–61. Royal Irish Academy/Discovery Programme, Dublin.

Grogan, E 1996 'Excavations at Mooghaun South, 1994', *Discovery Programme Reports 4,* 47–57. Royal Irish Academy/Discovery Programme, Dublin.

Grogan, E 2005a *The North Munster Project. Volume 2: The Prehistoric Landscape of North Munster.* Discovery Programme Monograph 6. Wordwell, Bray.

Grogan, E 2005b *The North Munster Project, Volume 1. The Later Prehistoric Landscape of South-East Clare.* Discovery Programme Monograph 6. Wordwell, Bray.

Grogan, E & Condit, T 2000 'The funerary landscape of Clare in space and time', *in* C Ó Murchadha, *County Clare Studies,* 9–29. Clare Archaeological & Historical Society, Ennis.

Grogan, E, O'Donnell, L & Johnston, P 2007 *The Bronze Age Landscapes of the Pipeline to the West. An integrated archaeological and environmental assessment.* Wordwell, Bray.

Guido, M 1978 *The Glass Beads of the Prehistoric and Roman Periods in Britain and Ireland.* Reports of the Research Committee of the Society of Antiquaries, London.

Guy, F 1893 *Guy's Directory of Munster Comprising the Counties of Clare, Cork, Kerry, Limerick, Tipperary and Waterford.* Guy and Co. Ltd, Cork.

Gwynn, Rev. A G & Gleeson, D F 1962 *A History of the Diocese of Killaloe.* M H Gill & Son Ltd, Dublin.

Harbison, P 2008 'The churches of medieval Clare', *in* M Lynch & N Nugent (eds), *Clare History and Society,* 1–26. Geography Publications, Dublin.

Hather, J G 2000 *The Identification of Northern European Woods.* Archetype, London.

Hencken, H O'Neill 1935 'A cairn at Poulawack, county Clare', *Journal of the Royal Society of Antiquaries of Ireland,* Vol. 65, 191–222.

Hencken, H O'Neill 1938 'Cahercommaun, a stone fort in Co. Clare', *Journal of the Royal Society of Antiquaries of Ireland,* special volume.

Hillson, S 1992 *Mammal Bones and Teeth.* Institute of Archaeology, London.

Hinton, D 1990 'Belt-hasps and other belt-fittings', *in* M Biddle, *Object and Economy in Medieval Winchester,* 539–42. Oxford University Press, Oxford.

Hull, G 2001 *00E0284, Archaeological Excavation N19/N19 Road Improvement Scheme, Ballycasey – Dromoland, Contract 1, Ballyconneely and Ballygirreen townlands, Co. Clare, AR 47/51, AR 48/50 & AR 49.* Unpublished technical report for Valerie J Keeley Ltd.

Hull, G & Comber, M 2008 'Caherconnell, Co. Clare, and cashel chronology', *Archaeology Ireland,* Vol. 22, No.4, 30–4.

Hull, G & Tarbett-Buckley C 2001 *Archaeological Monitoring and Excavation, N18/N19 Road Improvement Scheme, Ballycasey – Dromoland, Contract 1, 99E0350.* Unpublished technical report for Valerie J Keeley Ltd.

Hume, N I 1969 *A Guide to Artifacts of Colonial America.* University of Pennsylvania, Philadelphia.

IAWU 1993 *Excavations at Clonfinlough, County Offaly.* Irish Archaeological Wetland Unit, Transactions 2. Crannog, University College Dublin, Dublin.

Jeffrey, P 1990 'Burnt mounds, fulling and early textiles', *in* M A Hodder & L H Barfield (eds), *Burnt Mounds and Hot Stone Technology,* 97–102. Papers from the Second International Burnt Mound Conference. Sandwell, England.

Jones, C 1998 'The discovery and dating of the prehistoric landscape of Roughan Hill in county Clare', *The Journal of Irish Archaeology,* Vol. 9, 27–43.

Jones, C 2004 *The Burren and the Aran Islands. Exploring the archaeology.* The Collins Press, Cork.

Jones, C, Carey, O & Hennigar, C 2011 'Domestic production and the political economy in prehistory: evidence from the Burren', *Proceedings of the Royal Irish Academy,* Vol. 111C, 33–58.

Keeley, V 1999 'Iron Age discoveries at Ballydavis', *in* P Lane & W Nolan (eds), *Laois: History & Society. Interdisciplinary essays on the history of an Irish county,* 25–34. Geography Publications, Dublin.

Kenny, N 2010 'Charcoal production in medieval Ireland', *in* M Stanley, E Danaher, & J Eogan (eds), *Creative Minds,* 99–115. Archaeology and the National Roads Authority Monograph Series No. 7. National Roads Authority, Dublin.

Knight, J 1991 'Vein quartz', *Lithics,* Vol. 12, 37–56.

Lenihan, E 1990 'Ennis in the 1850s: the coming of the railways', *in* J Power (ed.), *An Ennis Miscellany*, 118–39. Clare Champion Printers, Ennis.

Lennon, C 1994 *Sixteenth-Century Ireland. The incomplete conquest.* New Gill History of Ireland 2. Gill & Macmillan, Dublin.

Lewis, S 1837 *A Topographical Dictionary of Ireland.* S Lewis & Co., London.

Lynch, L, Johnston, P & Kiely, J 2010 'Cremains and questions: Bronze Age burial at Derrybane', *Seanda* 5, 18–21.

Lynch, M 2002 *A Study of a Possible Mesolithic Landscape in County Clare.* Unpublished MA thesis, National University of Ireland, Cork.

Lynch, M 2008 'Colonel George Wyndham, 1st Baron Leconfield (1787–1869) and his estate in county Clare', *in* M Lynch & N Nugent (eds), *Clare History and Society*, 266–88. Geography Publications, Dublin.

Lynch, M & Jones, C forthcoming *Excavations at the Promontory Fort of Horse Island (Dunmore Head) in Kilbaha South, Co. Clare.*

Mac Niocaill, G 1963 'Duanaire Ghearóid Iarla', *Studia Hibernica* Vol. 3, 7–59.

MacMahon, M 1993 'The charter of Clare Abbey and the Augustinian "Province" in Co. Clare', *The Other Clare,* Vol. 17, 21–8.

McKeon, J & O'Sullivan, J in press *The Quiet Landscape. Archaeological investigations on the M6 Galway to Ballinasloe national road scheme.* NRA Scheme Monograph series. National Roads Authority, Dublin.

McKinley, J I 1994 *The Anglo-Saxon Cemetery at Spong Hill, North Elmham, Part VIII: the Cremations,* East Anglian Archaeology, No. 69. Dereham, Norfolk.

McKinley, J I 2000 'The analysis of cremated bone', *in* M Cox & S Mays (eds), *Human Osteology*, 403–21. Greenwich Medical Media, London.

Molloy, B 2009 'Knockcommane, Co. Limerick. Embanked ring-ditch. Site 4700.1a', *in* M, McQuade, B Molloy & C Moriarty, *In the Shadow of the Galtees. Archaeological excavations along the N8 Cashel to Mitchelstown road scheme*, 163–65. NRA Scheme Monograph 4. National Roads Authority, Dublin.

Molloy, K 1997 'Prehistoric farming at Mooghaun—a new pollen diagram from Mooghaun', *Archaeology Ireland,* Vol. 11, No. 3, 22–6.

Molloy, K 2005 'Holocene vegetation and land-use history at Mooghaun, south-east Clare, with particular reference to the Bronze Age', *in* E Grogan, *The North Munster Project, Vol. 1. The later prehistoric landscape of south-east Clare*, 255–87. Discovery Programme Monograph 6. Dublin.

Molloy, K & O'Connell, M 2012 'Prehistoric farming in western Ireland: new evidence from pollen analytical evidence at Caheraphuca, Co. Clare', *in* S Delaney, D Bayley, E Lyne, S MacNamara, J Nunan & K Molloy, *Borderlands. Archaeological investigations along the M18 Gort to Crusheen road scheme*, 109–21. NRA Scheme Monograph 9. National Roads Authority, Dublin.

Monk, M 2007 'A greasy subject', *Archaeology Ireland*, Vol. 21, No. 1, 22–4.

Moore, C 2007 'Right on track in Edercloon', *Seanda* 2, 20–1.

Mount, C 1997 *The Early and Middle Bronze Age in South-East Ireland. Aspects of social and cultural distributions*, Vol. 1. Unpublished PhD thesis, University College Dublin.

Mulligan, F 1983 *One Hundred Years of Irish Railways*. Appletree Press, Belfast.

Muñiz-Pérez, M, Bermingham, N & O'Sullivan, J 2011 'A multiperiod landscape in Treanbaun, County Galway', *Journal of the Galway Archaeological and Historical Society*, Vol. 63 (2011), 1–21.

Nally, D 2008 'Maintaining the marches: seigneur, sept and settlement in Anglo-Norman Thomond', *in* M Lynch & P Nugent (eds), *Clare History and Society,* 27–60. Geography Publications, Dublin.

Neilson-Marsh, C, Gernaey, A, Turner-Walker, G, Hedges, R, Pike, A & Collins, M 2000 'The chemical degradation of bone', *in* M Cox & S Mays (eds), *Human Osteology*, 403–21. Greenwich Medical Media, London.

Nugent, P 2008 'The interrelationship between population and settlement in County Clare in the seventeenth century: the evidence from the 1659 "Census"', *in* M Lynch & P Nugent (eds), *Clare History and Society*, 79–104. Geography Publications, Dublin.

O'Brien, P I D 1986 *O'Brien of Thomond. The O'Briens in Irish history 1500–1865*. Phillimore, Chichester, England.

O'Brien, W 1999 *Sacred Ground. Megalithic tombs in coastal south-west Ireland*. Bronze Age Studies 4. Department of Archaeology, National University of Ireland Galway, Galway.

O'Brien, W 2002 'Megaliths in a mythologised landscape: south-west Ireland in the Iron Age', *in* C Scarre (ed.), *Monuments and Landscape in Atlantic Europe*, 152–76. Routledge, London.

O'Brien, W 2004a *Ross Island. Mining, metal and society in early Ireland*. Bronze Age Studies 6. Department of Archaeology, National University of Ireland, Galway, Galway.

O'Brien, W 2004b '(Con)fusion of tradition? The circle henge in Ireland', *in* A Gibson & A Sheridan (eds), *From Sickles to Circles: Britain and Ireland at the time of Stonehenge*, 323–38. Tempus, Stroud.

O'Brien, W 2009 *Local Worlds. Early settlement landscapes and upland farming in south-west Ireland*. The Collins Press, Cork.

O'Brien, W in press 'The Chalcolithic in Ireland: a chronological and cultural framework', *in* M Allen, J Gardiner, A Sheridan, & D McOmish (eds), *The British Chalcolithic. Place and polity in the later 3rd millennium BC*. Oxbow, Oxford.

O'Connor, L 1991 'Irish Iron Age and Early Christian whetstones', *Journal of the Royal Society of Antiquaries of Ireland*, Vol. 121, 45–76.

O'Conor, K D 1998 *The Archaeology of Medieval Rural Settlement in Ireland*. Discovery Programme Monographs 3. Royal Irish Academy/Discovery Programme. Dublin.

O'Conor, K D 2001 'Housing in later medieval Gaelic Ireland', *Ruralia* IV, Supplement 15, 201–10.

O'Conor, K D 2004 *Medieval Rural Settlement in Munster*. Barryscourt Lecture No. VII, 225–56. Gandon Editions, Kinsale.

Ó Dálaigh, B 1987 'History of an O'Brien stronghold: Clonroad c. 1210–1626', *North Munster Antiquarian Journal*, Vol. 29, 16–31.

Ó Dálaigh, B (ed.) 1998 *The Strangers' Gaze. Travels in County Clare 1534–1950*. Clasp Press, Ennis.

Ó Dálaigh, B 2008 'A history of urban origins and village formation in county Clare', *in* M Lynch & P Nugent (eds), *Clare History and Society*, 105–37. Geography Publications, Dublin.

Ó Drisceóil, D 1990 'Fulachta fiadh: the value of early Irish literature', *in* V Buckley (ed.), *Burnt Offerings. International contributions to burnt mound archaeology*, 157–64. Wordwell, Bray.

Ó hÓgáin, S 1938 *Conntae an Chláir. A Triocha agus a Tuatha.* Oifig an tSoláthair, Baile Átha Cliath.

O'Kelly, M J 1954 'Excavations and experiments in Irish cooking-places', *Journal of the Royal Society of Antiquaries of Ireland*, Vol. 84, 105–56.

O'Kelly, M J 1962 'The excavations of two earthen ringforts at Garryduff, Co. Cork', *Proceedings of the Royal Irish Academy*, Vol. 63C, 17–150.

Ó Murchadha, C 1984 'Ennis in the seventeenth century', *The Other Clare*, Vol. 8, 65–8.

Ó Murchadha, C 1998 *Sable Wings over the Land. Ennis, County Clare and its wider community during the Great Famine.* CLASP Press, Ennis.

Ó Murchadha, C 2008 'The years of the Great Famine', *in* M Lynch & N Nugent (eds), *Clare History and Society*, 243–64. Geography Publications, Dublin.

Ó Néill, J 2004 '*Lapidibus in igne calefactis conquebatur*: the historic burnt mound "tradition"', *Journal of Irish Archaeology*, Vols 12–13, 79–85.

Ó Ríordáin, S P 1949 'Lough Gur excavations; Carraig Aille and the "Spectacles"', *Proceedings of the Royal Irish Academy*, Vol. 52C, 6–111.

Ó Ríordáin, S P 1954 'Lough Gur excavations: Neolithic and Bronze Age house on Knockadoon', *Proceedings of the Royal Irish Academy*, Vol. 56C, 297–459.

O'Sullivan, A 2001 *Foragers, Farmers and Fishers in a Coastal Landscape*. Discovery Programme Monograph 5. Discovery Programme/Royal Irish Academy, Dublin.

O'Sullivan, A & Condit, T 1995 'Late Bronze Age settlement and economy by the marshlands of the upper Fergus estuary', *The Other Clare*, Vol. 19, 5–9.

Pelham, H 1787 *The County of Clare in the Province of Munster and Kingdom of Ireland*. London.

Peterken, G F 1996 *Natural Woodland, Ecology and Conservation in Northern Temperate Regions*. Cambridge University Press, Cambridge.

Ponsford, M 1991 'Dendrochronological dates from Dundas Wharf, Bristol and the dating of Ham Green and other medieval pottery', *in* E Lewis (ed.), *Custom and Ceramics—Essays Presented to Kenneth Barton*, 81–103. APE, Wickham.

Power, J 2004 *A History of Clare Castle and its Environs*. Joseph Power, Ennis.

Raftery, B 1994 *Pagan Celtic Ireland. The enigma of the Irish Iron Age*. Thames & Hudson, London.

Raftery, J 1941 'The tumulus-cemetery of Carrowjames, Co. Mayo', *Journal of the Galway Archaeological and Historical Society*, Vol. 19, 16–85.

Read, C 2000a '35. Ballyconneely Middle/Late Bronze Age cemetery and ritual site 97E0042', *in* I Bennet (ed.), *Excavations 1999*, 10–11. Wordwell, Bray.

Read, C 2000b 'Neolithic/Bronze Age cemetery site at Ballyconneely, Co. Clare', *Archaeology Ireland*, Vol. 14, No. 4, 28–9.

Reimer, P J, Baillie, M G L, Bard, E, Bayliss, A, Beck, J W, Blackwell, P G, Bronk Ramsey, C, Buck, C E, Burr, G S, Edwards, R L, Friedrich, M, Gootes, P M, Guilderson, T P, Hajdas, I, Heaton, T J, Hogg, A G, Hughen, K A, Kaiser, K F, Kromer, B, McCormac, F G, Manning, S W, Reimer, R W, Richards, D A, Southon, J R, Talamo, S, Turney, C S M, van der Plict, J, Weyhenmeyer, C E 2009 'IntCal09 and Marine09 radiocarbon age calibration curves, 0-50,000 years cal. BP' *Radiocarbon,* No. 51, 1111-50.

Ryan, F 2000 'Ferns Lower, Ferns, Co. Wexford', *in* I Bennet (ed) *Excavations* 1999, 302. Wordwell, Bray.

Rynne, C 2006 *Industrial Ireland 1750–1930. An archaeology*. The Collins Press, Cork.

Schmidt, E 1972 *Atlas of Animal Bones*. Elsevier, Amsterdam.

Schulting R, Sheridan A, Clarke S R, & Bronk Ramsey C 2008 'Largantea and the dating of Irish wedge tombs', *The Journal of Irish Archaeology,* Vol. 17, 1–17.

Schweingruber, F H 1990 *Microscopic Wood Anatomy*. Swiss Federal Institute for Forest, Snow and Landscape Research, Birmensdorf.

Scully, O M B 1997 'Metal artefacts', *in* M F Hurley & O M B Scully, *Late Viking Age and Medieval Waterford. Excavations 1986–1992*, 438–89. Waterford Corporation, Waterford.

Scully, S 2009 'Glass beads', *in* M McQuade, B Molloy & C Moriarty, *In the Shadow of the Galtees. Archaeological excavations along the N8 Cashel to Mitchelstown road scheme*, 331–35. NRA Scheme Monograph 4. National Roads Authority, Dublin.

Silver, I A 1969 'The ageing of domestic animals', *in* D R Brothwell & E S Higgs, *Science and Archaeology*, 283–302. Thames & Hudson, London.

Simington, R C (ed.) 1967 *The Book of Survey and Distribution, Vol. 4. Clare*. Irish Manuscript Commission, Dublin.

Spellissy, S 1998 *The Ennis Compendium. From royal dun to information age town. A combined history and business directory for Ennis and Clarecastle*. Book Gallery, Ennis.

Tarbett-Buckley, C & Hull, G 2002 'Ballycasey to Dromoland road improvement scheme', *in* I Bennett (ed.), *Excavations 2000*, 15. Wordwell, Bray.

Taylor, G & Skinner, A 1783 *Maps of the Roads of Ireland* (2nd edn). Dublin.

Teacher, A G F, Garner, T W J & Nichols, R A 2009 'European phylogeography of the common frog (*Rana temporaria*): routes of postglacial colonization into the British Isles, and evidence for an Irish glacial refugium', *Heredity,* Vol. 102, Issue 5, 490–6.

Tierney, J 2011 'Rural settlement in the early modern landscape', *in* F Delaney & J Tierney, *In the Lowlands of South Galway. Archaeological excavations on the N18 Oranmore to Gort National Road Scheme*, 59–70. NRA Scheme Monograph 7. National Roads Authority, Dublin.

TVAS 2003 *TVAS Ireland Field Recording Manual*. Unpublished technical document for TVAS Ireland Ltd.

Tyson, R 2000 *Medieval Glass Vessels Found in England c. AD 1200–1500*. CBA Research Report 121, Council for British Archaeology, York.

Waddell, J 1998 *The Prehistoric Archaeology of Ireland*. Galway University Press, Galway.

Watts, W 1984 'The Holocene vegetation of the Burren, western Ireland', *in* E Haworth & J Lund (eds), *Lake Sediments and Environmental History. Studies in palaeoliminology and paleoecology in honour of Winifred Tutin*, 359–76. University of Minnesota Press, Minneapolis.

Westropp, T J 1900a 'The Augustinian houses of county Clare: Clare, Killone and Inchicronan', *Journal of the Royal Society of Antiquaries of Ireland,* Vol. 30, 118–35.

Westropp, T J 1900b 'The churches of county Clare', *Proceedings of the Royal Irish Academy,* Third Series, Vol. 6, No. 1, 100–76.

Wilmott, H 2002 *Early Post-Medieval Vessel Glass in England: c. 1500–1670*. CBA Research Report 132. York.

Wodan Database 2011 = Irish Archaeological Wood and Charcoal Database at www.wodan.ie

Zdepski, M 2008 'Iron-age bowl, information-age connections', *Bucks Woodturners*, February 2008, 6–8.

INDEX